Public School I Love You Not

Geoffrey Finch

Table of Contents

Dedication i

Acknowledgements ii

About the Author iii

Chapter 1 1

Chapter 2 37

Chapter 3 49

Chapter 4 72

Chapter 5 86

Chapter 6 115

Chapter 7 133

Chapter 8 159

Chapter 9 179

Chapter 10 195

Chapter 11 209

Chapter 12 223

Chapter 13 234

Chapter 14 257

Chapter 15 275

Chapter 16 289

Chapter 17 304

Chapter 18 318

Chapter 19 338

"Never give in, never give in, never never never give in except to convictions of honour and good sense."

-Winston Churchill

Dedication

This book is dedicated to my dear wife Jane for her encouragement and patience.

Acknowledgements

Thanks to Axel for his contractual expertise and Gustav for his moral backing. Thanks also to all those who have believed in this book and provided encouragement.

Special thanks to Galerie Paffrath for allowing the use of Die Eselsbank / On the Donkey Bench by Gustav Igler for the cover of this book.

About the Author

Born in 1949 during the continued aftermath of the Second World War, Geoffrey Finch survived ten years of boarding school, which successfully destroyed his desire to study. After leaving school, a brief spell in banking was soon exchanged for the world of computers. In this field, he enjoyed a ten-year stay in the Netherlands. A change of direction and location took him to former East Germany directly after the unification for five years before moving to Sweden, where he still abides with his Swedish wife.

Part I: Preparatory School

Chapter 1

The caravan was nothing to boast about. Painted cream with a green stripe round its middle, it was by no means new and not particularly large, but it sufficed to house the family whilst their new residence was being built. Standing on the caravan step, Geoffrey waved goodbye to his father George and brother David as they set off to school. George had married Thea as soon as the war was over and it wasn't long before their first son, David, arrived in 1947.

Avoiding piles of sand, bricks and other debris they wobbled off over the pavement onto the road on George's Corgi moped with David perched precariously behind his father. The Corgi, best described as a moped, although mopeds as such had not yet been invented, was a mini motorcycle left over from the war, during which they were dropped by parachute to strategic positions in the field enabling officers to move from A to B more quickly than on foot. How he came to acquire this will never be known, and although only designed for one adult, George had constructed an extra child seat behind his saddle. It was on this seat that David was now seated rather insecurely. The Corgi was cheap to run and George used it whenever he could instead of his Austin Somerset. Soon, however, the two-wheeled Corgi would be replaced by a vehicle with three wheels.

By now Geoffrey was three and half years old; the halves were always important at that age. When asked, “How old are you now, Geoffrey?” he would reply proudly, “Three and a *half*!” Like all small children, he of course had no idea what lay in store for him regarding his schooling and the notion that school, somewhere where David went every day, might be something bad or good never crossed his mind. Just now he was safe at home, albeit a temporary one, although later, for Geoffrey, even life at the proper house could be described as temporary. Later, when he became a little older, he discovered that their father had planned for both David and him to follow in his footsteps and attend Haileybury public school. George had a mind to continue a tradition since both his own father and uncle had studied there in 1886 and 1890 respectively, and he himself in 1932. Eventually, when Geoffrey’s younger brother Williams also went to Haileybury, it was almost one hundred years after their grandfather.

Father George had come down a rung or two from the grandiose of his ancestors. At the turn of the sixteenth century the Rt. Honourable Lord Heneage Finch was on the Privy Council to King Charles I but now, four centuries later, he lived in a caravan on a plot of land he had purchased in a village called Little Shelford situated on the smarter, south side of Cambridge about five miles from the city. Little

Shelford, as its name describes, was the lesser of the two Shelfords; Great and Little ran into each other with no clear division except for a road sign marking their names.

The caravan in which his family could live while their future home was being built was placed on the building site. Although it kept a roof over their heads, in retrospect it was primitive, to say the least. The caravan was parked towards the corner of the plot over what was soon to become the septic tank there being no communal drains at this time. Sometimes the tank became rather full and 'Boggy Joe' was called upon to come with his tank lorry to empty it. This involved lifting away concrete slabs covering the tank and exposing the dark brown morass topped with a paler frothy surface lurking within. It was not a pretty sight, not to mention the odour, and although told to keep away, Geoffrey couldn't resist a peek through half-closed fingers wondering just what he might see.

As it was not long after the war, there were still restrictions on the amount of building materials that could be used, so George had long discussions with Mr Wilsher, the builder, as to how they could maximise on his 'allowance'. The house itself was rather modern and almost ahead of its time being crowned with a flat roof, although instead of a crown it was more reminiscent of a 'flat hat'. George later rather regretted this as the storage space of an attic was sorely missed. While he was at work, Thea kept an eye on proceedings, supplying the builders with regular cups of tea. Thea was by no means unattractive, being quite petite and pretty and at the same time well-endowed in the breast department. Although being too little to understand, Geoffrey suspected that one or two of these chaps had a glad eye for Thea, especially one known as Ock, who suffered from a speech impediment (hence the name) and whose work was limited to hod carrying. All day long, the unmistakable sound of the builder's cement mixer filled the air and drowned out most conversations apart from anything else. During the filling in process of the foundations, David and Geoffrey, standing together watched avidly as the concrete was poured in. David, clutching his teddy bear, a rather unusual chocolate brown woolly animal, was particularly interested in the process and stood quite close to see better. Unfortunately, he didn't notice that his poor bear had slipped from his grasp and disappeared under the concrete mix as it was being poured onto the rubble footings, never to be seen again.

Life in the caravan was really rather basic, but George and Thea were young and there was always an end in sight. David and Geoffrey knew no better anyway. One end of the caravan was equipped with a table with seats on each side and the other end converted to a double bed. In the middle was a little gas stove. There was no electricity which meant the lighting was by a gas mantle and paraffin lamps. The table, being the only one, had to serve for everything; for Thea to prepare meals, for eating them, for David to do his homework, and even for bath nights. When it was bath night, a big galvanised tub was placed on the table and filled with warm water. In this tub, one by one, the brothers sat all scrunched up, knees to chin, while they were washed. For them, the luxury of a proper bath was not yet known. Inviting other children for birthday parties was of course out of the question, there being barely enough room for the family alone. Luckily, this only had to be endured for a few months, most of which were summer.

By the time Geoffrey had reached the age of four, the family had moved out of the caravan and into the house now known as 'Griffins'. The time had come for him to start school, which, being blissfully ignorant, he did without any trepidation – at this stage. His school, a private one, of course, went by the name of Islip House, and was situated in a terraced house at the start of the Huntingdon Road. Worn stone steps led up to its blue front door, and all the window frames were painted a matching blue. This little school was run by Miss Turner, a spinster, who treated parents with the same severity as her pupils, verbally anyway, as she only smote parents with words and not with a ruler. It was advisable to arrive at school exactly on time; not a minute early and not a minute late. Occasionally, George arrived outside the school a few minutes early which caused Miss Turner to open one of the upstairs sash windows, lean out and order him and the boys to "go away, you are too early" but on the other hand, if the boys came in one minute late they were scolded with "why are you late?" She was however dedicated to her teaching and mellowed considerably in her later years.

All said and done, it was a nice little school and it was indeed a school. Even though Geoffrey was only four, it was straight in at the deep end; no namby-pamby kindergarten or such. There were only two classes and only two teachers, one of these being, of course, Miss Turner, but she only taught the second class. She lived on the ground floor of the house with the two classrooms located above on the first floor. On entering the school, pupils were required to take off their outside shoes and change to an inner sort. In the entrance hall, straight ahead was the door to Miss Turner's living quarters and on the left were the stairs leading up to the classrooms. Having changed their shoes, they then made their way up the stairs being extra careful to only tread in the middle. The outer edges of the staircase were painted black, leaving a wide band of bare wood all the way down the middle of the stairs. It was absolutely forbidden to step on a painted area and if it should happen the offender suffered the wrath of Miss Turner.

The earliest recollection Geoffrey had of the first class was towards the end of a scripture lesson when all the children were asked to draw a picture depicting what they had just learnt. For filling in their drawing, coloured pencils were used. At home, Geoffrey had been taught that these were chalks, not crayons. Common people spoke of crayons. Geoffrey drew a green hill with three crosses. He didn't really understand what it was all about but anyway, he thought his picture was good; that was the last lesson before the Easter holiday.

The big class with Miss Turner was somewhat tougher. She taught everything, reading, writing, arithmetic, English, scripture, history and even 'music and movement'. 'Music and movement' was broadcast on the radio, so on these days, Miss Turner tuned in her wireless to the appropriate program, the children changed into their plimsolls and on cue, they hopped and danced around the classroom as instructed by the voice on the radio. At his next school, plimsolls became gym shoes and dancing became exercises.

By now, Geoffrey had made some friends at school and the inevitable exchange of birthday parties took place at regular intervals. Robert Wallis was one of his best friends who conveniently lived only a little farther along the

Huntingdon Road from the school. Robert's father owned and ran a big Jaguar garage on Mitchams Corner in Cambridge. Geoffrey suspected that his own father George was a little jealous, even though car dealers were considered as 'not quite top drawer'. He himself hadn't yet learned about such class distinctions. Occasionally, it happened that he and Robert were going to the same birthday party in which case Mr Wallis drove them in his Jaguar which even at that age Geoffrey found exciting. Compared to his father's little beige Austin A40 Somerset, it was indeed impressive; sitting on the leather backseat with his little legs dangling, feet not quite touching the floor, and with the quietness combined with the power, every minute of the journey was wonderful.

In many ways, George was an economical man; he wasn't stingy, just economical. Now that he had two young boys to take to school every morning, that being one too many for his Corgi moped, he upgraded from two wheels to three and bought one of the first Bond three-wheelers. The Bond was much cheaper to run than the Austin, so was used most often as the daily transport. This little three-wheeler barely qualified as a car, indeed it was classed as a motorcycle with a sidecar and the driver was required to possess an appropriate driving licence for such, which sadly for Thea, she did not. Mounted on the single front wheel was a BSA motorcycle engine which provided the power for the one wheel drive and thus, when steering, the whole arrangement would swing from side to side beneath the bonnet. Starting the motor was a feat in itself, there being a cable connected from the kick-start on the engine to a lever inside the car which had to be pulled very hard to bring the motor to life. This vehicle, one step better than a charabanc, was extremely primitive, but it did at least have a canvas roof so it kept the occupants dry in the event of rain.

Thea, not possessing a licence to drive the Bond, after practising with George a few times, arranged to take her test. It happened that on the same day, just a few hours before the test, she had been at the hospital to have a wart removed from her hand. This was all under control until it came to starting the car. Sitting ready in the Bond with the examiner squeezed in beside her and the preliminary questions out of the way, he said, "Now Mrs Finch you may start the vehicle." As instructed by George, she took hold of the lever and pulled as hard as she could. Nothing happened, no sign of life. She pulled again – and again. Unfortunately, these actions had rather disturbed the wound on her hand which had now begun to bleed. In the meantime, George, standing on the pavement observing progress, or lack of it, realised that she had forgotten to switch on the ignition and with much arm flapping, was frantically trying to signal to her to do just that thing. Inside the car, she pulled and pulled on the lever whilst the dressing on her hand became more and more soaked with blood, slowly turning from white to red. "I think perhaps we should postpone this today Mrs Finch and try again another day," said the examiner noticing the state of her hand. "No no, it's quite alright, it will start in a minute," said Thea, through gritted teeth, as at last, not a moment too late, she understood the meaning of George's theatricals on the footpath. 'Click' on with the switch, one pull on the lever and the Bond was underway. She passed her test.

In the summer, on sunny days, Thea drove with the roof down and the boys would sit on the very back edge of the vehicle with their legs in the small baggage space between the back of the only seat and the back of the car. This was extremely dangerous as there was little to hold on to, nothing to hold them in and no protection whatsoever. One fine sunny day whilst buzzing their way into Cambridge, the boys happily perched on the back with the wind raking their hair, another driver stopped them and didn't mince his words about how dangerous it was. Thea, rather taken aback, told him it was none of his business, but did see the error of her ways and that was the end of their fresh air rides.

Every morning in term time, each clutching his satchel, one by one, the boys climbed into the Bond – there were no doors – to make the daily trip to school. They squeezed in beside their father, three in a row, on the bench seat, taking it in turns to sit on the outside as that was more exciting. The vehicle was so low, that the road could be seen flashing by only inches away. On the whole, when it came to sharing or taking turns, very seldom was there any dispute between them, only occasionally if there was an element of unfairness were voices raised and very rarely did it come to blows.

Off they went hoping they would arrive exactly on time to escape a scolding from Miss Turner as their school day began. Every day the milkman delivered to the school a crate of milk in small, third of a pint size bottles, there being one for each pupil. When it was break time, around mid-morning, the children decanted the milk into their own mug kept in their satchels. When the break was over, and the mugs were empty, they were returned to the satchels unwashed. Inevitably, there were always just a few drops of milk left in the bottom of the mugs which, more often than not, found their way into the depths of the satchels. It wasn't long before this little spillage started its bacterial breakdown process and gave off a rather unpleasant odour. Inevitably, after a week or two, it became so bad that Thea was obliged to scour out the inside of the boy's satchels. As milkmen do, he always left the milk on the outside step so in the winter Miss Turner often considered the milk to be too cold for the children to drink. On these chilly days, she would place the crate in front of the gas fire, that being the sole heating for the classroom. The result of this was that one side of the bottle was warm and the other cold. When decanted, it was lukewarm and it was with great difficulty that Geoffrey managed to swallow it down. Thus began his dislike for milk.

Father George was an agronomist working at the National Institute of Agricultural Botany, better known as N.I.A.B. which in relation to the school was situated about a mile further up the Huntingdon Road. At lunchtime, all the pupils were required to leave the premises so Geoffrey and David would set out from the school and walk towards George's office. At about the halfway stage they passed Robert Wallis' house which for them was a kind of milestone demarking how far they had come towards N.I.A.B. Often, they spotted their father driving towards them, pop pop popping along in the Bond, dragging a hazy blue exhaust trail behind him. On these occasions they didn't need to walk all the way; for the little chaps, a whole mile was quite a stretch. Once back in the car, the trio puttered their way home for lunch which Thea had ready when they arrived and then it was back to school again for the afternoon lessons, exactly on time, of course. This was their daily routine except on Wednesdays when they were free in the afternoons with only their homework to do.

They were only together at Islip House for a short while before David was packed off to boarding school leaving Geoffrey to go to school on his own and fend for himself, but as he had friends at school he didn't mind too much, except for his fear of Miss Turner. He did miss his brother though, as now he had no one to play with at home. Back in the village, two new houses had been built next to Griffins, filling in their side of the street. Directly next door, a couple by the name of Westfield moved in, closely followed, one house further away, by Moira, a fiery Irish lady, together with her husband and daughter Josey. Josey was almost the same age as Geoffrey and although they sometimes met, actually playing together was a rare occurrence.

Like her mother, Josey was quite accomplished at telling fibs. One day, when Geoffrey was walking home from the bus stop in the next village, he bumped into Josey also walking the same way from her school. As they strolled along, chatting away, they were in disagreement over some trivial matter as children sometimes are. At the entrance to her driveway, they parted company and Geoffrey continued on his way to Griffins. He had hardly come in the door when the telephone rang which Thea answered, only to find herself on the receiving end to Josey's mother complaining vehemently in her broad Irish accent, "Thea, this is Moira. Josey just came in and to be sure I don't know what to think.

She showed me where Geoffrey just bit her arm. I'll not be after having such things happening to me daughter. What d'ya think is going on, ya must be after givin' him a good hiding and I hope he'll be round to apologise to poor Josey!" Fortunately, already familiar with Moira's ways, Thea believed Geoffrey when he exclaimed he had absolutely done no such thing. It transpired that, to get her revenge following the argument, she had bitten her own arm just before going into her house and then shown her mother the teeth marks saying, "Look what Geoffrey did." Later on, the truth came out and Moira was obliged to eat humble pie.

In the village, Griffins was halfway between the church and the pub and although big enough for a pub the village was too small to have its own school, so most children attended the school in Great Shelford, the next village. This school catered for all the children in the neighbourhood who did not have the same advantages as Geoffrey and David and mostly were from a working-class background. The two brothers were not encouraged to mix with them, and neither were they popular with the boys from the village of similar age. On one occasion, they had to take refuge behind the wall shielding their garden from the street whilst stones were cast at them. It happened that Gran, Thea's mother, was paying a very rare visit when one of these battles took place. With a sneer, she referred to the other children as 'horrid village boys' and would have nothing to do with them.

Meanwhile, at school, Geoffrey was learning his 'times tables' which still, to this day are firmly embedded in his head. In this respect, Miss Turner must have done a good job, even if sometimes she resorted to hitting her pupils over the head with a ruler crying, "blockhead, blockhead, blockhead," with each downward stroke.

Now that David was away at boarding school, Geoffrey was the only passenger in the little green Bond minicar so George frequently used to give a lift to a man called Robin, a teacher who lodged just around the corner in a gigantic gothic-style stone house called Kings Farm. On these almost daily occasions, Robin being somewhat larger than David, left only a small space between Robin and George into which Geoffrey had to squeeze. In actual fact, this was quite reassuring for him as he felt safer and secure being close up to George. Although the close contact was not something he was used to, he found it strangely comforting. It was small compensation for fatherly hugs.

One day in the middle of an arithmetic class, Geoffrey suddenly became aware that he urgently needed to go to the loo for number twos. However, his fear of disturbing Miss Turner in the middle of her lesson was so great that he was too afraid to ask to leave the room. So quite soon, no amount of clenching could prevent the inevitable from happening, and he was obliged to sit very uncomfortably for the rest of the morning with an unwelcome guest in his underpants. At last, it was time for lunch, and this day, George was in good time to collect him, so luckily for Geoffrey, he had no need to start walking to meet him and was able directly to squeeze between his father and Robin. Nothing was said on the way home for lunch, but the very second they walked in through the front door, Thea exclaimed, “Oh Geoffrey darling, have you filled your pants?” followed by, “George, good heavens, didn’t you smell it?” If Robin was suffering during the drive home, he had kept it politely to himself. For Geoffrey, however, it was directly into the bath and then a change of underwear and shorts before returning to school feeling nice and clean again. However, later that same afternoon, their neighbour Josey, now on speaking terms again, was having a birthday party and Moira had arranged for the children to be entertained by a magician. Unlike many, this conjurer was well accomplished at his art and all the children sat around him on the floor open-mouthed as he performed trick after trick. He produced colourful silks from an apparently empty top hat and Geoffrey was completely taken in by his ‘abracadabra’ wand which to him was indeed sheer magic. He was totally entranced by the show and when the conjurer suddenly found ping-pong balls behind his ear, his excitement became so great that for the second time that day he was unable to contain himself and his clean underpants suddenly were clean no longer, although this time not dirtied to the same extent as earlier. How was he going to get round this and avoid another scolding? Even at the age of six, he was becoming quite adept in the art of deceit as well as survival and as it happened his luck was in. When he got home, he discovered that he was all alone in the house. His mother was out and his father had not yet returned from his work, so as quickly as he could, walking with his legs a little wider than normal, he went upstairs and took out another clean pair of underpants and quickly changed so that his mother would never know. The problem now was what to do with the dirty ones caked with poo. He and David shared a bedroom in which they each had their own chest of drawers. While David was away at school, he had the room to himself and the best place he could think of was behind one of the chests of drawers, so he stuffed them into the small gap between the back of the chest of drawers and the wall. At the time it seemed easier to push the offensive underwear behind David's cupboard. So there they lodged and remained undiscovered for quite some time. Indeed, it wasn't until a few years later when George decided it was time to redecorate the boys' room, the chest of drawers was pulled away from the wall bringing to light the long-forgotten dirty underpants, which had now become a stiff, crispy dry clump. Fortunately, everyone was now a little older and George and

Thea decided that as so much time had passed, it was too late to punish Geoffrey who was rapidly learning how to save his skin and avoid punishment – a skill at which he later became quite accomplished.

By the time Geoffrey had started school, he had now gained a little sister, Clare, the latest addition to the family. As far as Geoffrey was concerned, she didn't get in the way too much and life went on more or less as normal. Both George and Thea must have been fairly healthily fertile as now there were three children quite evenly spaced in a relatively short space of time. Geoffrey had noticed his mother getting rather a large tummy, but at his age, pregnancy and babies was something of which he was totally ignorant, and adults could easily pull the wool over his eyes when he asked difficult questions. So when Thea's tummy became very big, she went away for a day or two and then came back with his little sister Clare; rather as if she had just been on a shopping trip.

Even though he always felt safe with this mother and father, he could never really say he was inundated with affection; similarly cuddling and hugging were a rare event and although he was happy, he always felt there was something missing. This would explain why he wasn't particularly jealous of Clare as nothing had really changed in the way of demonstrative affection since there was almost none to speak of anyway.

Quite often, to make his way home from school, he would take the number 112 bus to Little Shelford and occasionally if the times didn't fit, the 103 to Great Shelford. The latter meant he had to walk a fair stretch between the two villages. But for either bus, he first had to make his way to the bus station otherwise known as Drummer Street. Turning left from his school, he walked past the garage on the corner of Huntingdon Road, down Castle Hill, past the Round Church, on through the city passing Sainsburys, Woolworths, Marks and Spencers, George's bank Lloyds and at last left through a passage to Drummer Street. One day, through no fault of his own, he narrowly missed the 112 bus. Poor Geoffrey was in rather a state when he made his plight known to the first bus driver he saw in near proximity and who rather unwillingly told him to get on his bus as he was going roughly the same way. He explained that it would be possible for Geoffrey to hop off and still be in time to meet the 112 bus. The bus he was riding on was not in service, so apart from the driver and his conductor, he was alone. However, while he stood at the front, ready to jump off, the two men had decided that Geoffrey was a spoilt, privileged little boy playing truant. Luckily the journey was fairly short because they didn't hold back in giving him a good ticking off for the entire duration. No matter how much he explained that he had not been 'dilly dallying' on the way, his words fell on deaf ears and the two men continued their verbal bullying unabated. When he came home and related to Thea what had happened, she became quite angry and directly telephoned the Eastern Counties bus company to complain, but they were of course protective to their employees and nothing ever became of it.

Clare had now advanced a little in years and once a week, Thea would take her to a type of dancing school for very small children. These classes took place in a large house situated on the road that passed the backs of the colleges. It was not a particularly long way from Geoffrey's school and sometimes Clare's dancing classes would coincide with the end of his school day. On these occasions, he walked to meet Thea at the classes. The first hurdle was to cross over the busy Huntingdon Road but after that, the walk down Lady Margaret Road was easy. This was a pleasantly quiet area after the hustle and bustle of the main road and in the summer he could smell the hot pavement and some parts of the asphalt even became just a bit soft. Sometimes, after it had rained on the hot tarmac, it produced a truly wonderful smell combined with a misty coating of steam. The route he followed was mostly downhill and zig-zagged all the way, passing first a row of very old almshouses, all exactly the same, built of smooth grey stone with slate roofs. Even though all the doors were nicely painted, also grey, with shiny door knobs and knockers, it was always dark behind the windows. Every time he walked past, he peeked around to see if he could see anybody but there was never any sign of life in these houses and he began to wonder if anybody really lived there. He imagined old people being there in the winter of their life and was always glad when he had passed by.

However, as he strolled on down the meandering road, it took him past a rather fine Georgian house set back from the road with a big gate and gravel drive. In the garden stood a large chestnut tree whose branches reached out just enough to drop a few conkers onto the pavement for him to collect. The garden, with a high fence all around, was on a corner where the road turned right. For a boy of his height, the only way to see into the garden was through the gate at its corner. Here he followed the road round and walked on down the hill towards Madingley Road. He was soon to discover that this fine house was occupied by monks, as one day when passing he met a brother standing at the gate apparently watching the world go by. Thea explained later that the man was a monk after Geoffrey described him as wearing a sort of 'funny brown dressing gown' with a white cord round the middle. The monk struck up a conversation and enquired as to where Geoffrey was going and from where he had come. Geoffrey was in no particular hurry, and they had quite a little chat together. This became a regular feature of his walks down Lady Margaret Road, as almost every time he came to the corner, Brother Francis was waiting at his gate to chat with little Geoffrey. They became good friends and he always looked forward to pausing his journey and talking to Brother Francis.

On one particular occasion, after he had set off with his satchel on his back to meet up with his mother and sister, the heavens opened and he had no choice but to make his way in the pouring rain. This time Brother Francis was not standing at the gate. When he eventually arrived at Clare's dancing class, his mother was shocked to see such a sopping wet little boy. Even his satchel, made of material rather than leather, was soaked including its contents. But at least it washed away some of the rancid milk that had accumulated in the bottom. Fortunately, most of his homework exercise books were written in pencil so there was no ink to spread itself over the soggy pages.

Some years later, when Clare was old enough to also attend Islip House, the number of pupils had dwindled to just four or five and Clare was now best friends with Robert Wallis' younger brother Nigel. Nigel sometimes came home with Clare after school when they had half days and together they did their homework. One part of their English homework was a list of sentences with each sentence containing a blank. Into these blank spaces, they had to fill in the appropriate word from a list provided. The sentences were short and the words were simple, but when Nigel had worked his way down to the last sentence, the only word he had left with which to fill in the blank was 'fruit'. Somewhere along the line, he had made an earlier misfit resulting in his sentence reading 'Fruit house does your friend live in?' This being the last of his homework he wasn't inclined to see the error of his ways. But by this time Miss Turner had mellowed and he certainly would not suffer a whack on the head with her ruler.

Before Clare was born, when there was just David and Geoffrey and it was summer holiday time, George would pack up the little Austin, hitch up the caravan and off they would go to some seaside resort often down in Devon, where Thea's mother, Gran, lived. Thea's father, of whom she talked fondly, unlike her mother, had passed away before Geoffrey was born. Gran lived together with Thea's brother John, a confirmed bachelor, just outside Kingsbridge on his farm. Sometimes, the family would travel at night so the boys slept head to toe on the back seat which George had made a little wider by filling in the footwell between the back and front seats with various packages of holiday requirements to make it level. It was rather lumpy and the car rug was a little scratchy against the soft cheeks of the boys but the excitement overruled everything else so it didn't matter.

At their age, it was always exciting for the boys to go to Gran's, even though she was a little daunting. Everything seemed so big and rather old fashioned. If there was a front door, it was never used and to manage to come to the back door, which was guarded by Shep, a sleepy border collie, it was necessary to pass through a large barn where Uncle John housed his tractors, across a small courtyard and finally down a passage leading to the backdoor. The floor of the barn was just earth, hardened over the years from general use. Here and there it was stained with diesel and oil drops from the tractors, together with a scattering of straw amongst the farm machinery. There was always a special smell of farm and tractors in that barn which added to the excitement of being able to climb up onto the metal seat of one of Uncle John's Fordson tractors and drift into a fantasy world of pulling a trailer or ploughing a field. After the barn and courtyard, the passage to the backdoor was a walled-in flagstone path so well-trodden over the years that rain water collected in puddles where the sandstone had worn away.

Gran and Uncle John were rather well to do, so often when the family arrived, they were first greeted in the kitchen by the housekeeper Mrs Best. Here and there were jugs of milk or cream with beaded doilies hanging over them to protect the contents from flies; other edibles lay under wire-framed gauze covers. Built of stone with massive walls a metre thick, the house was always cool, probably remaining the same temperature in summer as in winter. There were dark spooky hallways and corridors with huge old oil paintings hanging. If Gran had not deigned to welcome her daughter and family on their arrival, it was with trepidation that they went upstairs to meet her in her room. Her room was at the top of a wide curving staircase almost as if ascending the turret of a castle. Fortunately, halfway up was a window so at least there was light to break the gloom. Here she would stay most of the time, venturing down for meals in the dining room. To a small boy like Geoffrey, the dining room seemed absolutely vast with an enormous table and an equally enormous sideboard. If he held his breath, there wasn't a sound to be heard except for the slow tick of an old clock on the sideboard. Gran and Uncle John dined here every day, each sitting at opposite ends of the great table. Uncle John was extremely deaf and had equipped himself with a deaf aid which most of the time he spent adjusting, so either it was whistling and screeching or he couldn't hear a thing. His deafness, combined with the fact that they had very little to talk about, meant that they each had a book to read while they ate. When the meal was over,

Uncle John would extract a pin kept in the lapel of his jacket and spend the next five minutes picking his teeth.

To Geoffrey, the whole house felt like an old stone castle. He overheard Uncle John complaining to George in his rather monotone voice, “You know George, when I wanted some rewiring done, the electrician tried to drill through the wall and even with his longest drill, he didn’t get halfway!” he chuckled mostly to his own amusement. Geoffrey sometimes wondered if there was even a dungeon below with iron rings in the walls to fetter wrongdoers and leave them to the rats, of which there were many.

Gran was a frail old lady but nevertheless, when she took Geoffrey by the wrist with her wizened hand, it was with a vice-like grip from which there was no escape. She may have been frail in body, but not in mind and indeed she possessed the ability to reduce Thea to tears with one ‘blow’ of her sharp tongue. Most Sundays, Thea made a phone call to her out of duty, but otherwise, they met so seldom that the boys hardly knew her. In Gran’s presence, they felt that they should be seen but not heard and must always be on best behaviour. Sadly, she was not one to show affection, so it was never reciprocated. This seemed to run in the family, although Geoffrey did not realise it at the time, and judging by the way she treated Thea, one could think that she did not know the meaning of love. Thea was raised by a governess so any maternal contact with Gran was severed from the very beginning, though she did speak more affectionately of her father. Similarly, as were her Sunday phone calls, the visits there were really only out of duty and for Thea to avoid a severe ticking off if Gran discovered, which she always did, that they had been in Devon without coming to visit her.

Nevertheless, it was always quite exciting for Geoffrey to ride on the tractors, watch the cows being milked, and even go fishing with Uncle John. His major passion was fishing and by all accounts, he was quite proficient, so sometimes they would all drive to Kingsbridge where Uncle John kept his boat and with all aboard, they chug-chugged their way out on the estuary. He was proud to show George a freezer full to brim with fish he had caught and since he caught more than he and Gran could eat, the freezer soon became full. His solution for this was just to buy another freezer and continue to fill that until that also became full.

On rare occasions, it was necessary to stay overnight in the house. Geoffrey did not relish this at all, as he was quite fearful of ghosts and monsters hiding in dark corners. Even on the brightest, hottest, summer days, it was always a bit dark with a slight chill inside and if the boys did have to sleep there, they always shared a room. So Geoffrey felt a little safer but still very small and vulnerable in the rather large cold bed. He lay as near the middle of his bed as possible and listened to every creak and crack of the old house. With his arms tucked tight under the bedclothes so they would not be caught by any wolf that might be hiding under the bed, his imagination ran riot, seeing shapes in the dark that weren't there and whispering to David for reassurance, "What's that over by the cupboard?" Geoffrey could see a scary form in the gloom.

"Where, I can't see anything," whispered David, as if by whispering, whatever might be there would be unable to hear!

"There, just near the door!" said Geoffrey again.

"It's nothing, just a chair. Now go to sleep." He always eventually dropped off to sleep.

Since George was an agronomist by profession, it pleased Uncle John to be able to show him round his garden, which was a rather fine Victorian style walled garden. Some years later, when both Gran and Shep the dog had passed away, Uncle John, now living there alone had acquired a cat which went by the original name of 'Pussy'. Pussy was his companion so when he took the family for a stroll to admire his garden, they were invariably accompanied by Pussy with Uncle John muttering away, "Come along, Pussy." He was a gentle, kind-hearted man, but having spent his life as a bachelor he really didn't know about children.

George's work was very biased towards agriculture and he had many contacts in that branch. Consequently, he knew many farmers in the south of England which enabled him always to find a friendly farmer who would allow him to place his caravan in one of his fields. As long as there was a tap not too far away from which they could fill their water cans, then everyone was happy. Every time the cans needed filling, George called out "water boy" and David and Geoffrey would take the containers and make their way to the tap to collect water. Going to the tap with empty cans was easy but Geoffrey was a little smaller than David and his stick-like little legs would wobble away as he struggled with the now heavy, filled can. Before George had modified the sleeping arrangements inside the caravan, the boys slept in a tent pitched next to it. It was a rather antiquated tent with no groundsheet and hemp ropes that shrank when wet. Every time it rained at night, George had to come from his bed and loosen the ropes before they pulled the pegs out of the ground. Sometimes they shared the camping field with the farmer's cows but usually had a whole field to themselves or maybe just one or two other campers, all keeping their distance from each other.

During a stay at one of these fields, another rather large caravan arrived or endeavoured to, as the entrance to the field was not at all wide and there was very little room to make the turn in from the typical devonshire lane. Even with the van uncoupled from the car and with everyone helping, pushing and pulling and turning it this way and that, it just would not pass through the gate. All the adults helping made their own suggestions as to how to get it through until eventually, one man said to the owner of the caravan, "You know how to solve this don't you?"

"No, how?" he replied, keen to finally get his van into the field.

"Get a smaller caravan," said the helper. The owner was not amused.

Together, the family enjoyed their holidays finding uncrowded shores by the sea, mostly within walking distance of the caravan. Both George and Thea liked to enjoy some privacy and disliked crowded beaches. This was never a problem as there was always plenty of room to spread their groundsheet and rug on a stretch of golden sand above the seaweed residue deposited by the latest tide and without any interference from noisy neighbours. Some beaches were small and enclosed by cliffs and rocks, while others were long open stretches of dunes and sand. Often, the path to these beaches led over loose-sanded dunes, which made it hard work for Geoffrey's little legs with sandals full of sand. Going downhill to the beach, he ran faster and faster until the slope of the dune made him run more quickly than his legs would carry him, resulting in a headlong tumble in the sand; but that was all part of the fun. On the rocky beaches, he and David would spend hours gazing into salty rock pools looking for prawns and small crabs that they could seldom catch; or sifting through the tide's debris in search of cowrie shells. They saved their shell collections until they were back home again and then used them to decorate 'useful' little boxes for Thea in which she could keep her jewellery. Most years, she would be given new ones which would remain on her dressing table for a suitable period before quietly disappearing. Somehow David always seemed to find slightly better shells and make a slightly better box. This could be attributed to his being a little older, but playing second fiddle to David seemed to follow Geoffrey throughout his life. Quite often, the holiday destination was a little place in Devon called Woolacombe where George knew a farmer well and who had boys of similar age to David and Geoffrey. As it was nearly always harvesting time when they were there, they were able to 'help' with the harvest, although it was probably more of a hindrance than a help since none of them was strong enough to lift a bale of straw, but it was, however, wonderful for them all to climb and jump and hide around the haystacks while they were being built.

Just for a change, one summer, George decided to try Southwold for their holiday. It turned out to be anything but a success. He could not be blamed for the weather, but it rained almost every single day. For most of the time, David and Geoffrey were confined to the caravan, where they spent their time sitting at the table with colouring books. Quite quickly, they had finished the books they had brought with them, so every day, George took them into the town to buy another one each, in the hope that there would be sunshine the next day. But it rained and rained, and before their holiday was over, there wasn't a colouring book to be found in the whole town that the boys had not already completed.

As the family increased in size, George purchased a slightly larger caravan and modified the seats to convert into extra bunks so that the whole family could sleep inside, making the tent redundant. The upper bunks were level with the windows on each side, so when it was particularly warm weather, Geoffrey often lay with his head half out of the window. One evening, as he lay there enjoying the night air, Thea decided to have a good wash all over. The easiest way to do this was outside, so thinking everybody was asleep, she crept out of the caravan carrying a large plastic bowl of water to carry out her ablutions. Geoffrey, still wide awake, was suddenly confronted with the luminous figure of his stark-naked mother, which opened his eyes even wider.

"*Mummy!*" he exclaimed, surprising Thea so much that she dropped the bowl and scuttled inside again. She was more careful the next time an all-over wash was due.

The nocturnal slumbers of the family were frequently disrupted by the added hazard of snoring. George was a heavy snorer, frequently keeping everyone awake. No amount of shouting at him helped, often making it necessary to climb out of bed and shake him awake. David's solution to this was to have his shoes available beside his bunk, and if and when his father started snoring, he could throw them at him to wake him up. This worked, except that when George was struck by a flying shoe, he stuck his head up demanding, "What is going on?" When David told him that he was snoring, he grumbled, "It's not me snoring. It's you throwing shoes around!" Not many nights passed without the casting of a shoe.

Eventually, the holidays would come to an end, and after George had dug a large pit in which to empty the contents of the Elsan loo, and everything had been packed and stowed away, George would hitch up the caravan. With mixed emotions, they would head in the direction of home. There were alternative routes for the way back to Cambridge, one of these being via the infamous Porlock hill, which once and once only, George unwisely chose. The caravan, although not particularly large, was rather on the heavy side, and the

Austin was not gifted with an abundance of horsepower, so as they started the ascent and the hill's incline became steeper and steeper, progress became slower and slower until the poor car could go no further. The slower the car, the longer became George's face as he leaned forward, almost pressing himself against the steering wheel, willing the little Austin to climb just a bit farther. Finally, having changed gear down to the lowest, the car finally succumbed and came to a grinding halt. Now they had stopped, and not only was there no chance of going any further forward, but it was also nearly impossible to hold the car and caravan on such a steep incline without it running back again. It was as if the Austin had a will of its own with the sole intention of rolling backwards. The nervous sweat started beading on George's forehead, Thea had turned a ghostly pale, and the boys sat silently in the back, sensing the tension and that all was not quite as it should be. "George, George, what are we going to do?" Thea cried in panic as she envisaged the whole equipage descending backwards down the hill out of control. Out of control, it almost was at that moment. The nervousness spread to David and Geoffrey, who had now become too frightened to utter a sound. Slowly and carefully, while practically standing on the brake pedal, George eased the caravan backwards so that one corner of the van lodged against the grassy bank, and it was unable to move further. With the handbrake on as hard as it would go, he stepped out of the car and, whilst surveying the situation, spotted a Jaguar climbing up the hill towards him, and he bravely flagged it down. As luck would have it, the Jaguar was equipped with a tow bar, and not without some difficulty, they managed to disengage the Austin and couple the caravan onto the Jaguar, which sailed to the top of the hill with no problem whatsoever.

So were their summer holidays, and for Geoffrey, at that age, they were happy days, mainly because he was happy doing things he liked doing, but not from any emotional aspect. Although he felt safe with his parents around him, and he knew they cared about him, there was still a singular lack of demonstrative love. Love was an unmentionable thing in the family. The children just had to try to believe that their parents loved them and that there was love there somewhere. The result of this was an emotional block from an early age which was very soon underlined when it was time for boarding school, but in the meantime, Geoffrey could still enjoy home life for just a little longer until that time when the division between child and parent began.

The summer months passed all too quickly, even though at that age he was never really aware of days and weeks; only when he was reminded that he should start school again next week or in two weeks, or so far ahead it didn't matter. But soon, it was really going to matter, and every day was important. Going back to school at Islip House was never a big issue; it just happened, and the routine would start again. Most important was knowing that at the end of each day, he would be at home again. They always got up in the morning at the same time regardless of whether there was school or not, and the breakfast procedure never changed. Porridge oats in the winter and cornflakes in the summer, the former task usually assigned to George. Although that was the only cooking he ever performed, the rest of the cooking was left to Thea. Had Geoffrey known what lay ahead, he would have made the most of his time at home, but change was just around the corner.

Chapter 2

"Come along, boys, we must go up to Great Shelford and choose your tuck at Miss Motts," called Thea to the boys. The time had come for Geoffrey to start his first term at boarding school. He remembered that when choosing sweets for David, it was always done the day before he had to go away to school, so it just underlined the fact that today was his last full day at home. But since it was his very first term at boarding school, Geoffrey was half excited and half in trepidation since what lay ahead for him was still an unknown quantity.

All boys were obliged to take with them 'tuck', that being a quantity of sweets and chocolates that would be rationed out to them during the school term. Buying these sweets was in itself quite enjoyable but would have been much more fun if it hadn't been yet another signal that home life was about to end. Miss Mott's shop, with a lovely curved bay window, was not very big, but it was full to the brim with everything small boys could want, and Geoffrey often used to look in the window to see if she had any new Dinky toys or any other interesting items. Once inside, it was difficult to see Miss Mott. With her being on the short side and perhaps a little rotund, she rather disappeared out of sight behind all the big glass jars full of sweets that she kept on the counter at eye level for the very purpose of tempting her customers.

The school, to which Geoffrey was being sent, was situated near Aldenham and had originally been a rather fine three-storey country house wrapped in ivy and wisteria with white pillars embracing the main entrance. The outbuildings that had once housed coaches and horses were now classrooms and changing rooms for sport. When Thea announced to neighbours and friends that "Geoffrey's starting at boarding school now", it made him feel quite grown up, but at the same time, something inside him was giving him an unwelcome feeling. He was now eight years old, and this first time going to boarding school was the only time in his whole school career that he did not fearfully dread it.

One by one, the days had disappeared, and the time when he would be separated from his parents drew nearer and nearer. As each day passed, he mentally counted the days he had remaining. Although he never said a word to his mother and father, within himself, he was in turmoil. They had already been through the school uniform process, which meant visits to Eaden Lillys, a rather old-fashioned department store in Cambridge. Although the trying on of new school clothes was the first reminder that boarding school lay ahead, it was still far enough away for him not to start having butterflies in his stomach. In the shop, it was always the same assistant who helped them; a very pleasant man with a slight eye disorder which caused him to shake his head from side to side when trying to read the size on the label of a garment Geoffrey was wearing. The misfortunes of others should not be mocked, but when the clothing ordeal was over, they always found it amusing enough to have a little laugh together afterwards.

The school provided parents with a list of clothes that their sons were obliged to take to school. Every piece of clothing must be labelled with the child's name, and everything packed in a trunk also bearing the child's name. All items on the list must be ticked off by the parents to confirm their existence, and then the list placed in the trunk for Matron to make her own control. Apart from the school tie, there were grey flannel shorts in the summer and grey corduroy shorts in the winter. Long grey socks with a red band round the top in the winter and short grey socks in the summer. There were thick, rather scratchy vests and underpants in the winter and thinner cotton vests and pants in the summer. They had grey flannel shirts in the winter and short-sleeved Aertex shirts in the summer. For sport, there had to be football and rugby shirts and shorts and similarly white vests and shorts for gym; football boots, cricket boots and gym shoes; lace-up shoes, sandals and wellington boots.

And of course, proudly worn, a red blazer with an embroidered emblem on the breast pocket together with a matching red cap with the same embroidery. 'Proudly worn' was only for the first time or two, the novelty soon wore off, and all it achieved was to arouse contra sentiments. As David was a little older and a little bigger than his brother, Geoffrey was often fitted out with the clothes that David had grown out of, resulting in David having most of the new clothes.

The big day loomed nearer, and privately Geoffrey began to think about the school. He and David never really discussed either the school or feelings, so Geoffrey never knew what was going on in David's head as school approached. Neither did David ever relate anything unpleasant about the school, so for the first term, Geoffrey was blissfully unaware of how it was going to be. He was soon to discover for himself what life at boarding school was like. A strange, uneasy feeling started when he realised that he was eating his last supper at home, soon to be followed by the last time in his own bed, cosy and warm. The countdown had changed from days to hours, and on the day that they were going back to school, Thea packed their trunks, together with a small overnight case for pyjamas, hairbrush, toothbrush and washing items. On their beds, she lay out their school uniforms, into which they changed before departing, discarding their holiday clothes for a number of weeks to come. On these awesome days, George came home early from work, drank his cup of tea and loaded the trunks into the car. Most often, he drove the boys to school alone, since saying goodbye to them at school was invariably much too emotional for Thea, so whenever possible, she stayed at home and wept in private where she would not be seen by them. But this being Geoffrey's first term as a boarder, Thea came along as well to see him settled in for his first night.

The journey took about forty-five minutes, and having previously travelled the route with his brother, Geoffrey was familiar with all the landmarks that signalled their proximity to the school as they approached nearer and nearer. Sitting in the back, the boys became more and more subdued as they sunk both deeper in their thoughts and deeper in their seats as if trying not to see where they were. The lump in Geoffrey's throat became bigger and bigger until the final swing into the driveway took them the last hundred yards to the front of the school, where they crunched to a halt. The gravel drive formed a loop enabling vehicles to drive round and return the way from whence they had come. Enclosed in the centre of the loop with a couple of flower tubs was a teardrop-shaped piece of grass aptly named the lozenge. Usually, there were many boys arriving at the same time, but new boys were required to come a little earlier so that parents and masters could meet, and their offspring introduced.

Passing through the main entrance, they came into a large wood-panelled hall with an elegant wide staircase leading from the left up to the landing overlooking the hall. Even the doors leading from it were of the same dark oak, and after Miss Turner's little school, the sheer size of everything reciprocated in Geoffrey feeling even smaller than he did already. Both David and Geoffrey were of lesser stature, so when in the presence of the headmaster, Geoffrey sensed that he diminished even further. There were polite cups of tea and talk of "he's going to love it here" while he was encouraged to make friends with other new boys. One other new arrival went by the name of Jack Helm, and it turned out that he became Geoffrey's best friend for the duration of his years at this school. He, poor chap, lived in Scotland, so he was only able to go home when there was a long 'exeat' which happened just once each term. Although George and Thea were already fairly familiar with the layout, there followed a quick tour round the main part of the school, which included being shown in which dormitory and in which bed Geoffrey would sleep. Nearly all the beds in his dormitory were occupied by new boys, but nevertheless, there was a notable absence of teddy bears or any other cuddly toys, these being strongly discouraged as they were ‘big boys now’.

While George took David off to find his dormitory, Thea helped Geoffrey unpack the few things he had in his case.

“The beds don’t look very comfy,” said Geoffrey, but otherwise, he was mostly silent. Together, they found the bathroom; cold lino floor, a row of white basins and a single bath across the end. Thea found a peg marked ‘Finch G.’

“Look here, darling, this is where you can hang your towel, and look, here’s your mug for your toothbrush and toothpaste,” she said, trying to sound cheerful. Everything seemed alien to him. Although he endeavoured to drag it out for as long as possible, he knew that soon his parents would head for home, leaving him behind, and now this awful moment had finally arrived, and it was time to say farewell; no tears, please.

“Bye-bye darling, I’ll write every week; you’ll soon settle in and make lots of new friends,” said his mother, trying to control the tremble in her voice and hold back the welling in her eyes. A quick hug from both, and they headed to their car. Geoffrey, feeling very small, stood and waved while a sense of abandonment took hold of him as the car crunched its way on the gravel round the lozenge and disappeared out of sight around the corner. His waving had become more and more feeble, and his arm lowered slowly to half-mast and then dropped to his side as the truth of the moment sank in; that would be the last he saw of them for what would seem like an eternity. Feeling totally alone and deserted, he slowly turned and followed David back into the big hall; but he did not cry.

"You must be Finch minor," said a female voice behind him. So that was going to be his name from now on, and David presumably was Finch major, he thought. He found he was being addressed by a young woman wearing nursey type clothes who turned out to be the assistant matron. She slept in a room adjacent to his dormitory, so she was able to take care of any nocturnal crying or nightmares. He was glad about this, not because he was going to cry, although he felt like it, or have a nightmare, but because she was much nicer than the matron.

"Come with me," she said as he followed her into another rather dark, wood-panelled room looking out onto the driveway. This room, furnished only with a number of long tables and benches, turned out to be the dining room. There was one door in the corner and another larger door, through which they had come, leading in from the hall. The latter was reserved for masters only; boys had to share the other smaller door together with the kitchen staff when they brought food to the serving table.

"Here's a sandwich and some milk, and after that, it will soon be your bedtime," she said, and although he could tell the time – he did not have a watch – it seemed awfully early for bed. It still felt as if it was late afternoon. There were other new boys also nibbling at their first taste of school food and looking shyly at each other, not quite knowing what to say or indeed wanting to say very much as they were all inwardly suffering the desperate loneliness that had been thrust upon them. For some boys, this took quite a few days to overcome, and there were one or two who never ever really became used to boarding. Geoffrey met up with Jack again, which momentarily helped to ease the situation; he seemed quite cheerful, so he must have been made of sterner stuff than Geoffrey.

"Are we in the same dorm?" asked Jack.

Geoffrey wasn't quite sure what a 'dorm' was but, guessing, he replied, "I think so; Mummy said that's where all the new boys are going to sleep."

While being shown around the school, he was led from room to corridor to staircase and back again; everywhere seemed to smell of new paint. At least he now knew how to find his dormitory, which was just as well, as at that moment, he was startled by a very loud bell that started to ring, and he was told it was time to go up to bed. So along a corridor, up a stairway, this way and that along another passage, and there was the dormitory. His was the most junior dormitory in which there was only place enough for six beds. One window overlooked the school's main play area where older boys still played after the juniors had 'lights out', their cheerful cries and playful noise keeping the young ones awake.

The beds were a far cry from the one Geoffrey was used to at home, the head and foot being of tubular steel once painted black but now chipped with bare shiny steel on the corners where the paint had been worn off over the years by endless small hands. Between each end was a rectangular frame with a network of small chains and wires stretched across it, held tight with springs all around the circumference. On top of this was a thin grey and off-white, striped mattress stuffed with horsehair. Geoffrey had been right about 'not looking very comfy' because comfort did not come into the description. It could be assumed that the lack of springs helped to discourage bouncing on the beds, which was strictly forbidden, but 'bouncing' was perhaps rather optimistic anyway. There was a small blanket under the bottom sheet and a larger blanket over the top sheet, all tucked in neatly with a thin pillow at the head. Vertical bars in the bedhead prevented the pillow from falling off the end. Each boy had his own travel rug, which was the final layer lain over the top. Since these tartan rugs, chosen by the boys themselves or their parents, were all different, it made every bed individual, so apart from helping the boys to keep warm, it marked the ownership of each bed.

"Clothes off, except for your underpants and into the bathroom. Wash your face and hands and brush your teeth and then come and show me before getting into bed," came orders from Matron. Geoffrey went into the bathroom with some of the boys who had undressed first and quickly found his toothmug, towel, and flannel amongst all the others. He soon discovered that it was advantageous to be one of the first into the bathroom as there were more boys than basins, thus avoiding standing around half-naked, waiting for your turn. As he stood there at the basin, he was quick to learn that the practise was to hold the towel between his legs while he washed his face and hands and cleaned his teeth. All the while, they were watched over by Matron's eagle eye. Back in the dormitory, he put on his pyjamas and then brushed his hair in front of a mirror where all the labelled hairbrushes lay. "Come here, Finch, let's have a look at you." Geoffrey went over to where Matron stood, and even though she was not very tall, she still made him feel small. She inspected his hands, both sides, and tweaked his ears to check behind them before eventually dismissing him with 'alright, into bed with you'. At last, he could climb into his bed, at which point he discovered how hard and basic the bed was. Cosy it was not.

It did not take long for Geoffrey and all the boys to become familiar with the procedure. This first night, however, was a little more relaxed as everything was new to all of them, but they were very soon expected to follow all the rules obediently. The curtains were drawn, and the barred window opened. When they were all in bed, they were allowed to talk for a few minutes before lights out. Since they were so early in bed, lights out was rather ineffective as it was still the end of summer and full daylight outside. After a few days, when lights out had in principle taken place, then the whispering started, but on this first night, Geoffrey and the other boys were only occupied with their own homesick thoughts. Now, as he lay there in the fading light, the truth of the situation and the sense of loneliness really made its mark. He thought of his sister Clare tucked up in her cosy warm bed at home, receiving a goodnight kiss from Thea. While he lay curled up in the unforgiving bed in unfamiliar surroundings, his mind dwelled on all the nice, simple things of home and how much he was missing everybody and everything. To begin with, a few stifled sobs could be heard, but after such an emotional and stressful day, all the boys were tired out and soon, the only sound that could be heard was the steady breathing of a group of seven and eight-year-old boys. As Geoffrey eventually drifted off to sleep, he wondered what lay in store for him the next day.

Chapter 3

Suddenly he was startled awake by the loud ringing of a bell, a sound he came to love and hate. As he opened his eyes, he became acutely aware that this was not his room at home where he usually woke, but instead, alien surroundings greeted him; those were not his curtains, and what is that bed next to his? These thoughts rushed through his head as the reality struck home, and he unwillingly remembered where he was. One of the beds was occupied by the dormitory captain, a senior boy who came down from the 'top dorms' which were situated one floor higher, his duty being to look after the new boys and see to it that there was no mischief. So now he instructed them to go and wash, brush their teeth and hair and then get dressed, after which he showed them how their beds should be made. First, the bottom sheet must be pulled tight so that all the wrinkles disappear, and after this stage has passed inspection, the top sheet and blanket can be drawn over and the rest of the bed made. If a boy's bed was not satisfactory, neat and tidy with 'hospital corners', it was pulled apart, and the victim must start all over again. Finally, when all the boys had made their beds, they were obliged to stand by them ready for inspection before forming a line ready to go down to breakfast.

The way down was via the back stairway, which was much narrower and with a tighter curve, so the boys had to remain in a line, two abreast not being possible. As Geoffrey approached the dining room entrance, he was greeted by wafts of the breakfast that was about to be served. These were not the friendly smells of breakfast at home and did not inspire a great appetite, especially this first morning when he was already feeling rather nervous and homesick. The table for new boys was nearest the entrance door, and they were quickly shown where they should sit. At this point, Geoffrey did not know it, but it was important to choose the mealtime neighbours he wanted, as from this day on, they would be his table companions for the rest of the term. The tables were long, as were the benches on either side and for the seating, there was a rotation system meaning that every Monday, each boy had to move one place to the left. Since the two boys at the end of the table had easy access in and out, their duty was to serve the rest of the table, and because they were at the end of the table, first one side and then the other, they were on serving duty for two weeks. At the head of the table, there was always a master placed to watch over his fellow diners. Since the boys moved round one place per week, each boy ended up sitting next to him a few times during the term; one week on his left and one week on his right. This first morning, by luck, Geoffrey ended up sitting in the middle of the bench, but later on, when his turn came, he found out how it was to sit next to a master. Depending on the master, this place made mealtimes rather stressful and uncomfortable as when it happened, it was necessary to be on absolute best behaviour with best table manners. The school was very strict about table manners, and even though seated in the middle, he hadn't survived many meals before he felt a master's knee in his back for not sitting up straight and when he put his knife and fork down at an angle wider than ninety degrees he was reprimanded with a smack on his head. He soon learned to cope with it, but what he feared most came later when seated at the senior 'top' table and placed next to Mr Pont, the headmaster. The result of this was two very uneasy weeks, and it was accentuated by the fact that boys must always leave a clean plate. Everything they were served had to be eaten. It was bad enough at the lower tables when seated next to a master, but next to the headmaster, it was impossible to surreptitiously hide anything that couldn't be eaten. The downfall of many boys was the school cabbage which for the majority was served far too often. Most boys managed to choke it down one way or another, however much they disliked it, except for one boy who was quite incapable of swallowing it. It was a sad situation for him because the rule was that boys were not allowed to leave the table until their plate was empty and on more than one occasion, only when it was time for the evening lessons was he allowed to give up the battle with the stone-cold cabbage. Beside his plate, resembling a miniature green armada, was a half-full glass of water with a thousand small pieces of cabbage floating around following his attempts to wash down each minuscule mouthful with water. It was advantageous to be on good terms with the boys serving so that they could be persuaded to squash unwanted remnants between two plates when no one was looking. For Geoffrey, although cabbage was not his favourite, it didn't present a big problem. However, meat was a different story. He was already a little fussy about meat in as much he had difficulty coping with any 'nasty' bits. Unfortunately for him, much of the meat served at school was not of the choicest cuts, containing endless gristle, fat and sometimes 'pipes' wobbling unappetisingly in the air defying him to eat them. When any of these 'tasty morsels' ended up on Geoffrey's plate, that was his undoing, and no matter how hard he tried or how small he cut them up, they just would not go down 'the little red lane'. If such an event occurred when seated next to the headmaster, then he really was in trouble. The only chance he had was if the headmaster left his seat to chastise another boy or make an address to the school, then there was an opportunity to secretly hide the inedible offal. Otherwise, he remained at the table, struggling with his food for long after everyone had left.

On this first morning, those problems had not yet arisen; all the little boys found a place at the junior table, the bottom rung of the hierarchy, and waited to see how their first school breakfast would taste. The whole room remained standing, so Geoffrey and the other new boys did likewise, and when it was decided that all the borders were present, the hall was hushed, and a voice was heard to say grace "*For what we are about to receive may the Lord make us truly thankful,*" (but not so thankful when it was cabbage or meat). He soon discovered that the voice belonged to the head boy, and the very moment he finished his recital, the hall filled with a loud scuffling noise as all the boys simultaneously seated themselves on the benches and began chattering. Just beside the entrance door was a sturdy table covered with a plastic tablecloth on which all the plates and bowls stood ready to be filled from a giant steaming metal cauldron. Behind the table stood an elderly woman and a taller sterner looking middle-aged woman wielding a ladle. The elderly woman was Mrs Pont, the headmaster's mother, the other being Mrs Webster, the joint headmaster's wife, and the two of them were invariably on serving duty, which meant slopping food onto the plates borne by the boys serving the tables. Out of the steaming cauldron came a ladleful of grey coloured gruel they called porridge, followed by a swish of milk and topped off by a spoonful of brown sugar. The amount of sugar varied a lot and the unlucky ones sometimes only received a minuscule helping, but anyway, every little bit helped to make the porridge more edible. The consistency of the porridge varied from day to day, sometimes really thick and lumpy and other times thinner and runny, but both were nearly always lumpy; it all depended on the mood of the Spanish kitchen staff that morning. The thick porridge could almost be cut with a knife leaving a shiny, smooth surface, and for those boys who were only used to eating cereals for breakfast, porridge came as quite a shock, but most became used to it quite quickly. Luckily, this first morning was without incident, but a rather unpleasant accident took place a couple of weeks later. As Geoffrey and the other boys began to tuck into their porridge, to which they had now become accustomed, there was one poor chap called Woolley who was not feeling so well. He was situated on the opposite side of the table and fortunately, not directly opposite Geoffrey because after he had eaten a few mouthfuls of his porridge, nausea overtook him, and quite suddenly, he clapped his hand over his mouth in an attempt to hold back the vomit that was surging its way upwards. His hand failed to block anything, but it did create a fountain of half-digested porridge, which squirted over the table only to land in the bowl of the boy opposite. This, in turn, was nearly enough to make the recipient regurgitate his own breakfast. After the mess was cleared up, it was not surprising that most of the boys had lost their appetite.

But this first morning was rather more peaceful and after a rasher of bacon and a slice of bread thinly 'buttered' with margarine by Mrs Webster, all washed down with a mug of brown liquid they called tea, it was time for the closing grace. As everybody stood up again, a hush took over the hall as the head boy recited, "*For what we have received, may the Lord make us truly thankful, Amen.*" So was Geoffrey's introduction to school food with his successful completion of the first meal, but there was worse to come.

Following a brief address by the headmaster, all the boys filed out of the hall the way they had entered. A left turn out of the door took them along a short corridor to the 'passage'. The passage, glistening with new paint, led from the back door, past the kitchens, then the model club and all the way down to the recreation room on the left with the headmaster's study on the right. It was strictly forbidden to run along the passage, although its smooth red-tiled floor and its sheer length invited boys to do so. Now, however, on arrival at the passage, directly opposite the door to the kitchens, it was a right turn through the back door, up some steps under a covered way and out into the 'yard'. The yard was the main free time recreation area, and in the mornings, all the boys played there before first assembling in their squads and then going to Chapel. It was roughly a small quadrangle, although not exactly square. Two sides were buildings, and the rest walled in, except for an opening which, once upon a time, had been the entrance for the horse-drawn coaches. The surface of the yard was made up of large square concrete slabs, making it ideal for roller skating, but also rather easy for knees to be skinned when falling. Every day after breakfast, whilst the yard was in full swing with the morning's commotion, the boys and their activity was watched over by the headmaster, who always stood on the same spot at the head of the yard. The headmaster, Mr Pont, was a rather suave yet domineering character. Always well dressed, most often clad with a smart blazer with gold buttons and immaculately pressed grey trousers or cavalry twills, he had a commanding air about him. Sporting a thick moustache and slick black hair, he nearly always smoked his pipe while he stood there, often tapping it out on the heel of his highly polished shoes, and although most of the boys did not exactly fear him, his dominant posture made Geoffrey feel the vulnerable weak little eight-year-old that he was. Throughout his time at the school, he never looked upon Mr Pont as a fatherly figure, and he never felt there was anyone who could possibly be any sort of parental replacement. He soon discovered that it was always advisable to keep in his good books, which he later found out was easier said than done.

As a new boy, he was feeling rather alone and lost, having no idea what was coming next and just now, he luckily did not have time to think about home. He at least had the fortune to have his brother David there, whom he managed to locate amongst all the other boys. He felt a little safer when in his company. David told him that soon the bell would ring, and then he must line up in his squad, "You're in Stanton, the same as me, and you must stand over there. I'll show you when the bell rings," he said. The school was divided into five squads, and he and David were both in Stanton squad. Each squad was distinguished by different colours, theirs being red.

Hanging near the corner of the form room block was a bell with a long rope attached. Whoever was assigned to ring the bell had to pull the cord repeatedly, causing it to clang so loud that it could be heard over the whole school. Sure enough, the bell soon rang for Chapel and immediately, all the boys stopped playing and lined up in their squads. As instructed by David, Geoffrey went to where Stanton squad lined up, and he was quickly put in his place by the squad leader. Each squad comprising two rows of boys started with the most junior at one end of the front row, working up to the most senior at the other end of the back row. One rank higher was the squad leader, whose duty it was to see that all members of his squad had brushed their hair and washed their hands before meals or lessons. While standing there, he felt glad that it was still early autumn, so it wasn't too cold on his skinny little legs protruding from his short trousers.

Short trousers were all year-round attire, regardless of the temperature, the only difference being corduroy for winter and grey flannel for summer. During the colder months, it was commonplace for small legs to become extremely chapped and sore. The soreness was eased by smearing in Vaseline provided by Matron; it was not unknown for the headmaster to help the more senior boys with this task.'

The majority of the boys were boarders, but during the short period before Chapel, the dayboys also arrived, mostly driven to school by their parents, but one or two came on bicycles. Although the dayboys were rather scorned by the boarders and considered a trifle wet, they secretly envied them, being able to go home every evening and especially at weekends when school finished on Saturday. They never needed to miss the warmth of home and the love and care of their parents or endure the long-term loneliness.

This morning, worship awaited them as they filed two by two out of the yard and up to the chapel situated a little way behind the gym and junior classrooms. Geoffrey's parents were not particularly religious but were raised as good Christians, so he had been to church in the village a few times, although mostly only at Christmas and Easter. Inside, the chapel seemed really quite small compared to the church at home, but nevertheless, it was big enough for all the boys, the staff and sometimes a few parents. Once again, the most junior went in first and were ushered to the front pews. The daily services were quite a quick affair, just a hymn, a lesson and a prayer and then out to the classrooms. Once he became used to the daily procedures, he found that the few minutes in Chapel always gave him a little time to reflect on what lay ahead in the way of lessons and, worst of all, tests. He should have been having religious thoughts, but instead, when he was feeling particularly lonely, he said a prayer asking to be taken away. Sometimes, if he knew that the first lesson after Chapel was going to be a test or something he feared, he was thankful for the time spent in Chapel delaying the awful moment. The routines established with the different subjects and teachers meant that the boys nearly always knew when they would be subjected to a test. However, this being the very first day of his boarding school life, he was only busy trying to take in everything that was happening around him and concentrating on finding the right hymn in his hymn book, how to place the kneeler properly, when to stand and when to kneel, and so forth.

When the service was over, they were herded from the chapel down the path towards their classrooms. Classes one, two and three were in a building separate from the others. Classes were referred to as forms, and most new boys naturally started in form one, that being the lowest. But unknown to Geoffrey at the time, George had aspirations for him to achieve a scholarship to public school, which would save him considerable expense. This meant that Geoffrey started directly in form two. Amongst all the rest of the boys in his form, there was only one other new boy, presumably also considered to be bright enough to miss out form one. It was the second or third term for all the other boys who had progressed from the first form. He never knew whether he was placed in class two because he was considered bright or whether it was purely for George's financial benefit later.

Every form had a form master except for the first two forms, which had a form mistress. Being used to Miss Turner helped him feel slightly less apprehensive. She introduced herself and then, one by one, each of the boys, before informing the class as to who would be teaching the different subjects, one of which was Latin. Geoffrey thought this was quite exciting as it was something completely new to him, even though at this stage, he could not understand the use of it. Later, of course, it became obvious and actually quite useful. Anyway, so he started with 'amo, amas, amat, and it turned out that Latin was about the only subject he managed to cope with without too much chastisement. When asked by Mr Price, the Latin master, "Finch, decline the verb amo!" he was able to stand up and recite "amo, amas, amat, amamus, amatis, amant,"

"Good, sit down." Said Mr Price. Ironically, the very word he was declining was what he sought most – love. Once all the introductions were made, and after a mass of other information drummed into the class, their first real lesson began. Luckily it was arithmetic, soon to be known as maths, which was one of his stronger sides, so he made a good start and found his level in the class.

Cling clang, cling clang, the bell rang to signal the end of the lesson and the start of the morning break, whereupon the whole class departed to the covered way beside the yard. Geoffrey followed along to find there were two tables, one with some rather basic buns and another with crates of milk in small bottles with silver aluminium tops similar to Miss Turner's. This form of sustenance, milk and a bun, was a ritual that took place every morning, winter and summer. In the winter, it was not unknown for the milk to freeze, so the boys had to hold it in their hands to try to defrost it so that it became drinkable. The milk was drunk through straws, but on one occasion, a boy found the aluminium top of his bottle was half open on one side and no longer properly sealed. When the poor boy tried to push in his straw, it would only go a little way, so after poking around, he found the obstruction was a drowned mouse that had entered the bottle headfirst and was unable to come out again. Fortunately, this was not a common occurrence.

After finishing his milk and bun, he wandered around the yard feeling rather lost, as till now he had not made any real friends. Many boys were still renewing their friendships from the previous term, so activity was running at a low level this first morning. Depending on the time of year, there were various different activities that took place in the yard. In winter, if there was a good frost or even snow, the boys made slides, polishing up a stretch of icy concrete with their shoes until there was an adequate length on which to slide. It was, however, an extremely hard landing for anyone who happened to fall, which was not uncommon. In summer 'French cricket' was popular using a cricket stump and a tennis ball, whereas in the autumn term everybody played 'conkers', including even some of the masters. When the chestnut trees shed their fruit, the ground around the tree was always littered with lovely shiny brown, glistening chestnuts, otherwise known as conkers. Some had blown down before they were properly ripened, still encased in their slightly prickly green shells, and when opened, the exposed fruit was often a creamy white colour. Pockets were filled with conkers, boys always trying to find the biggest and the best. When it was the season for playing conkers, the school provided the boys with skewers and string. The skewers were used to make a hole through the middle of the conker, which was then threaded onto a length of the string knotted at the end to prevent the conker from sliding off.

Two persons were needed to play the game, which required one to hold his conker dangling on the end of his string while the other person swung his as hard as possible with the intention of smashing the hanging conker to pieces. After each swing, the roles were reversed until, eventually, one conker would disintegrate, and the other became the winner. Every win with the same conker was reckoned, so every brown nut had a score; the better and harder the conker, the higher the score. Mr Thomas, a history teacher, always saved a few conkers from the previous year and rumour had it that he even soaked them in vinegar before baking them in the oven to make them extra hard. The resulting item was almost indestructible, the soft inside having shrunk to a wizened little lump which was loose and rattled inside the hard, outer shell. After a while, the brown outer shell would break away in small pieces leaving a knurly little lump on the end of a rather dirty, worn-out piece of string, but nevertheless invariably carried the highest score. Geoffrey was quick to learn how to play and found it fun, but there were drawbacks too. If the attacker was not particularly accurate when swinging his conker, it did happen that the other participant was quite painfully smitten on the knuckles or fingers by a flying brown chestnut. Every time a conker was smashed to bits, those bits fell on the ground, so quite soon, the yard was covered with small brown pieces of conker, creating quite a dreadful hazard when roller skating. Many a boy came to grief when his wheels jammed on pieces of conker, causing his skates and feet to stop dead beneath him.

When it was frosty in the winter, Mr Pont would ring the bell early and make everybody jump around doing exercises before filing into Chapel. Often, during this short walk from the yard, bully boys walking behind Geoffrey found it quite entertaining to flick his sticking out ears which already hurt from the freezing cold.

Cling clang, cling clang, the bell decreed the half-hour break to be over, and it was back to the form room for two more lessons before lunch. In Geoffrey's form, the desks were in pairs with his place a little off-centre, halfway back. Until now, anyway, it seemed that Miss Turner's teaching had not been in vain as he was able to keep up with all the other pupils even though this was form two, so the early days in the form room passed without any undue harassment or misery. Cling clang, cling clang, now it was time for lunch. Geoffrey was buoyed along with the rest as everyone crammed into the washroom to wash their hands and then battled to stand before the mirror to comb their hair after first attempting to dry their hands on a roller towel that soon became more wet than dry. Before going into the dining hall, everyone assembled in their squads for hand and hair inspection by the squad leader. Hands were held out in front with palms up and then turned over for scrutiny of the backs.

When the squad leader was satisfied, then they must be held behind the back in a 'stand at ease' position. Geoffrey soon learned that it was not advisable to present dirty hands; otherwise, the offender must, in front of the whole school, cross the yard and go and wash them again. On returning, the rewashed little hands had to be presented to the duty master standing at the head of the yard. The effect varied, since some thick-skinned boys were not so sensitive, but for Geoffrey, whenever he was the target, it was the worst thing that could possibly happen, and he just wanted to shrivel up and disappear, but there was nowhere to run, nowhere to hide. Added to this, there was no home to go to later to relate what had happened and unload the sorrow, which now just had to be bottled up inside.

Squad by squad, the whole school filed into the dining hall, trying to distinguish the smells emanating from the kitchens to give an early warning as to what would shortly be served for lunch. Once again, the grace "*For what we are about to receive may the Lord make us truly thankful*" and then the room filled with the noisy chattering of boys. When everyone had finished eating, and all the plates cleared away, except of course for any boy who was still struggling to swallow his food, the headmaster called for silence and he then made an address, issuing instructions for the afternoon's sporting activities. One day, just as he was holding forth, he stopped abruptly and commanded a boy to stand up. All eyes focused on the individual. What had he done? The boy's name was Morley, and he had the misfortune to be a nail biter and just at that moment, he was occupied with trying to bite off a small piece of what little still remained. "I see you must still be hungry, Morley," boomed Mr Pont, "Come here!" and then as an afterthought, "and bring the mustard pot with you."

"Yes, Sir," answered the terrified boy as he extricated himself from between his two neighbours on his bench, regretting that his unfortunate habit had got him into so much trouble.

"Show me your hands," he ordered, and Morley meekly obeyed, thrusting them out palms up.

"Turn them over, and let me see your fingers." As he inspected them, he said so that the whole room could hear, "Just as I thought, well, let's see if you are still hungry." Whereupon he smeared a thick layer of mustard onto each of Morley's fingertips.

"Now chew your fingernails!" ordered Mr Pont.

Morley studied his fingers for a moment before he gingerly put one finger to his lips, but the mustard burnt his mouth, and he grimaced. "That's it, and all the rest of them," came the command. Morley licked and spluttered, desperately looking for a glass of water to ease his burning mouth, “Now sit down and don’t ever let me catch you chewing your fingernails again.” He learned his lesson, as did most of the boys in the room at his expense.

When lunch was over, a rest period followed before games, games being some form of sport. Geoffrey was shown into a large recreation room where every boy had a locker, locker being rather a misnomer as they were not lockable. He was told to take a book to read and advised that there was no talking. The parents of some boys paid for their sons to have extra fruit to increase their vitamin intake, so at the start of the rest period, those lucky boys collected their orange or apple. ‘Tuck tins’ were also allowed during the rest period, so for those fortunate enough to still have something left in their tuck tin, they could take it with them to their place and enjoy one or two of their rationed sweets. Every boarder had a tuck tin with his name written on it on a piece of sticking plaster, that being Matron’s answer to labels. Tuck played a very important role in prep school life, and waiting for refill day was like waiting for a salary to come onto a bank account. Tuck tins came in all shapes and sizes, whatever empty container Matron could lay her hands on, and in these, she put a few sweets from each individual’s main supply. Wednesdays and Sundays were ‘tuck’ days, so on these days, as soon as breakfast was finished, everybody rushed up the back stairway and placed the now, of course, empty tins on a table in Matrons 'surgery'. After lunch, they were ready for collection, refilled with rations for the next few days. It always seemed to Geoffrey that Matron was rather stingy, because there never seemed to be many sweets in his tin and the temptation was to gobble them up all at once, but most boys learned to eke them out so that they lasted until the next refill; this saving trait stayed with him for the rest of his life. Since none of the boys had any money, their sweets served as a substitute for currency as they could be used to 'swap' toys or sweets with other boys.

Cling clang, cling clang, rest time was over and time for games. In the summer, cricket was played, but this term games meant football which was something new for Geoffrey. At Islip House, there were no games. Such activities were beyond Miss Turner. But now it was into the changing rooms where there was a row of pegs above a bench. By each peg was a name and under the bench was a place for football boots. Football clothes were already hanging on the peg ready for action and likewise boots, mostly all shiny and new, under the bench. Feeling very self-conscious in his baggy shorts, he followed the others out onto the slightly sloping football pitches behind the school, and there he learned the rudiments of football. There were other pitches, which were level and of better quality, at the front of the school, but these were reserved for matches against other schools. The boys with the lowest standard of football were correspondingly taught by the teachers with the lowest standard, but it didn't matter to Geoffrey as he knew no better. It soon started to become clear as to which boys had a modicum of skill or bravery when it came to ball control or tackling. Geoffrey's friend Jack showed some admirable ability which he developed, enabling him to later become goalkeeper for the first team. Geoffrey himself was a little better than the average and the following year played for the colts team; he could boast that he was tested to play on the wing for the first team, but in the end, they chose another boy, the son of the art master, who could run a little faster than Geoffrey. Although it didn't count for much, he was well appreciated in the 2nd XI, but the first team would have been best. After always being in second place to David, it seemed to him that he was somehow destined to endlessly be second best.

His introduction to football was soon over, and after washing his hands and knees, it was back into ordinary clothes before a short spell of recreation time when boys could rollerskate or indulge in other activities before tea. Tea comprised a bun and a mug of the same brown liquid called tea, served in faded yellow hard plastic mugs which seemed to be unbreakable; Geoffrey never saw one break in all the years he was imprisoned there.

Cling clang, cling clang, time for the afternoon lesson. Geoffrey had started to find his way around now, so everything wasn't so alien. He had his places to sit for lessons, for meals and for Chapel, and he had his locker where he could put his tuck, books, maybe a dinky toy or two and any other private items. Although the lockers were not lockable, strangely enough, there was no stealing.

At last, the bell signalled that the last lesson of the day was over, and it was time for supper. When grace was said, food served, and they were allowed to talk, Jack would start to relate the story of a film he had seen on television at home. Geoffrey did not have a TV, so he listened in awe and enjoyed Jack's stories. After each holiday, he would have some new stories to tell and although Geoffrey was slightly jealous of Jack having TV when he and his family did not, each mealtime was like a new episode of a television series. "*For what we have received may the Lord make us truly thankful*"; supper was over, and it was out to the yard for a short playtime before bed. Back in the dormitory, the 'going to bed' began with undressing down to vest and pants, then into the bathroom to wash and brush teeth and hair, all the time supervised by Matron, who did not hesitate to dish out a good smack if there was any fooling around or disobedience. Pyjamas on and into bed; now, the loneliness felt strongest. Always when alone in bed, the feeling of abandonment struck deepest. Thoughts of home brought silent tears; it was not done to be seen crying because of homesickness. Nevertheless, sniffs and snuffles could be heard around the dormitory as all the small boys went through the same sorrowful feelings. For some boys, it was worse than others, depending on the amount of love and warmth they received at home. Although Geoffrey knew that his mother and father cared for him, simple gestures such as a hug were few and far between, with very little love demonstratively shown, even though it was probably there somewhere. However, he was still desperately missing home, and as he lay there all alone staring at the ceiling, he wondered why, if his parents loved him, they sent him away to this misery; it all seemed so contradictory.

Chapter 4

The first days went slowly by, and with each day passing, the pain became less as the settling in process began to establish itself. Luckily the term started in the middle of the week, so there was only a couple of days until the weekend. When Saturday came, it was lessons as usual, but only the morning lessons, so at midday, they were finally free; free from lessons anyway. The lucky day boys went home and enjoyed home life until Monday morning. Borders, however, did not have this option unless an 'exeat' had been requested. Three times a term, boys were allowed an exeat which meant they could go home if they lived near enough, or if not, just out somewhere for the day; for the day actually meant just a few hours. An exeat could be on a Saturday or a Sunday; on Saturday, boys were not free until the lessons were over, so this was already lunchtime, and then they had to be back in time for bed in the evening. For new boys, the most junior, bedtime was six o'clock, so after an hour to drive home and an hour to drive back again, there was very little time at home, and every second was precious, but at least Geoffrey was with his parents. The alternative was Sunday, but again, boys had to attend the morning chapel service before they could leave and then return in time for the evening service. However, now was the first weekend at school, and Geoffrey wasn't going anywhere.

This first Saturday afternoon, they were free to play. Once the term was underway, there was often a football match against another school, and all the boys were required to don their wellington boots and duffle coats, stand at one side of the pitch and cheer for the school. At half-time, the boys watching were obliged to run around the pitch while the players sucked on slices of orange. Primarily, this was to keep them warm, but it also helped to keep them out of trouble, saving any embarrassment in front of the guest school. The opposite side of the pitch was reserved for the headmaster, other staff, and parents who came to watch their son's sporting activities. While they all stood there, the line of boys was patrolled by prefects strolling up and down. If they thought a boy was not paying attention, they asked, "What's the score, Finch?"

"Um, two-nil to them?" replied Geoffrey hesitatingly, in his uncertainty more asking and stating.

"Wrong. Boot cleaning!"

If the wrong answer was offered, there was a good chance of being sentenced to boot cleaning. After the game, the boots of the opponents were collected, and those boys to be punished had the onerous task of cleaning all the mud from the eleven pairs of boots. This task was, of course, carried out in their playtime. Boys soon learned to pay attention to the game. These matches did, however, give

Geoffrey a chance to spend some time together with David, but between them, there was never any talk of home or homesickness. Never did Geoffrey have anyone to confide in as to how much he missed home; this in itself only added to the awful loneliness.

But anyway, one Saturday afternoon, when they were standing together talking and not paying attention to the twenty-two boys running around the pitch chasing after a football, David asked Geoffrey, “What would you do if my eyes got masses of sand in them?”

“I don’t know,” came the expected answer from Geoffrey.

“I’ll show you,” said David, and went on, “you have to *lick* the sand away like this.” He then proceeded to demonstrate to Geoffrey how it should be done using him as the patient. Unknown to them, they were being watched by the headmaster on the other side of the playing field and from what he could see, it looked suspiciously as if they were kissing, which in front of the parents in all likelihood embarrassed him enormously. But in retrospect, knowing what came later, it probably also rather excited him. Inevitably, word soon came that the brothers Finch must report to him in his study after the match. Not knowing why they were to report, they could not invent any excuses in advance, and they wondered what was in store for them.

Outside his study door, they waited in trepidation for what seemed like an eternity before finally they were summoned. Entering his study, knowing that punishment awaited, was in itself not for the faint-hearted. In they went with knees atremble, into the fumes of tobacco and aftershave, to be severely reprimanded. The headmaster sat at his desk in a revolving wooden office chair in which he swivelled to face them as they entered. In one corner of the room was a tall pot that might normally hold umbrellas, but in this case, it housed less friendly articles, namely his canes. He ordered them to demonstrate again what they were doing on the football pitch, not only for their embarrassment but also possibly for his own enjoyment. Mr Pont dealt them a mighty scolding, but only verbally, so Geoffrey considered himself lucky that he wasn't leaving the room with a very sore behind from a beating with one of his canes. In school terminology, being beaten was known as 'getting the cane'.

During this first Saturday afternoon, there was no football match, so Geoffrey played under the cedar tree. Just nearby the lozenge was a very old and very big cedar tree whose wonderful twisting branches were like arms ready to embrace the boys, inviting them to swing and climb as a small child climbs on an adult. Its gnarled roots popped up above the ground here and there and made for a small boy's fantasy to run wild. All sorts of roads and bridges for their dinky toys could be made with the assistance of mother nature. In the summer, many hours were spent making small highways and excavations under the cedar tree. This wonderful tree also lent itself kindly for climbing, but if a boy wished to climb the tree, he must first ask permission from the master on duty. Junior boys were only allowed to climb the lower branches until they advanced in years when they were permitted to climb as high as they liked, or indeed dared. There was one exception, however, and that was Pearcey. Geoffrey found out that Pearcey, who started the same term as himself, had been involved in an accident with a car and had been lying unconscious in hospital for a number of days. Generally speaking, he was fine, except for his balance, which was no longer one hundred per cent coupled with a very slight shake in his hands. For this reason, it was absolutely forbidden for Pearcey to climb the cedar tree.

But boys will be boys, and one Sunday afternoon, while Geoffrey was quietly driving one of his dinky toys around his road complex by the trunk of the cedar tree, Pearcey, being an adventurous chap, disregarded his climbing ban and decided to have a go anyway. One branch hung quite low over the ground, and it was fun just to straddle it and bounce up and down to see if it could be made to hit the ground below. This branch was so popular with the boys that the top surface had become polished shiny from a multitude of small bottoms sitting on it. It was always the starting point when climbing the tree and thus was also the natural starting point for Pearcey. Needless to say, it was also the ending point too. Simultaneously there was a thump, and a crack, and a cry, causing Geoffrey to look up and see what had happened. There lay Pearcey on his back in the dusty earth where a hundred sandals had scuffed below the branch. The fall had knocked the wind out of him, and his back was hurting him most, but what he was not yet aware of was his arm which was well and truly broken. Just as Geoffrey looked over to see what had happened, Pearcey tried to push himself up using his damaged arm. Geoffrey saw the broken bone stretching the skin from the inside as he pushed on it to try to sit up. With a cry of pain, he collapsed back onto the earth again. At the same moment, Mr Pont, having seen what happened from the house, came bounding over, collected the boy up in his arms, who was now in a half faint and rushed him back to the house. Not long after, an ambulance arrived at full speed and crunched to an abrupt halt in front of the main entrance. Pearcey was quickly whisked away, not to be seen again for a few days until he reappeared with his arm encased in a plaster cast.

Geoffrey never ceased to be amazed how Mr Pont always seemed to be there when such an incident occurred.

He obviously kept his eyes open and was always aware of what was happening around him. On one occasion, when Geoffrey was seated next to him at the senior table, Mr Pont suddenly launched himself from his chair, rushed across the dining hall and was just in time to catch a boy who had fainted and was falling backwards unconscious from the bench. He gathered him up and took him out in one fell swoop. Similarly, one hot summer day, his elderly mother passed out in the dining hall while serving. Mr Pont was also there to catch her just as she fell. One thing could be said for him, he had a talent for spotting anything untoward.

More often than not, when they had free time, they would play outside, roller skating in the yard, climbing the cedar tree or building a camp in a little wood in the school grounds. Sometimes there was a film show, which was always an excitement and something to look forward to a good while ahead. When there was going to be a film, all the boys assembled in the library where chairs were arranged such that the bigger boys sat towards the back with the younger, smaller boys being seated on the floor at the front. At the back of the room, a projector was installed, and at the other end, a screen made from a bedsheet was pinned to the oak-panelled wall. The thick curtains were drawn, and the lights extinguished, ready for the start. All rather primitive, but the young audience didn't know any better, and it didn't deter their excited anticipation. When all was quiet, and everybody was seated in place, the projector was set in motion. It didn't always get started properly the first time, but soon enough, after a lot of whirring and clicking, the film countdown, usually out of focus, could be seen on the screen. Always in black and white, the film finally started after a certain amount of refocusing. Tarzan films and Laurel and Hardy were always popular, along with westerns starring John Wayne; Geoffrey sat through 'Where the river bends' at least twice. Usually, there were only two or three films in each term, and as this was the first Saturday, there was no such entertainment.

Supper time came and went, and it was soon time for bed again. Always at bedtime, when not preoccupied with other activities, the loneliness took hold in its magnitude. Even when surrounded by other boys during the day, the loneliness was never absent but whilst lying alone in a hard bed, in a dormitory where the silence was only broken by the sniffling of other homesick small boys, the thoughts of home became almost unbearable. Geoffrey tried to look forward to the next exeat, but term had only just started, so it was so far away as to be almost irrelevant. How could he bear this? He longed for someone to talk to, in whom he could confide. Eventually, sleep would take over.

The first Sunday morning came, and Geoffrey awoke thinking about what he would be doing at home and what his mother and father would be doing. He imagined them sitting at the breakfast table with the chairs rearranged to compensate for the empty places where he and David would have been sitting. On Sundays at home, they always had sausages for breakfast, lovely browned fat sausages from the local butcher; now, there would be two less. No routine spoonful of malt or 'Haliborange' vitamin C pills today; he wondered if they were thinking about him. Back in the reality of school, on Sundays, they had an extra half hour in bed before the bell signalled time to get up. Breakfast as usual, and after a short play period, it was time for Chapel. Following the usual lining up in squads, they 'crocodiled' up to the chapel two by two. Sunday services were always longer, fully-fledged services, usually with a guest preacher from elsewhere, but occasionally Mr Webster, the joint headmaster, took the service. Often a few parents also attended if they were taking their son out for the day. The parents waited outside the chapel entrance while the boys filed in, and as they passed them, they might catch a waft of a mother's perfume. This only helped to remind him of nicer homely things instead of the alien smells of fresh paint and classrooms. It was strange how all the rooms at school had different smells; the classrooms, the gym, the chapel, the dormitories, the library, the billiard room, the dining room, the art room and the model club all had their own special identifying smell, but none of them were like home.

The Sunday morning service always seemed too long, especially if that particular day had been chosen for an exeat. But this being the first Sunday, there were no boys going out that day. There were hymns and prayers, a sermon and another hymn. Luckily Geoffrey had learnt the Lord's prayer by heart so was able to recite it, or it could be said ‘mumble it softly’. He was not so familiar, however, with the creed, but neither were any of the new boys. Bowing his head at the appropriate moment was not something with which he was familiar. When they were on their knees praying, he would silently ask Mummy and Daddy to ‘please come and take me away’. His prayers always seemed to fall on deaf ears and go unanswered. When the service was over, and they left the chapel, those boys who were about to enjoy an exeat would rush to their parents for a hug and a cuddle and off to the car as fast as possible, smiling with happiness, and joy written all over their faces. They were real, happy smiles, unlike those during school time.

After Chapel on Sundays, it was letter writing time for everyone, except of course for those who were enjoying an exeat. Boys were obliged to write a weekly letter to their parents, so they all assembled in the big recreation room where the boys had their lockers. In Geoffrey’s locker, he had his writing paper along with a book or two, his dinky toys and his tuck tin, which at this moment was waiting for his sweet ration from Matron. Out came his Basildon Bond writing paper and envelopes, and after finding a place to sit, he wrote his letter. Carefully at the top, in his best handwriting, he wrote the school address, and then 'Dear Mummy and Daddy', always the same, followed by a few lines describing what had happened and what he had been doing during the week and finishing 'with love from Geoffrey'. As his writing worked down the page, the neatness deteriorated, and the lines became less and less level. All letters were checked by the master on duty before they were allowed to be sent, so Geoffrey took his letter for approval, and the master pointed out any mistakes that he must correct. Once it was accepted, boys were then permitted to make a private addendum, which was not for the eyes of anybody else. There were not many Sundays that Geoffrey didn't add words to the effect 'I am so unhappy here, please take me home'. It must have been devastating for his mother to read this week after week when his letter arrived.

Every day, after lunch, was a rest period which meant sitting quietly reading a book, except on Sundays when the book was exchanged for the Bible, from which all boys had to read, mark, learn and inwardly digest a specified passage.

Junior boys had easier passages to read, but for the senior classes, the last period on Monday afternoons was a test on the piece of scripture they were required to read. These tests took place in the same room where the letters were written. All the senior classes assembled together with their exercise books and pens. When Mr Pont decided that everybody was present and correct, one after another, he fired questions at them, allowing just enough time for the answers to be written. At last, the questions came to an end, but still, there was worse to come. As he went through the questions one by one, he would randomly pick any boy for the answer and that poor boy was not expected to give a wrong answer. If it should so happen, he was chastised in front of the whole assembly. Sometimes when he sat there, Geoffrey knew he had a wrong answer and was petrified that he would be the one to be selected to give the answer; to his chagrin, it often was so. Still, it was not over. When they were finally through with all the questions, Mr Pont would go around the room asking each boy individually how many correct answers he had. In this way, there could again be more embarrassment in front of all the other boys if he did not have a good score. The temptation was to lie, but a spot check, which certainly did happen, could result in even greater chastisement. Later on, Geoffrey came to dread these Monday evening tests, and the more he dreaded them, the worse he performed.

Mondays were bad enough but waiting until the evening was like having the sword of Damocles hanging over him.

For the moment, as a junior, Monday evenings were not so fearful and went by like most other evenings, except for the occasions when it was time for clean underwear. This happened only once a week, as it was assumed that little boys did not suffer unduly from body odour. However, the procedure was such that at bedtime, after they had undressed, their dirty vests and pants were placed in two separate piles in the middle of the dormitory floor. When they were ready for bed with their pyjamas on, they were instructed by Matron to stand at the foot of their beds. The first time this happened, Geoffrey wondered why, but this soon became clear. Matron, ignoring the vests, went straight to the pile of underpants, picked up a pair, spread the waistband and looked inside. This was inspection day.

If a boy was unlucky enough to have not wiped his bottom adequately and left some tell-tale marks in his underpants, Matron looked at the name tag sewn on the waistband and summoned that boy over. She then sent him to the bathroom with his underpants to wash them by hand. Of course, each boy recognised his own underpants and knew in advance if they were clean or dirty, so it was just a matter of time before he saw Matron pick up the offending item and then he knew what was coming. From these performances, all the other boys knew who had made a mess of their underwear. As soon as Geoffrey became familiar with these proceedings, he did his utmost to make sure he would not be embarrassed in front of the rest of the dormitory or teased thereafter by boys chanting 'dirty pants, dirty pants'. Consequently, he always monitored the cleanliness of his underpants and should there be any indiscretion, he did his best to clean it in advance. His method for this was by first locking himself in a toilet cubicle, and then with the help of some wet toilet paper, he did his best to clean away any tell-tale streaks. Luckily this was not so often necessary, but nevertheless, these inspections, like scripture tests on Monday evenings, also became a trauma for him. The underwear inspections became a 'hang-up' that subconsciously developed from this period of his life and never left him.

Chapter 5

With every day passing, he became more familiar with the school routines. And as he mentally ticked off each day, it brought him a little nearer to his first exeat. Soon he could begin to count down the days, but he was never quite sure exactly when he and David were going out, so it was really just a case of surviving until the great day actually arrived.

His very first time out was on a Sunday, and the chapel service that morning seemed to drag on and on whilst his excitement grew and grew. At last, they came out of Chapel, and he rushed round to the lozenge by the front entrance to see if mother and father were there. George had now exchanged the Austin for a larger vehicle, that being a dormobile. What a surge of delight passed through him as he saw the dormobile waiting with his father sitting behind the wheel smoking his pipe. He did not care that most parents arrived in their Jaguars or Alvis' whilst they only had a Bedford dormobile dubbed by Mr Pont as the ice cream van; they named it Polly after mother explained 'poly' meant many and this vehicle could hold many. He was not ashamed of it, and he was probably just as happy to be going home in his van as the other boys were in their Rovers. Just being with his father was enough; for the moment, his loneliness was gone. He and David sat side by side on the front bench seat as they eagerly looked forward to coming home in time for lunch at Griffins. At last, they came into the village, and as they turned into their street, they could see the curved walls with the blue gates marking the entrance to their driveway. At least on their street, no two houses were the same, but theirs was the only one to have such a fine entrance. Most houses just had a break in their front wall through which the owners could drive in and out. Although the gates were never closed, George liked his privacy and had planted a beech hedge behind the wall, which was already taller than most people. Later, this hedge grew a good deal higher than the wall, so they were well protected from prying eyes.

George swung Polly into the entrance and scrunched to a halt in front of the house. This was the moment for which they had been waiting. Thea, who had been busy preparing lunch, came to the door to welcome them whilst at the same time untying her 'pinny', as was her habit whenever anyone came to the door. The emotion of being home again was unforgettable; the delicious aromas of a home roast joint as opposed to the smells that wafted from the school kitchen, the feeling of security when in the familiar environment of home, his home, touching all the familiar things; for the moment it was all so wonderful. It was strange how home now seemed so small after the size of all the rooms at school, but things remained unchanged, still in their places just as they were when they drove away a few weeks ago.

Sunday lunch had always been a special lunch, always a roast of some sort. This Sunday was no exception with roast beef, roast potatoes, brussels sprouts and of course, delicious gravy. No need to worry about any nasty bits that he couldn't eat, and anyway, if there were any, there was no need to worry about leaving them. After lunch, he went up to reunite with his room or the ‘boys’ room’ to which it was referred since David and he always shared a room. There was his cosy bed waiting for him, but it was going to be a few weeks yet before he could enjoy snuggling down in it again. There were all his models and dinky toys; maybe he should take that truck or that tractor back to school this time, he pondered. And that's a nice book, he could show it to Jack. How nice it was to be at home again.

Just as he started to become engrossed and really enjoy being with all his toys in familiar surroundings and not thinking about school, Thea called out to say it was time for tea. She said, “We must have an early tea, darlings, so Daddy can get you back to school in time.” With those words, his stomach turned inside out with just the thought that he must go through the abandonment barrier again. This time he also knew what awaited him; the hard bed with thin blanket and mattress, the hard benches to sit on, and worst of all, no one to love him. But so it was, and after tea, the dreaded moment arrived. Following a quick goodbye kiss from Thea, they reluctantly climbed into Polly again. It seemed as if they had only just got out of the van and now were back in it again. Off they went with a sad wave goodbye. The first landmarks of the journey were almost friendly as they signalled there was still a good distance from school, but soon they became less and less welcome as he knew how close they were coming, until inevitably George turned the dormobile into the school driveway.

Slowly and rather unwillingly, Geoffrey stepped out of the vehicle. George wanted a quick chat with Mr Pont to see how he was getting on, so he and David followed him into the hall where Mr Pont, immaculate as ever in his gold buttoned blazer, awaited them. As they stood there in the middle of the hall on the polished parquet floor discussing Geoffrey and his progress as if he wasn't there, Geoffrey squirmed and studied his shoes. The only good thing about this little meeting was that it prolonged the moment before his father, his last contact with that other world, would leave again. According to the headmaster, he was doing well and had settled in nicely. Little did he know, thought Geoffrey. It wasn't long before George made his exit; a quick hug and a kiss, and off he drove, not to be seen for another few weeks. His father was never very demonstrative with his affection, and it wasn't long before the kisses stopped and just a quick hug sufficed. Later that too disappeared, and all that was left was a rather formal handshake.

Now it was time for the evening service in Chapel. This service, every Sunday evening, was for Geoffrey the most painful and emotional experience, and if he had been out for the day on an exeat, it was even more devastating. Invariably the chosen hymn was John Ellerton's 'The day thou gavest Lord is ended'. Mr Webster sat at the organ and played the introduction. Geoffrey did not take much notice of the words of most hymns, except for this one and the moment it started, the lump in Geoffrey's throat became so big he felt he could hardly breathe; not a sound could he utter as in vain he tried at least to mouth the words. As if he needed reminding that the day and the weekend was over, he was back at school away from his mother and father and tomorrow there were lessons again. He began to realise that he was destined to live a life of uncertainty. All manner of thoughts came to the surface at this moment, mostly all the forthcoming events he dreaded. Just now, he was really only missing home, but when he was a little further up the school, all the things he dreaded added to his plight and at the top of the list of things he feared most was the Monday evening scripture test.

Eventually, the days turned to weeks, and weeks turned to months, and as the end of term approached, so did his birthday. Because it was at the beginning of December, it always fell in term time, unlike the rest of his siblings who could celebrate at home. Apart from Mr Pont wishing him a happy birthday, it was more or less just another day except that Thea usually came to the school in the afternoon with some presents and a birthday cake. It was, of course, wonderful to see his mother again, if only for an hour, but as usual, he also had to say goodbye again. At least it was only a short time before the end of term, which took away some of the pain.

Whenever there was a birthday, there was always a cake. Many boys with wealthy parents had fancy cakes from Harrods made like a football pitch or a billiard table. At supper time, birthday cakes were duly shared out, first of all to the headmaster, then to all the boys at the birthday table and lastly to any other friends who sat elsewhere. Needless to say, it was a real treat to have such a cake, so everybody was suddenly your best friend. Thea did her best with her homemade cakes, although on a couple of occasions, it was a trifle embarrassing for Geoffrey. Once, as a surprise, she wrapped some little elephants in grease-proof paper and baked them in the cake. For every birthday, Mr Pont always came into the dining hall for the sole purpose of being offered a slice of the cake. When Geoffrey offered his cake to Mr Pont, it happened that just the slice he chose contained one of these elephants, which disappeared into his mouth with his first bite. Not knowing what it was, he surreptitiously and politely removed it from his mouth. Having thought that his mother had by mistake left the piece of paper in the cake mix, out of politeness, he kept quiet about it and discarded it elsewhere. When another elephant turned up in another slice, he realised his mistake and retrieved it from the waste bin. On another occasion, the middle of the cake was not quite properly baked, which resulted in many boys struggling to digest it, and sadly the following supper, nobody was interested in what was left of his birthday cake, and all the best friends suddenly weren't anymore.

At last, joy of joys, the end of term was in sight, and the school started practising Christmas carols and rehearsing the school pantomime. In addition, there were form plays performed by every class. The performance level of the various classes reflected the level of interest shown by the respective form masters. Different masters specialised in different subjects, but each class had one master appointed as form master. One year it was the music master who was appointed as Geoffrey's form master. He endeavoured to make a short play out of the 'cockles and mussels' Molly Malone song. Since singing was not Geoffrey's best asset, he was given the role of both Molly Malone and her ghost.

All he had to do was shout 'cockles' and then 'mussels'. The rest of the class sang the song, and at the appropriate moment, after they sang 'Alive alive'oh, alive alive'oh, crying…' then Molly shouted 'Cockles', and 'Mussels' and the chorus would finish with 'Alive alive'oh' once more. This should have been quite straightforward. The living Molly would slowly wheel a wheelbarrow, apparently full of cockles and mussels, across the stage and back again while the rest of the class dutifully sang the song. When Molly had sadly passed away, and it was time for her ghost, it was the same procedure again, but this time it was the ghost who wheeled the wheelbarrow. In rehearsal, it was all relatively easy and went rather well. However, the rehearsals were done without costumes. When it was time for the actual performance, Mr Mills, the music master, produced an old bed sheet with which he planned to transform Geoffrey into a ghost by throwing it over his head and tying it round his middle. There was, unfortunately, a drawback in that when mummified in the sheet, he could see absolutely nothing, but all he had to do was walk straight across the stage guided by his wheelbarrow. So, the curtains went up, and the song began. Everything went smoothly, according to plan, and playing the part of the still-living Molly, he wheeled his wheelbarrow slowly across the stage and shouted 'cockles' and 'mussels' at just the right moment. Having traversed the stage and now back again in the wings where he started, Mr

Mills quickly threw the sheet over his head and tied it loosely around the middle. Unfortunately, after his return from the first crossing, the wheelbarrow was now facing the wrong way, but with the sheet over his head, he was unable to see that the handles were at the other end. However, his main objective right now was to be out on the stage at the right moment to shout his lines. Not only could he not see, but it was necessary to fumble through the sheet to try to grasp the wheelbarrow. The audience found it hilarious as he endeavoured to push the wretched wheelbarrow backwards across the stage whilst wrapped up in a sheet. Not enjoying being ridiculed, Geoffrey had difficulty in sharing their humour and added to this, it gave cause for some severe teasing by the other boys.

At last, the end of term arrived; his trunk was packed and his little brown overnight suitcase on which George had stencilled his name, lay on his bed ready to go home. The excitement was almost too much, breakfast was nigh impossible to swallow, and the idea that at last, he would be back in his lovely cosy home for more than just a day was overwhelming. This sensation, a mixture of anticipation, excitement and pleasure, never changed throughout his school career, and to this day, Geoffrey still experiences these same feelings when returning home from travelling.

Back at home, after the autumn term, it was usually only a day or two before Christmas, which raised the excitement level again. Never a thought just now, that the days were already disappearing before it was back to school again; that was a long way off. On Christmas Eve, everyone was busy doing their last-minute Christmas shopping and wrapping presents ready to be given the next day. Thea was busy in the kitchen preparing the turkey and making ready the Christmas pudding. She always made these puddings some weeks in advance, and at the time of making them, each member of the family, one by one, made a wish while they stirred the pudding mix. The mix, being rather stiff, required two little hands to make a successful stir with the wooden spoon.

When bedtime arrived on Christmas Eve, Geoffrey and David would each hang an old sock at the end of their beds, ready to be filled by Father Christmas. Before they started at boarding school David and he were firm believers in Father Christmas, and a week or two in advance, they wrote a wish list of presents they wanted on a piece of loo paper and sent these lists up the chimney. Loo paper was used as it was nice and light, so the heat of the fire lifted it quickly up to the heavens above. Occasionally they failed to catch the upward draught and fell back into the flames, which very quickly engulfed them. New lists were duly written as it was very important to tell Father Christmas what they would like. When it was time for David to start boarding school, George and Thea considered it might be best to tell him that actually, Father Christmas didn't exist. They didn't want to spoil his fantasy, but it was purely to avoid any unnecessary teasing if other boys thought that he was still a believer. Once the news had been broken to David, it, of course, wasn't long before David brought Geoffrey up to date. Believers or not, lying in bed in the dark, he and David talked and talked; sleep was far from their minds as they were anxious to stay awake long enough to catch Father Christmas filling their stockings which they had hung on the ends of their beds. Eventually, there came shouts from the sitting room below, "Stop talking, boys!" They lowered their voices to a whisper but that was short-lived as the volume soon escalated to the same level again. "Go to sleep, boys!" shouted George again. Eventually, they both fell asleep which at last allowed their father to creep in and fill their stockings. To save filling them in the dark in situ, he actually had the matching sock of each of their pairs which he and Thea had filled beforehand, so all that was necessary was just to exchange the socks.

Sometime in the night, they were woken by their own excitement, and David called across to Geoffrey, "Geoff, are you awake?" which, of course, if he wasn't already awake, he now was. "Has Father Christmas been?" he asked.

“Yes, I think I can see balloons!” Geoffrey’s imagination was running wild. Even at this hour, the excitement meant that all they wanted to do was to discover what lay in wait in their stockings, but George had given them express instructions not to open anything until the morning. But ‘morning’ to the boys was not necessarily ‘morning’ to their parents.

“Is it light outside?” asked David,

“I can't see any light,” replied Geoffrey, since there wasn't even a hint of moonlight, but David was determined that it was time enough.

“Yes there, between the curtains, I'm sure that's light,” he said and climbed out of bed to peer through the curtains. After a moment or two, he continued to try and justify himself and said,

“Behind the Westfield’s, there is a bit of light!” And that was enough to convince him that morning had arrived, and they could start opening their stockings. There is nothing much darker than a moonless December night and the fact that it was only four o'clock in the morning did not deter them. So, without any further ado, they put on their bedside lights, scrambled to the end of their beds and took hold of their stockings. These were always filled the same way, even seventy years later when, out of tradition, George made a stocking for Thea, his method never differed. At the very bottom of the stocking was a 'half-a-crown' and a tangerine, followed by some small toys while the top was adorned with some crackers and two or three balloons. On this particular Christmas morning, David had a clockwork boat which he was quick to wind up and test. The ensuing noise when the propeller was released directly woke their parents who slept in the bedroom next to theirs.

"What is going on, boys? It is far too early to get up. Go back to bed at once and wait until the morning – and no more talking!"

Thankfully, since it was Christmas, George didn't vent his wrath to its full extent.

At last, it was morning, and like every winter morning George came in, drew the curtains and switched on the electric fire. On ordinary days the boys climbed out of bed and sat in their pyjamas huddled in front of the fire. On frosty mornings there was often ice on the inside of the windows. But this morning there was no ice and he and David were far more occupied comparing the contents of their stockings. They excitedly showed their parents what Father Christmas had given them, oblivious to the fact that they of course knew exactly what they had put in their children's stockings. But their main present, which provoked the most anticipation was yet to come. First, though, was breakfast. Never did they devour their breakfast so quickly as on this day knowing that all their best presents were waiting for them. When breakfast was cleared away and all the Christmas gifts were placed on the table, they, first of all, tried to guess what was inside the wrapping by feeling the shape. Then they began opening, quickly creating a mass of wrapping paper and cartons with cries of "Oh it is just what I wanted!" and "Thank you, Mummy, and thank you, Daddy." George was busy trying to make a note of who gave what to who, so that when it came to writing the thank you letters, they thanked the right people for the right presents. Amongst the presents they could always rely on an envelope from each of their grandmothers containing a little money; at this stage, a one-pound note, later to grow to a five-pound note as they became older and to keep up with inflation. In their thank you letters they could relate to Gran or Granny what they had spent it on or what they were still planning to buy.

Days passed much too quickly, and it was not long before the first real reminder came when they had to try on school clothes to see which ones still fitted. But still, there were a few more days of freedom before the return to school. No matter how hard he tried to forget that the day was nearing, the thought was always there in the back of his mind. Having survived his first term, he now knew what was coming, which made it even worse and just the idea of going back provoked a dreadful ache in his stomach. However, another visit to Miss Motts for their tuck supply and back to school it was. Usually, it was only his father who drove him back to school often accompanied by his sister Clare. This always made him insanely jealous when he saw her sitting snugly and smugly next to father as they drove away leaving him alone. But this time both George and Thea travelled with them, which probably made the moment of separation even worse and he just could not hold back the tears.

"Be a brave boy now, darling. There'll soon be an exeat." Said Thea, also trying not to cry. It probably upset his mother as much as it did himself.

Now he was in another dormitory and tomorrow he started in the third form. Many of the same boys from the last term were also in this dormitory so that made it a little easier as at least there were some familiar faces and they could chat a little about what had happened in their holidays. There was his bed in the corner, he recognised it at once by the colours of the travel rug. A different washroom now and new places for mugs and towels. Quickly he said his prayers and climbed into the cold hard bed. The first night was always the worst. How he longed for home. Curled up tight to keep warm, sleep eventually overtook him.

Form three was an unwelcoming room with a high ceiling and always a little chilly. Owing to its location, sandwiched between the gym and the boot locker room, never could a ray of sunshine find its way in, which seemed to reflect on the atmosphere of this class. The luxury of female teachers had passed. From now on, it was only masters with varying degrees of strictness. Every boy had his own desk in which he kept all his exercise books and textbooks. The slightly sloping top was hinged at the front just behind a ledge on which pens could be laid. When this top was lifted all the way up, by bending forward as if looking for something within, a boy could hide behind it and be out of sight of the master. This was useful if contact with one's neighbour was needed. Boys in this class were not old enough to dare to misbehave or 'lark around', but they were also too young to endure the harshness of the masters. Back in form two, there was never any mental or physical abuse, but now things were different, and it was not unusual to be chastised with the sharp edge of a ruler or just a hard hand to the head.

In Geoffrey's class was a slightly overweight boy called Dawson who was not in the best of health because he was suffering from a rather unpleasant boil on the back of his neck, probably due to the lack of vitamins in the school food. Just to tilt his head forward caused him a great deal of discomfort and indeed pain. Unfortunately for him he was rather near the bottom of the class so often had bad marks and frequently was unable to answer questions directed at him by masters. Latin certainly was not his best subject and when he failed yet again to give the right answer the master called him out to treat his backside to the sharp edge of his ruler. To receive this punishment, it was necessary to bend over so that the grey flannel of his shorts was drawn tight across his buttocks. Naturally, he protested, complaining that because of his boil it was too painful to bend forward. Sadistically, the master quickly realised that to make him do just that, was a more effective punishment.

"Bend over, boy!" he demanded.

"No, please, Sir, it hurts."

"That's the meaning, now bend over."

"Please, Sir…"

"Bend over!" shouted the master, whose patience was over.

With cries of pain, he finally bowed forward, causing the boil to erupt. With tears running down his face and the contents of the boil running down his neck, he was dismissed from the class and sent to Matron to have it dressed.

Having graduated from the second form, where he managed quite well being in the top half of the class as opposed to the bottom half, Geoffrey now found it was much harder to hold his own, and some subjects were particularly difficult. Probably Miss Turner's teaching had held him in good stead up to the level of form two, but now everything was new and not so easy. The fact that all the other boys in his class were a year ahead of him only added to his struggle. But his father was still hoping for him to win a scholarship.

The only lesson, if it could be called a lesson, that he really enjoyed was PT. He later learned this stood for physical training; a far cry from 'music and movement'. In the gym were two climbing ropes, a gymnastics box horse, a springboard, medicine balls and mats for forward rolls and other groundwork. He never did know how the medicine balls earned their name but for him, they were just medicine balls. It didn't take long before he discovered that PT was something at which he was one of the best. How or why, he didn't know but it just came naturally to him; he could climb the ropes, do forward rolls, or spring from the springboard over the horse. He was never afraid to try, unlike some of the heavier boys who ran full tilt at the box horse but at the last minute were too frightened to make the jump, and like an equestrian refusing a fence they unsuccessfully endeavoured to stop, resulting in an enormous collision with the box horse. Anyway, he was always delighted when he knew he had PT as one of the day's lessons. It was an escape from the agony of sitting in a classroom.

It wasn't until higher up in the school that they were taught by Mr Pont. His lessons were the most dreaded of all.

Mr Pont taught mathematics, more easily referred to as maths, and if you weren't one of his favourites or were not so good at maths then your life was far from pleasant. In the meantime, however, Geoffrey worked his way through the fourth forms with varying degrees of misery, as his struggle to keep up became harder and harder. Sometimes he was so terrified by the forthcoming lesson or test that at whatever cost it just had to be avoided. One ploy he used was to hide in the lavatories until the lesson was over. Naturally, he was soon missed in the class, so eventually, while he sat locked in a cubicle in his self-imposed solitude, he heard the outer door open and a voice call his name "Finch are you there?"

"Yes, Sir," he replied timidly, immediately recognising which master it was.

"What are you doing there?" he asked. Normally that would be a rather stupid question, but not in this instance.

"I've got a tummy ache," he lied.

"You better come out and go to Matron," came the order.

"Yes, Sir." So he pulled up his shorts, flushed the loo unnecessarily and came out.

"You must tell us if you have a stomachache. You can't just go and hide in the lavatory!" He was actually a bit sympathetic. By the time Matron had finished with him, having not surprisingly been unable to find anything wrong and sent him back to the classroom, the lesson was at an end, and his mission was accomplished. Unfortunately, this ploy could not be used too often.

Although hiding in the lavatory was more of a 'one off' situation, he found that illness was a very useful means of avoiding school. During his struggling days which seemed to be most of the time, waking up on a Monday morning and contemplating what lay ahead became a trauma. The result of this was that he invented earache on rather many Monday mornings. During this period though he actually did have a problem with earache and sore throats, the result of which being that nearly the whole of one school holiday was taken up with the removal of his tonsils. However, having decided that it was necessary to act sick on a particular Monday before it was time to get up, he lay with his ear pressed down on the pillow so that it might appear a little inflamed. Even though it wasn't particularly comfortable, he kept this going until the day's first bell rang signalling time for the boys to wipe the sleep from their eyes and start the day. This was the crucial moment when he had to say that he was not well. The dormitory captain then summoned Matron who took his temperature. This was difficult to cheat but invariably his symptoms were accepted, and he was told to stay in bed. Later on, the doctor came and used his various instruments to look into his ears and down his throat. Because he often did have a little inflammation, the doctor, playing it safe, sentenced him to bed for a couple of days and off games for a couple more. So were many Monday tests avoided. If a stay in bed for more than a day was necessary, the patient was moved into the sick room. Unfortunately, or perhaps fortunately he spent a fair amount of time in there which was good for him but not particularly helpful for his schoolwork.

After the Easter holiday, both mother and father took him back to school. Standing in the corridor outside his new dormitory the dreaded time for goodbye finally arrived. Up until now stiff upper lip had always prevailed and tears were kept at bay, but this time he could not control them; they just welled up and ashamedly he clung to his mother and cried. Eventually, after much consoling, with Thea also working hard to hold back the tears and hide her emotions, they both departed and left Geoffrey sitting on his bed preparing for bedtime.

This term, his bed was in the 'blue' dormitory, which meant yet another washroom with a new set of pegs on which to hang towels and clothes and a new tooth mug, all correctly labelled 'Finch minor'. At last, all the uncertainty was put aside and along with his dormitory comrades they climbed into bed. One bed remained empty which belonged to the dormitory captain. He, a Jewish boy named Levine, arrived just as they were all about to fall asleep, but in the half light, and with one eye they peeked out from under their blankets and watched him get ready for bed. As Levine undressed, Geoffrey could not help noticing that his underpants were very different to his own, not at all loose and flappy. Perhaps that was what older boys wore, he thought to himself, but why he noticed this, he did not know. Since the dormitory captain was from the top dormitories his bedtime was later than the boys under his watch, so by the time he was in bed, sleep had overtaken the younger boys.

In the middle of the night Geoffrey suddenly awoke and without warning, as he turned onto his front from his curled up, foetal position, his stomach decided to disgorge its contents and he threw up, filling the bed with vomit. The combination of the poor springs and thin mattress meant that the bed sagged in the middle forming a kind of trough causing the vomit to collect in the middle and run slowly down to where he now desperately tried to avoid lying. Directly, Levine the dormitory captain, summoned Matron. After changing the sheet and with a new pillow and clean pyjamas it was back to bed. All this took place in semi-darkness with everybody trying not to disturb the rest of the sleeping children. Morning came, Matron took his temperature and ordered him to stay in bed until the doctor arrived. This was a good start to the term.

Geoffrey languished in bed listening to all the familiar but forgotten noises of the school starting up for the first morning’s breakfast. Lying alone in the dormitory with all the other beds empty made him feel even smaller and lost than ever. Unlike a bedroom, the dormitory was so big and cold and not the least bit cosy. It wasn't until halfway through the morning that the doctor arrived to make his examination. After listening through his stethoscope to Geoffrey's chest from the front and then again on his back and feeling his tummy, he made his diagnosis. Geoffrey had measles. The onslaught of the sickness lay behind his inability to hold back the tears the evening before. Where he had picked up this disease was not to be known, but for the school, it was not a welcome beginning to the term. Everything must be done to prevent an epidemic. Consequently, no time was wasted in moving him into isolation in the sickroom. In order to stop it from spreading throughout the school, it was decided that he should be sent home again until fully recovered. In one fell swoop, his sadness was replaced by gladness and he could scarcely believe his luck that already he could go home again. Matron came into the sick room and told him that his mother was going to come and collect him the next day. Geoffrey was so elated he didn’t think he could possibly wait so long, and if it hadn’t been for the measles he would have been jumping for joy, but the measles had sapped much of his energy so it wasn’t long before exhaustion took over and he fell asleep. The next morning, he went through all the normal sick room procedures, temperature taken, wash, clean teeth, brush hair and back into bed for school breakfast on a tray. All was going well, and his excitement level was rising in anticipation of the arrival of his mother. However, halfway through the morning, Matron came into the sickroom and in her unsubtle way, announced to Geoffrey, "Finch, I'm afraid you won't be going home after all. Your sister has chickenpox, so you don't want to go down with that as well now do you?" Poor Geoffrey could hardly believe his ears; in seconds his whole world had fallen apart and he was utterly devastated. All the excitement and anticipation disappeared instantly, and he burst into tears. He cried and cried but there was no one there to console him. Slowly the shock of the terrible news began to wear off as he struggled to get used to the idea that he was not going home. His mother tried to make up for his dashed hopes by sending him a postcard every day. Now it was only these that brought a little happiness to him and even though they reminded him of home, he couldn't wait for their arrival every morning and he read them over and over again, but they were a poor substitute for recuperation at home. Eventually, the doctor decided he was better and that it was safe for him to return to normal school life again.

As he moved up through the school, lessons became harder and school life became tougher and tougher. In the fourth forms, his French teacher was Mr Brooks. Mr Brooks or ‘Brooky’ as he was commonly known, was a rather portly figure who smoked heavily. He always had with him a round tin of ‘Players Senior Service’ untipped cigarettes which he smoked endlessly throughout the lessons. Whenever entering the classroom his tin of cigarettes was the first thing he placed on his desk. As with most of his classes, Geoffrey was nearer to the bottom than the top; he was certainly not one of the best at French and his failure to answer a question that Brooky considered easy, invariably resulted in him being chastised and made an example of in front of the class. After one such chastisement, which took place just before lunch, it also happened that by coincidence Brooky was the master sitting at the head of Geoffrey's table that lunchtime. At one end sat Brooky and at the other end of the table sat Geoffrey still reeling from being ridiculed. His presence inspired Geoffrey to say to the boy next to him “I hate Brooky, I'd like to hit him.” Out of spite, this boy repeated it to his neighbour saying “Pass it on, pass it on” and so it went from boy to boy all the way down the table until it finally came to the ears of Mr Brooks himself. In return, he sent a message back to tell Finch that he must come and see him in the library after lunch. A little while later, lunch over and doing as he was told, he stood there obediently waiting in the library. It wasn't necessary to wait long before Mr Brooks came in and said “Now Finch, what did you say you wanted to do?”

"Nothing, Sir," replied Geoffrey.

"That's not what I heard. I'll ask again, what did you want to do?"

Barely audibly, he said, "I want to hit you, Sir."

"Speak up! What did you say?" he demanded with his dark smoker's voice, the effort nearly prompting a fit of coughing.

"I want to hit you, Sir," replied Geoffrey, a little louder this time.

Opening his jacket, revealing his tobacco reeking shirt stretched tight over his large stomach, he ordered, "Hit me then!"

There he stood, towering over Geoffrey with his stomach at eye level, demanding to be hit. To hit someone without provocation was not something Geoffrey had encountered, and he was baffled as to how he could escape this situation.

"Hit me!" he ordered again.

Tentatively Geoffrey threw a feeble punch at the great expanse of shirt holding in his stomach. Even before his tiny fist had made contact, he was dealt such a blow he thought his head had been knocked clean off. Through the ringing in his ears, Geoffrey heard him ask, "Do you want to hit me again?"

"No, Sir," he spluttered through his tears as he desperately tried not to cry.

"Good, then never let me hear such nonsense again and now go away." Geoffrey ran out of the library as fast as he could and with his head still resounding from the smite he was dealt, he took himself away to a quiet corner to recover.

So Geoffrey slogged his way through the lessons graduating slowly from class to class. The fourth and fifth forms were situated upstairs in what was once an old coach house, converted into classrooms. The partitioning walls were very thin made primarily of hardboard supported by wooden ribs. When a voice was raised by a master in one classroom it could be heard clearly from one classroom to another. All the classes had black boards and white chalk and it was not uncommon, most often when drawing a line, for the chalk to create the most fearful screech which was almost worse than scraping fingernails down the board. For wiping the board clean there was a special 'board duster' which actually was just a wooden block with thick layered felt fixed on edge on one side which performed the actual cleaning. The English master, Mr Davids, was mostly quite a calm unaggressive man, but only up to a point as the rest of the class found out during the course of one lesson. It happened that Mr Davids was also quite an accomplished cricketer with a very powerful throw. During one of his lessons, a pupil was not paying attention and was duly reprimanded. The boy in question did not seem to take heed of the scolding and continued with his non-attentive activities. Now this made Mr Davids become quite angry and finally he raised his voice and shouted at the boy. However, this still had no effect, and shortly after, for the third time, the boy carried on misbehaving. When Mr Davids addressed him again the boy was so engrossed in his other activity that he did not even hear and neither did he answer. That was enough. Mr Davids' limit had been reached. He picked up the board duster and hurled it at the boy. Whether he meant to hit the boy or not, it was lucky that the board duster missed; it crashed into the thin wall with such force that it made a hole, almost right through. Had it contacted the boy's head it probably would have knocked him unconscious.

It was in the English lessons that Geoffrey started with a little surreptitious cheating. In the main, English was one of his better subjects but sometimes, if it didn't go so well, Geoffrey had developed a method to improve his situation. Often Mr Davids would give them a little test which meant that his questions were verbal, but the answers were to be written in the exercise books. When it was finished, they answered the questions round the class according to the answers they had written down. Finally, they counted up their correct answers and reported these to Mr Davids.

Answers were written in ink with a fountain pen, but correcting, which the boys did themselves, was made with a pencil. Each boy had his own desk, at the front of which was a groove to stop pens or pencils from rolling away. Geoffrey realised that if he made a little puddle of ink there, just as the test was finishing, it was then possible to dip his pencil into the ink and adjust his answers accordingly. This worked quite well until it came to exam time at the end of term, when such cheating was not possible, and he had to rely on what he had learned. Mr Davids was always surprised that Geoffrey's exam results were far below those he had apparently achieved during the term.

Chapter 6

In the fourth forms, it had become more and more difficult to keep up. The more he struggled the further he fell behind. The further he fell behind the more he feared every lesson and the more he longed for home. But home was a long way away. His only contact with home was via his Sunday letters which contained even more reports of bullying, misery and 'please take me away' messages. In return, every week he received a letter from his mother; hardly ever from his father and it was nearly always the same; a few lines of home news and then a quick ending with 'from your loving Mummy'. As a child, Thea had been naturally left-handed but under the control of her governess, she was made to write with her right hand, reverting back to her left hand after she had finished school. After changing from one to the other and back again the result was a very special script. To make matters worse, the lines of her letters always sloped downwards on the right, and progressively so as she continued down the page. The end result was not easy to decipher but nevertheless, Geoffrey could barely wait for their arrival even though it always seemed they had been written in a hurry and that they were seldom more than one page.

In the meantime, Mr Pont was still trying to keep Geoffrey up to scholarship level which meant that he had to struggle on, in classes a year ahead of his level. Classes were made up of around fifteen pupils and in most subjects, Geoffrey was seldom higher than tenth and mostly nearer to the bottom. Some of the masters were of the belief that information could be beaten into boys. On many occasions, Geoffrey's head was the recipient of a wallop from a master's hard hand especially that of Mr Whitely, who wore a heavy ring which substantially increased the pain. He had a habit of setting a test and then patrolling around the class looking over the shoulders of the boys. If he didn't like what he saw, he questioned the boy's answer and then invariably delivered a mighty blow to the boy's head. On other occasions, if a boy was unable to give the right answer or was found guilty of some other misdemeanour he was made to stand on his chair. The chairs, made of tubular steel were rather unstable, making it really quite difficult to stand still, which in turn could provoke further punishment. If the ignominy of standing on the chair was not enough then sometimes the victim was required to pull up a trouser leg of his shorts exposing the fleshy part of his thigh which was then struck with a resounding slap, hard enough to leave a clear imprint of the hand that dealt the blow.

For some boys, history lessons with Mr Thomas were enjoyable, but not for Geoffrey. Mr Thomas, also known as 'whisker', due to the mass of long hairs protruding from his nose, mostly droned on and on, relating to his pupils the dates of various battles or treaties, but very little as to what they were about, so Geoffrey never understood the significance of all these battles or even what a treaty was. The result of this was that very little stayed in Geoffrey's head. To supplement his efforts to inspire the boys into remembering all these historical dates of apparent importance, he would test them with his 'cards'. This meant a mass of grubby pieces of cardboard were produced on which he had written various questions such as 'what date was the battle of Agincourt?' The questions went round the form and when a correct answer was given then Mr Thompson would flick the card and send it spinning towards the boy. At the end of the lesson, each boy counted how many cards he had which usually for Geoffrey was not many. The only thing that he found interesting was when Mr Thomas related about being a prisoner of war. Prisoners were occasionally allowed to send letters home, but all their letters were vetted by the Germans so that no strategic information was divulged. In order to convey information back to their homeland, the British prisoners devised certain methods and codes. When prisoners planned to try to escape they disguised the letters S K P when they were allowed to send a letter to their family or friends. The guards did not realise that this meant 'escapee'.

Geography with Commander Bentley was even more boring. With terrible squeaking of the chalk, setting everybody's teeth on edge, all he did was draw maps on the blackboard, sometimes to show rivers and sometimes to show cities. The boys were meant to copy these and then be able to reproduce them from memory. If he had made the topics even remotely interesting, then they were far more easily remembered, such as when he told about two major towns in France being like a Frenchman's trousers, namely Toulon and Toulouse.

In his efforts to make Geoffrey improve his class work, Mr Pont put him on a report system known as 'satis' reports. This meant that after every lesson, the unfortunate owner of a 'satis' book needed to obtain comment and signature from the appropriate master. There was always hope that the master would write 'satis' or even something better, but more often than not, it was something like 'must try harder'. For those boys who were not performing so well in the classroom and especially those already on satis reports, Friday lunch times were something to be feared. As lunch drew to a close, Mr Pont would make his entrance clutching his paperwork at the ready. He would make his address, inform everybody of forthcoming events or any new rules and then lastly came the moment everybody dreaded. From his papers, he pulled forth a list of names and then announced, "I want to see the following boys in my study after lunch." If your name was on the list, it was time to start becoming nervous. One such Friday, Geoffrey's name was there as usual, but Geoffrey was already on a satis report from the previous week, and this week, it did not read well, with most comments reading 'poor' or 'must do better'. With his report in his hand and his skinny little knees knocking with fear, Geoffrey waited outside Mr Pratt's office. "Next" came the call from inside, and he ventured into the lion's den. Mr Pratt's room smelt of tobacco and aftershave, and there was just a trace of cigarette smoke hanging in the air. He sat in his swivel chair with his back to the door, and as Geoffrey entered, he gestured that he should come and stand beside him. Never ever did a boy sit.

"Let me see your satis report," he said, taking it from Geoffrey's hand. As he thumbed through the pages, reading day after day all the 'unsatis' remarks, his moustache bristled, and he said, "This is not good enough, is it Finch?" as if to obtain Geoffrey's approval for punishment.

"No, Sir," he replied.

"What are we going to do to improve this?"

"I don't know, Sir," said Geoffrey shakily.

"And what's this?" he paused while he looked to see who had written it, and then continued, "from Mr Thomas, 'does not pay attention'?"

"But I was, Sir," Geoffrey retorted.

"Not according to Mr Thomas. It strikes me, you are not trying hard enough. If you want a scholarship, you must do better, Finch; let's see if this will help you to pay attention and try harder. Bend over the chair." In the corner of his study stood an umbrella stand, and from this, he pulled out a cane, a thin, flexible item. The headmaster moved behind Geoffrey and told him to stay still. As he clutched onto the chair, not quite knowing what to expect, all of a sudden, with a swish, he heard the cane cutting through the air a fraction of a second before striking the little round spheres of his buttocks. Luckily, he had been allowed to keep his shorts and underpants on, so he had a little protection, but when the cane struck, the sting, which came a split second after the contact, was vicious, and he let out a yelp. Again, the swish and again the sting; all Geoffrey wanted to do was rub his backside. Never had he ever been beaten like this. Even his father on occasion had spanked him with his hand but never as hard, and when he did, his mother would say to him, "Not too hard, George, not too hard." But the humiliation was greater than the burning on his behind, and as he tried to rub the pain away, he burst into tears. He blubbed. Mr Pont put away his cane, came over to him and gave him a cuddle. At this moment, Mr Pont was his worst enemy, so even though he was deprived of affection, he was loathe to be cuddled by his chastiser. Just then, all he wanted was to be held and loved but not like this; now he was confused. To be beaten like that and seconds later to be cuddled by the same person just didn't make sense. This was his first taste of being beaten, but unfortunately, not his last.

At about this time, he was perpetually at war with Pearcey, whose arm was now fully recovered. He was forever trying to bully Geoffrey both physically and mentally, and being the larger of the two, much to Geoffrey's chagrin, he was usually fairly successful with the physical bullying. The two boys were always fighting, and Geoffrey was nearly always the one who came off worst. This continued week after week until eventually Geoffrey had so much anger built up inside that he had to find a way to get his revenge. In the end, he asked Mr Dorsey, the PT master, if they could have a boxing match. This was duly arranged, and soon after, during a break between lessons, Pearcey and he and their respective supporters assembled in the gym. Benches were set out to form a boxing ring, and Mr Dorsey gave each of them a pair of boxing gloves which their 'seconds' laced up for them. Now they were ready for the big fight.

Geoffrey had no boxing skills whatsoever, and thanks to Pearcey's earlier car accident, neither was boxing one of his pastimes. However, with Mr Darcy as judge, it was 'seconds away, round one', and the two ill-matched boys started slugging away at each other. Geoffrey didn't know if the onlookers were cheering or not, but whilst engrossed in the fight, all he heard was a ringing in his ears when Pearcey landed a punch. Pearcey was just a little overweight, so he already had an advantage over Geoffrey's skinny little frame, and apart from being of greater stature, he also had a longer reach. It was not long before Geoffrey was on the receiving end of many more blows than he had delivered. While he attempted to land punches to Pearcey's nether regions, Pearcey had no problems bashing away at Geoffrey's unprotected head. Bang, suddenly a punch landed fair and square as Geoffrey took a direct hit on his nose, which started it bleeding and caused his eyes to water so much that he could barely see his target. *Pling, pling,* the bell signalled the end of round one, and as he sat in his corner with his eyes watering, Geoffrey was determined to be brave and not lose face, so he made a point of saying to his seconds, "I'm not crying, it's just because of my nose." He was, in fact, on the verge of tears, and some of the moisture in his eyes was not only due to the punch. So they punched and clinched and bashed away for two more rounds until Mr Dorsey diplomatically declared it a draw. Once their gloves were removed, they shook hands, and strange as it may seem from that moment on, Pearcey and Geoffrey were best friends.

During this battle through the fourth forms, living on a knife-edge, the terms came and went, and the exeats came and went, but far too seldom. In the middle of the summer term, a long weekend exeat was scheduled for the whole school. How lovely Geoffrey found it to be home for more than one day. Even though no matter how hard he tried just to enjoy the moment, and obliterate school from his mind, sometimes the thought of returning to school life just popped into his head and completely upset the enjoyment of being at home, particularly now, while he was still floundering around at the bottom of the class, suffering punishment after punishment. Always at the back of his mind was the daunting thought of hard benches and thin mattresses.

So as the day to return to school approached, Geoffrey decided to use the sickness ploy as a means of prolonging the exeat. Some hours before he was supposed to leave, he went up to the bathroom. Anyone standing in the garden, if they looked up to the bathroom window, could see who was there, and it was part of Geoffrey's plan to be seen in the bathroom. His father, as usual, was busy in the garden, so Geoffrey hoped he would spot him there, which would add some weight to his claims of feeling ill. After a little while of acting sick in the bathroom, he went back downstairs and found his mother.

"Mummy, I'm not feeling very well. I feel really sick," he lied.

"Oh darling, when did this come on?" she asked.

"A little while ago, I was in the bathroom. My tummy feels funny."

"We better put you to bed and see if it gets better," she said, probably knowing it was all concocted. So the last few hours of his freedom were spent tucked up in bed with the curtains drawn in the middle of a lovely sunny afternoon. But even this was better than going back to that dreadful institution.

Sometime later, Thea returned to his bedroom and opened the curtains.

"How are you feeling now, darling?"

It happened that he had actually developed a bout of heartburn. As this was the first time in his life he had experienced heartburn, he replied, "A bit better now, but I have a sort of burning in my throat."

"Oh, have you, darling, I wonder what that can be. I'll talk to Daddy, but I think you better stay at home another day," she said as she felt his brow. With this news, he was elated. Another day at home, how wonderful. His fake illness had worked even though he suspected that they – his mother and father – knew all along there was nothing wrong with him. Or perhaps, as he was often troubled with sore throats and earache, they considered it best to play it safe and give him the benefit of the doubt.

At about this stage in his early school years, it was decided that owing to these endless bouts of colds and sore throats, Geoffrey should have his tonsils removed. In actual fact, this should have been done quite some years earlier. So, at the very start of one Easter holiday, he was bustled into the Evelyn nursing home, a private nursing home situated on the way into Cambridge. As in many things, his father was thorough about making sure that should any of the family be in ill health, they would be taken care of in the best possible way. Consequently, it wasn't necessary to place Geoffrey in a crowded ward in an ordinary hospital; he could enjoy the benefits of a private nursing home. It all happened rather fast, into the nursing home late one afternoon, and although at this stage he felt fine, he was put to bed in a room shared with another boy. That boy had already been through the ordeal and was going home the next day, but now Geoffrey was being made ready for the little operation in the morning. Morning came, and when it was his time, everything happened rather quickly; the doctor and a nurse came into the room, and with a few words of encouragement that it wasn't going to hurt and that he should count to ten, they stuck something into his arm. He had hardly managed to count as far as two before an extraordinary black buzz filled his head, and he was gone. The next thing he knew, or, as he was still semi-comatose, of which he was vaguely aware, was that he was apparently still in the same bed in the same room. His instinct was to sit up, but his efforts were thwarted by an assortment of hands pushing him down again, telling him it would be alright. Then oblivion overtook him again. The second attempt at waking up was rather more successful, except this time, he was acutely aware of the most horrific sore throat he had ever experienced. There were nurses by his bedside assuring him the worst was over and in a day or two, he could go home again. Still groggy from the anaesthetic, he turned onto his side and answered the nurse with a deposit of bloody vomit beside his pillow. This not being enough, he turned the other way and made a second deposit on the other side of his pillow.

The boy next to him had disappeared off home, having made a quick recovery as was normal following a simple tonsils removal. However, for Geoffrey, things weren't going quite so well. He had a fever that was persistent and would not subside, and to begin with, the wounds were reluctant to heal, resulting in a constant taste of blood in his mouth as off and on they bled a little. Unlike an ordinary hospital, the rules for visiting were far more relaxed. This meant that Thea could come and visit in the afternoons for as long as she liked. She always brought David and Clare with her as they were too young to be left alone, but Geoffrey was happy that they came, and he always looked forward to their daily visits. After nearly a week, it was decided that he was well enough to go home. For most children, two or three days was all that was needed to be back on their feet and well on their way to a full recovery.

Normally Geoffrey and David shared their bedroom, but to avoid them disturbing each other, Thea had made up the bed in the spare room ready for him. When he arrived home, there was his bed with a bottle of Lucozade on the bedside table; everything was much cosier than in the nursing home. A continued stay in bed was ordered, but he wasn't feeling up to running around anyway. During the afternoon the next day, there was a persistent taste of blood in his mouth, and as he lay back on his pillow, he could feel a constant trickle down his throat. He called out for his mother and complained that apart from his throat hurting, he thought he was going to throw up, whereupon he did just that. But what came up was almost only blood, so suddenly the nice clean eiderdown was covered by a dark red bloody mess. For humans, blood is very indigestible, and in this case, the sheer volume was too much for his stomach, which very soon rejected it. George immediately telephoned Mr Wilsden, the specialist surgeon who had removed his tonsils, and recounted what had happened. In some respects, he supposed he was lucky because it wasn't long before the doorbell rang, and there was Mr Wilsden with his black case of instruments and all the things a doctor needs to deal with a small boy's missing tonsils.

With the help of a torch and a spatula to hold down Geoffrey's tongue, the doctor peered into his throat. He didn't say a lot, only mumbled something about clots. He fixed onto his head a surgeon's lamp that allowed him to have both hands free, and then took from his instrument box a long pair of tongs with which he reached down Geoffrey's gullet, far too far for his likings as it caused a considerable amount of retching. After poking around for what seemed like an eternity, he pulled out two large lumps of coagulated blood. As Geoffrey lay back, all pale and feeble, Mr Wilsden spoke to his mother and father, and apart from something about injections, Geoffrey thought he heard a mention of the nursing home. Anyway, the next thing he knew was the bedclothes were drawn back, and he was told to turn onto his front. He had no idea what was happening until some hands pulled down his pyjama trousers, and Mr Wilsden stabbed a hypodermic syringe into his right buttock. Geoffrey managed a little 'Ow' but was almost beyond caring. As if this wasn't enough, he was ordered to stay put and directly there was another shot into his left buttock, producing another 'Ow'. This was just too much, and try as he might, he couldn’t prevent the tears from bursting forth. Whilst being comforted by his mother, they told him that he must return to the Evelyn nursing home. This did nothing to quieten his sobs which only increased as he protested that he really, really, really didn't want to go back there.

His father lifted him out of bed and wrapped him in a blanket. This was the last time he remembered being held by his father.

His protests, of course, came to nought, and back to the nursing home it was, but this time he had his own room. Following all the commotion and the injections, Geoffrey was only half engaged as to what was going on around him, and soon he was tucked up in the hospital bed and falling asleep. The following morning, Mr Wilsden made his visit and once more peered down his throat. Unable to follow the medical jargon, Geoffrey had no idea what was awaiting him, but it soon became apparent that his daily medication was to be more injections into his poor little backside. Every morning he waited in fear of these, and every morning, the nurse asked which side it was to be that day. Once it was over, he could relax until it loomed before him the next day, but his posterior was beginning to hurt after being punctured by endless needles. Geoffrey was not one to complain, but now that he could no longer sit comfortably in bed, he felt he must say something, so the nurses brought a special rubber, ring-shaped cushion to put under his perforated posterior.

While confined to bed, he was required to pee into a special type of plastic container, which was, of course, an ordinary male bedpan. Being rather shy, Geoffrey was desperately nervous that a nurse might enter the room while he was busy making use of the bottle, so he waited and waited, not daring to get caught in the act until eventually, he thought his bladder would burst. At last, in the afternoon, when Thea arrived with David and Clare, he asked them to stand guard outside his door while he used the bottle. What a relief as the stream went on and on, but he had waited so long that now he was scared that the container would overflow as he filled it up. In the end, he had to stop before he felt that he was really ready, but he certainly felt rather more comfortable. In the end, he doubted that the bottle would have overflowed, but it was certainly very full.

Some years earlier, Geoffrey had been given a model farm, and slowly but surely, he had built up a collection of tractors, combine harvesters and other farm machinery, together with all sorts of little farm animals. To help pass the time in the nursing home, he asked his mother to bring his farm collection so that he could play with it. One day when he had all his animals out on parade, amongst which was a family of pigs, a nurse entered his room, and when she saw the collection, she was especially intrigued by the tiny little piglets, one of which she borrowed to show her colleagues. After this, Geoffrey's ego was boosted by a constant stream of different nurses who came in to admire his animals.

When Geoffrey was readmitted to the nursing home, George had taken the trouble to bring Thea's portable radio. Portable was a rather optimistic description as anybody moving it needed to be some sort of weight lifter. It was only portable in as much there were no cables attached. The family had not yet equipped themselves with a transistor radio, so this contraption was no small device and was powered by an exceptionally heavy battery. But it did help to break the silence, and Geoffrey became quite adept at twirling the tuning knob until he could listen to the BBC light programme. He soon became familiar with 'Woman's Hour', 'Edmundo Ross' and 'Family Favourites' amongst others.

After a rather boring week confined to bed and with his bottom now like a pin cushion, he was at last allowed to return home. More than half his school holiday had been spent in hospital, and now there were only a few days left before it was time to go back. Although to begin with, he was rather wobbly on his legs and had to take things gently, he was soon back in good health and rushing around as a boy of his age should. Sure enough, the end of the holidays arrived and far too soon, the dreaded return to school was imminent. At least now, he wouldn't need to spend so much time in the sick room.

Chapter 7

Mr Pont was waiting for them when Geoffrey and his father scrunched to a halt in their dormobile on the gravel drive around the lozenge. As always, when returning to school, Geoffrey had a huge lump in his throat at the idea of being left alone again. Mr Pont and George discussed together what was going to be best for Geoffrey's future and, as usual, talked about him as if he wasn't there. Now that he was rid of his tonsils, they didn't expect him to miss too much school through sickness and to ensure his entrance to Haileybury, the public school where David had now started, they finally realised what a desperate struggle it was for him and that it would be best to abandon the idea of a scholarship. So instead of moving him up, it was decided to keep him back in the same class as before, where he now would be joined by his contemporaries of the same age group. Apart from discussing Geoffrey's future, somewhere along the line, George's work came into the conversation. It happened that at that particular time, George was heavily involved with developing Brussel sprouts to become the nice and small, and compact item they are today. Mr Pont was not entirely convinced, "What's this I've heard, George, that you have made a cabbage more like a tennis ball?" he asked.

"Yes, that's right, at the Plant Breeding Institute, we've managed to make a Brussel sprout nice and small and compact," replied his father, "and I tell you what, next time I bring Geoffrey back, I'll take one in a match-box for you, then you can see for yourself!" This he duly did on Geoffrey's first exeat.

At last, things took a turn for the better and instead of floundering around, out of his depth at the bottom of the class, he was now enjoying being at the top end of the class. 'Satis' reports were a thing of the past, and Friday lunchtimes were no longer to be feared. However, other events started to take place.

In the Latin classes, they were learning scanning, which Geoffrey mastered rather quickly, and French, still with Mr Brooks, was much easier now, as he could remember a substantial amount that he had learnt the previous year. Mr Brooks, or Brooky, still smoked his Senior Service incessantly. His habits never changed, when he entered the classroom, before planting himself in the chair at the master's desk at the head of the class, he placed his round tin of 'Players' cigarettes on the desk, took one out, tapped both ends on his thumbnail and lit it. Now the lesson could begin. Apart from the fight Geoffrey had with him the previous year, in the main, Brooky was not unkind, but when provoked, he could show a turn of anger, as he did when Robson, a rather disorganised boy, was unable to find the right textbook in his desk. Brooky rose from his seat, which he disliked having to do anyway, and walked round to where Robson sat. When he saw the utter mess in Robson's desk, he lost his temper. He opened the window, took the desk and emptied the contents out into the yard. The classroom was upstairs on the first floor and amongst his books was his 'tuck tin' although this time it was a glass jar. Inevitably, on collision with the concrete yard, it smashed into a thousand fragments. The resulting pile outside consisted of textbooks, exercise books, broken glass, an old conker, pieces of string and some sweets. Robson was busy for the rest of the lesson tidying up the mess.

Brooky, albeit unwittingly, managed to create a nickname for Geoffrey's friend Robert Wallis who had also come to the same boarding school from Miss Turner's Islip House. Apart from being rather shy, poor Robert suffered from a stutter, although in this instance, it was of no significance. During one of Brooky's lessons, one by one, he had his pupils read French out loud from a textbook. When it was Robert's turn, the name Mme Leroy appeared in his text. Not being familiar with the shortened version of Madame, he read out Mme as 'Mimi', and from that moment on, Robert was known as Mimi. Unhappily for Robert, he suffered from failing kidneys, and in spite of his mother donating one of her own kidneys, it was not enough to save his life and sadly, he later passed away. At his young age, death was unfamiliar to Geoffrey, to whom, ironically, it seemed just part of life. Because of Robert's medical instability, his mother, Mrs Wallis, sometimes paid him a special visit during the week. Owing to their earlier friendship Mrs Wallis often also greeted Geoffrey. On one such occasion, a short while before she was due to arrive, Mr Pont called Geoffrey into his office to see that he looked respectable. In order to smarten him up a little and see that he was looking his best, he had him undo his shorts and reorganise his vest and underpants, all the while discussing with his secretary whether or not it was best to tuck his vest into his underpants or leave it outside. After some experimental tucking and untucking, he finally considered his attire was sufficient to meet Mrs Wallis.

For mathematics, Geoffrey now had the honour of being taught by Mr Pont, and headmaster or not, he was not someone to fool around with. He was strict to the extreme, and if, on occasion, he was in a bad mood, it was not unknown for him to bring a cane into the classroom hidden down the leg of his trousers. It was a sad moment for the first boy who was slow to answer a question. Quick as a flash, he whipped out the cane and thrashed it down on the desk with a swish and a mighty thwack. The swish was all too familiar to Geoffrey's ears after his earlier beating, but the noise of hitting the desk was rather louder than the sound made when striking his bottom. This frightening action only further reduced the victim's ability to think straight, and quivering with fear, he had no chance to answer any question, which most often resulted in the boy having to bend over the desk to receive a couple of strokes of Mr Pont's cane. And he was not allowed to sob, even when his behind stung too much for him to sit down again.

On Sundays, all the boys were free after morning Chapel and again in the afternoon after lunch. One such afternoon the boys were playing a game they called 'Kollyocky', a more advanced form of hide and seek. When it was Geoffrey's role to do the seeking, he was looking for a boy he thought was hiding in a cellar that housed some of the school boilers. Leading down to the cellar was an old worn concrete stairway, and rather than venture down the steps in the semi-darkness, he stood at the top and leaned down the narrow stairway clinging onto the door frame at the top of the steps. Hanging there by his fingertips, he called down to the boy he suspected was hiding there. Unfortunately, he was hanging onto the hinged side of the doorframe, and the boy he sought was not down there in the darkness. He was, in fact, right behind him. To avoid being seen by Geoffrey, he slammed the door closed. As the door crushed his fingers, Geoffrey let out a mighty scream that could be heard from miles around. By chance, Mr Pont was on duty in the yard just around the corner and was rapidly on the scene. A quick look at his flattened fingertips, and he ushered Geoffrey to Matron. The most squashed of all his fingers was his long finger from which the skin was also grazed off. Matron bandaged up the worst of the damage, and he soon reappeared back in the yard to resume his playtime, although now rather subdued.

One of the first lessons the following Monday morning was a maths lesson taken of course by Mr Pont. Geoffrey's fingers were a lot better, although his long finger still hurt a little. Just for a moment, Geoffrey was distracted and wasn't paying proper attention. Mr Pont, who missed nothing, was quick to address him,

"What's the matter, Finch? Are you not with us today?"

"My fingers are throbbing, Sir," he replied quickly, using that as an excuse for not paying attention.

"Oh, are your fingers thwobbing?" he mocked, repeating Geoffrey's words in a drawn-out way and went on, "go and stand in the corner and see if they get better there." Humiliation was something that made Geoffrey suffer most, and standing in the corner hurt more than the pain in his fingers.

Sometimes when Mr Pont was in a better mood, then everything flowed more easily, even too easily. It was not uncommon that after teaching his class something new, he would test them by writing some sums on the blackboard, and the boys wrote their answers in their exercise books. One by one, each boy, in turn, was summoned up to the headmaster's desk with his exercise book, where he had to stand while his answers were checked. Often while Geoffrey stood there beside his chair, inhaling the doft of tobacco and aftershave, Mr Pont's hand would slyly glide up the trouser leg of Geoffrey's shorts. This became an all too common occurrence. Even though his fingers stroked and squeezed his little buttocks, being only eleven years old, Geoffrey believed it to be nothing more than some sort of sign of affection, of which he was starved. If nothing else, he took it as a signal that Mr Pont liked him, and it was very important to Geoffrey to be liked. A trait that stayed with him for the rest of his life. Innocently he thought that maybe he was one of the headmaster's favourites. The bottom fondling continued until he had finished his exams to Haileybury, and there were no more exercise books to be corrected. Presumably, Mr Pont was quick to find replacement buttocks to feel.

In the dormitories, there was a bath night schedule which mostly meant every third evening. When Geoffrey had graduated to the top dormitories, one night while sitting in his bath, it happened that Mr Pont decided to take a stroll around all the dormitories as he sometimes did. As Geoffrey sat there in his bath washing himself, Mr Pont entered the bathroom and told him to stand up, which of course he did, not wishing to disobey. Mr Pont approached the bath and squatted down beside it so that Geoffrey's private parts were at his eye level. He then started poking around Geoffrey's little penis and testicles. After a short while, he said, "I thought it looked a bit sore there, but it seems to be alright." Whereupon Geoffrey sat down again and continued washing, being glad there was nothing wrong 'down there'. Mr Pont walked out of the bathroom.

In the summer term, when it was warm enough, it was customary for all the boys in the top dormitories to indulge in an early morning swim before breakfast. This was something they had to do; there was no option. Mr Pont was in charge of the senior boys who slept in these dormitories, and he was always there to wake them up and make sure that everyone hurried down to the swimming pool. However, there was a special rule for these morning dips; all boys were obliged to swim naked. For whose benefit this was will never be known, but Mr Pont, clad in a silk dressing gown over his pyjamas, was always there to keep a close eye on proceedings.

Apart from swimming, the other summer sport was cricket. It turned out that Geoffrey was fairly adept at fielding in the slips, as well as bowling, to the extent that he was selected to play for the 'colts' team. Probably he had inherited a modicum of ball skill from his father, who, it was reported, had been quite good at cricket. For his last summer, although not quite good enough for the first team, he was appointed captain of the second eleven and was even awarded his half colours in spite of his somewhat mediocre batting, which was never much to boast about. When there was an 'away' match, the team, togged out in whites, along with all the cricket pads and bats, were loaded into a minibus and driven off to meet their opponents at the other school. Occasionally they won an away match, so on their return journey, as the team approached the front of the school, they sang with great gusto, "We won because we won, because we won…" thus making sure the rest of the school knew of their success.

Geoffrey's bowling average was really quite respectable, but sadly his batting was not. During his period as captain, by his own choice, more often than not, he was the opening batsman. So it was when he opened the batting against Heath Mount School. After the first few balls from the bowler, which he gallantly defended, the bowler bowled a wide. Thinking that now he had a chance to hit a four, Geoffrey took it upon himself to make a rather wild left hook. He missed the ball completely but owing to his bat being rather heavy for his little arms, he was unable to control its momentum, and it continued its journey onto the stumps behind him. There it was, he was 'out for a duck'. Not a good example from the captain. After the tea break, Geoffrey's team were fielding quite successfully and had bowled out the first few of their opponent's batsmen. One batsman, however, was hitting too many runs, so in his role of captain, Geoffrey appointed another bowler in the hope he might be more successful. He was not aware, however, that his new bowler was in dire need to spend a penny but was too afraid to disrupt the proceedings and ask to go. Just as he was preparing himself to bowl, his nice white cricket trousers suddenly changed colour to become a trifle see-through, adhering themselves to his thighs as they became soaked by his uncontrollable pee. He still managed to bowl, albeit rather ashamedly, but actually, with a certain degree of success and being a sunny day, his trousers dried off quite nicely. Sadly though, on this occasion, there was no singing on the return to school.

The end of the summer term was best of all because Geoffrey knew that what lay ahead was endless weeks of holiday away from school. In addition, he would be having his own holiday somewhere by the sea, even possibly in France. But like all holidays, long or short, the end arrived and once again, it was time to see which winter school clothes still fitted and then pack trunks and tuck boxes.

While David and Geoffrey were now at different schools, they nearly always started and finished their terms on different days, so sometimes it was David, and sometimes it was Geoffrey who went back to school first but being alone at school made the return even more painful. So his last year started with Mr Pont's continued bottom fondling and an occasional hug. Now in the fifth form, many of the boys were reaching puberty, but for Geoffrey, this did not happen until he had started at Haileybury, so until then, his voice remained a rather high-pitched treble.

Once again, it was back to the hard beds and smell of newly painted corridors, the school routines and the frequently unpalatable food. In the dining hall, Geoffrey now sat at the top table, and it was always at the head of this table that Mr Pont ate his meals. The weekly rotation system of seating meant that as the boys worked their way round the table every so often, they ended up sitting first on Mr Pratt's right side and then on his left. Geoffrey already knew that these places made it extremely difficult to hide any inedible food, particularly pieces of meat, making some mealtimes very difficult to endure.

Mr Pont also had the ability to make a spectacle of an individual in front of the whole school, and this he did to Geoffrey on more than one occasion, indeed once to the extent that he gained a nickname with which he was teased for the rest of his days at that prep school. Before Chapel one morning, when the whole school was assembled in the yard with all the boys standing in their squads, he asked Geoffrey, “Finch, when is your maths lesson today?” Geoffrey suspected he needed to know himself at what time he had to teach them, but by some insight, Mr Pont knew that Geoffrey hadn't properly studied the lesson schedule on the noticeboard, so Geoffrey could only answer, “I don't know, Sir.”

“What do you mean, ‘you don’t know’, haven’t you looked at the board?”

“Yes, Sir,” he lied.

“Then when is your maths lesson?” he demanded again.

“I don’t know, Sir.”

“Then go and look at the board again, and don’t come back until you can tell me,” he ordered.

So while the whole school waited for him, he ran to the form room block where the notice board hung and tried to study the schedule. Panic-stricken, knowing that everybody was waiting just for him, he couldn’t see the wood for the trees and could not take in anything. Eventually, he calmed down enough to see that maths was scheduled for his form 5b after the morning break. He ran back out into the yard with everybody waiting to see what happened and reported to the headmaster.

"The third lesson, Sir," he panted.

"Oh good, you can read then. Don't forget to look at the board in future, you 'barnechute'!" How, or from where, he came up with this name will never be known, but now the whole school had heard it, and from then on, he was called a 'barnechute' with boys chanting at him 'barnechute, barnechute'. Slightly more endearingly, it was later shortened to Barney.

During a week when he had the misfortune to be seated beside the headmaster, he took a dislike to Geoffrey's runny nose. He was ordered to stand up and leave the table, go to the corner and wipe his nose clean before returning to his seat. As soon as a boy stands up during mealtime, all eyes are upon him to see what is going on. To do as instructed under the gaze of the whole school was almost more than he could bear, but there was no alternative and do it he must.

As they neared the end of the winter term and Christmas was in sight, it was again time for the form plays and, this time, even a pantomime. The school was to perform 'Jack and the Beanstalk'. Instead of having an acting part, Geoffrey's role was personal assistant to Mr Pont, who was both the director and producer. This meant that during all the rehearsals and indeed the performances, Geoffrey had always to be on hand to do this or that, fetch this or that, and any other errands that Mr Pont wanted him to do. In his innocence, he was unaware of any ulterior motives on the headmaster's part and having fallen into the trap of wanting to please and be liked, he ran around after him like a little puppy. As rehearsals progressed and Mr Watson, the art master, was busy painting the scenes, it was eventually time to try on some costumes. The role of a peasant was played by a boy called Barnett, and part of his clothing was a cross between tights and very tight-fitting trousers without any fly opening at the front. Whilst all the boys were busy trying on this and that, Barnett, having wriggled and squeezed his way into his trousers, appeared boasting a large wet stain on the front. He was shamefully trying to hide it but owing to the material, it was painfully obvious for all to see. Not knowing any better, Geoffrey thought it strange that he had peed in his pants, but of course, he later realised it was not that at all, Barnett, having reached puberty somewhat earlier than himself, had become overexcited by the tightness of his trousers.

Eventually, all the acts started to fall into place, but not without a good deal of shouting from Mr Pont. At last, it was matinée and apart from the occasional prompt when lines were forgotten, everything went smoothly. The big night was saved for the parents. The gym, which was now used as the theatre, was packed to the point of overflowing. Mr Pont had Geoffrey running hither and thither, collecting forgotten pieces of costume, looking for his script, helping change the scenes and hoisting the beanstalk until, at last, down came the final curtain. As the whole cast was enjoying taking a bow, Mr Pont pushed Geoffrey onto the stage to join them so his part did not go unnoticed, and he could enjoy a moment of appreciation.

The pantomime was closely followed by the carol service. Geoffrey had always thought that he could sing quite well in his own little treble way, but a while earlier, to his chagrin, Mr Mills, the music master, had been totally unimpressed with his singing voice and had dismissed him as absolutely not chorister material. Relegated to the congregation, he was selected to read a lesson. He practised and practised, but nothing could alleviate his nervousness. The chapel was decorated with holly and extra candles and near the altar was a nativity scene with Joseph and Mary and baby Jesus in a little manger being looked upon by a donkey. The scale of the ass did not quite match the rest of the setting, standing taller than Joseph and Mary, but it did not seem to matter. The parents arrived and filled all the pews towards the rear of the chapel. Extra chairs had been brought in, and all were quickly occupied. Geoffrey's pew was just in front of the parents, and his seat was on the outside next to the gangway. This meant it was necessary for him to walk a few paces to the front of the chapel in order to read his lesson.

Right at the front was a small lectern placed precisely in the middle of the chapel. This was where the lesson readers were required to perform their duty. The service opened with a solo rendering of 'Once in Royal' with the choir and congregation joining in after the first verse. As the carol approached its last few lines, Geoffrey's time had arrived. He stepped out from his pew and made his way to the front, and stood behind the lectern. Shaking like a leaf, he began to read; luckily, his voice was relatively steady, but the same could not be said for his legs. Had he been wearing long trousers, he would have been a lot happier. As it was, his knobbly little knees, exposed for all to see, were trembling like aspen leaves. He was so desperately aware of them shaking away under his shorts that his concentration was divided between the scripture he was trying to read and his efforts to stop his knees from knocking. He struggled on, and with enormous relief, he was finally able to say, "Here endeth the first lesson," whereupon he wasted no time in returning to the safety of his seat.

At last, the end of term arrived. The excitement, not only within himself but running through the whole school, created an air of energetic gladness. The chattering at the breakfast table reached a crescendo like never before, and it was hard to eat any breakfast on this wonderful morning. Nothing happened fast enough, including the last Chapel service, which seemed to take an eternity. Directly after Chapel, all the boys rushed out to see if their parents had arrived. The driveway in front of the school had become a melee of Jaguars, Rovers and Alvis'. Mothers and fathers, in between hugging their dear sons and talking to various masters, were loading trunks and overnight cases into the boots of their cars. George was there in Polly, the dormobile, and they wasted no time in pushing Geoffrey's belongings into the back. A quick goodbye to one or two friends with a "See you next term," answered with a "Bye Finch," and after his father had ignited the Gallaher & Lyle tobacco in his pipe, they were off on their way home at last. What euphoria, not only to go home for more than a weekend but also with Christmas only a few days away.

They arrived home just in time for lunch, and Geoffrey quickly changed from his school uniform into his home clothes which increased the sensation of being really away from school. Just to be home and enjoy touching familiar things, discovering again his toys that had been put away for so long and being able to enjoy the smell of home filled him with such happiness and thankfulness. It was still a little empty, though, without David, who had two more days at school before his term ended. After lunch, George returned to work, and Thea unpacked his trunk.

During the last few days of term, Geoffrey had been dreaming of being at home and making a Christmas present for his father. Now, at last, he could pursue this, and so it was directly into the workshop where he started sawing and hammering away to make his gift; this time a pipe holder. Later on, after tea, he wasted no time in switching on the radio so that he could listen to David Davids introducing 'Children's Hour'. Before he knew it, a day had passed, and it was time to go and fetch David from Haileybury, so George and he left in good time to collect his brother after the morning chapel service. Geoffrey's school had seemed big, but even though he hadn't yet started at Haileybury, he found the sheer size of everything somewhat daunting, especially knowing that in only a couple of terms, he too would be waiting to be collected together with David. There he was, his big brother, although, like Geoffrey, he was smaller than most of his contemporaries, waiting with his trunk and tuck box. Now the family was complete again, for two or three weeks anyway, and with David at home, they could send their Christmas lists up the chimney to Santa Claus. The two brothers, each armed with a sheet of Bronco loo paper, wrote their wish list and dispatched them up the chimney. Even though they both knew that Santa did not really exist, it was still fun, and they sort of felt that maybe something magical just might happen. David also had made a Christmas present for his father. This time it was a toolbox with three drawers that was specially designed to fit under the driver's seat in Polly. Since father had played a major role in measuring and drawing up the plans, it was not going to be any big surprise, but David was still going to paint it at home, so that part would anyway be a surprise. Unfortunately, there was something not quite right with the paint, so when Christmas Day arrived, it still had not dried. George was, of course, very pleased with it, more so than with Geoffrey's pipe rack, and after scraping off the still-wet paint, it was fitted into its place where it stayed forevermore.

Christmas came with the usual excitement, unwrapping all their presents and opening the yearly envelope from Gran containing a pound note. Mostly the present from their mother and father was something unexpected. Sometimes the shape enabled the children to guess what lay inside, but usually, it was always a wonderful surprise. Invariably, Boxing Day was scheduled for a drive to George's mother, Granny, where an annual reunion took place with the whole gang of other relations, including Geoffrey's cousins Carole and Charles.

Granny lived in Brentwood in a big house called Laurel Hill, together with her brother Phil. From the road, the drive made a big sweeping curve upwards through an abundance of laurel bushes to the house which stood above the road. As it curved left towards the house, it passed a grass tennis court on the right. Granny's hall was a huge room with a big open fireplace and a brass gong for informing residents that a meal was served. Uncle Phil's golf clubs always stood there in the hall, although Geoffrey never saw him take them out to play. Centrally placed in the hall was a wide staircase dividing into two smaller staircases on either side, leading to various bedrooms and bathrooms. To the left of the staircase was a passageway that led to the kitchen and scullery, and on the left, where the passage began, was a door to the vast dining room. Sometimes they spent the whole Christmas period at Granny's together with all the relations from George's side of the family. Even though Laurel Hill was enormous, it still ended up being full to the brim and sometimes David, Geoffrey and cousin Charles were obliged to sleep in an outhouse which Granny called the Dutch barn. The ground floor of this building comprised a garage and potting sheds with their bedroom situated on the floor above. The only form of heating upstairs was a small open fire. Everything was just a little damp, and even though Granny and Uncle Phil had done their best to warm up the room by lighting the coal fire well in advance, it did little to improve the indoor climate. Even the bedsheets didn't feel quite dry when climbing between them. The fire was kept burning all night which may have helped to lessen the chill in the room, but it was still reminiscent of school, although here was a level of excitement instead of fear. Charles and David were of similar age, and both were a couple of years older than Geoffrey. Two years at this age was quite significant, so he always felt rather small and shy when they were together. When it was bedtime, both sets of parents saw to it that they were tucked in properly and that the fire was well made up with plenty of coal, although most of the warmth from the fire went up the chimney, warming any nocturnal birdlife. With a "Not too much talking now boys," the parents left them alone to go to sleep.

Boys will be boys, and soon there was the usual joke telling and laughter. Charles farted and stuck his head under the blankets exclaiming "Ah Bisto!" and again "eggy bisto!" to best describe the odour of his flatulence. The talking and joking went on for a while until Charles, who seemed to know what to do about the fire, which impressed Geoffrey, jumped out of bed and threw on a last shovel of coal. Geoffrey was falling asleep by this time, and the next thing he knew was that there was a stocking with crackers and balloons hanging on the end of his bed, clearly the sign of a visit from Santa. So began Christmas Day at Granny's.

The next morning, back in the main house was a lot of hustle and bustle as breakfast was about to be served, after which, the whole family should go to church. Everybody was wishing everybody else a happy Christmas as, one by one, they all slowly appeared for breakfast. In Granny's dining room stood an enormous dining table at which they all sat, having helped themselves to the different dishes placed on the sideboard. “When can we open our presents, Daddy?” Geoffrey quietly asked his father. “After church,” he replied. It seemed like an awfully long wait. Eventually, when breakfast had been cleared away, overcoats, hats and scarves were donned, and everybody went off to church.

At last, the church service came to an end, and back in Granny's hall, the big moment had arrived. “This is from Mummy and I,” said George as he gave Geoffrey a long, quite heavy parcel. Geoffrey looked at the tag hanging on the parcel, which read ‘To Geoffrey, Happy Christmas from Mummy and Daddy’. Eagerly he started unwrapping; the boys had learned not to just rip and tear but to open presents carefully. As more wrapping paper was removed, he realised what it was; a ‘Pogo’ stick. He never could have guessed. “Oh, thank you, Mummy, and thank you, Daddy,” he cried as he quickly started to try it out. It didn't take him too long to master the technique, so the rest of the time at Granny's was spent hopping up and down on the Pogo stick, counting all the hops. Of course, David and Charles were also eager to try it out, so there was soon a competition to see who was able to make the most hops without stopping.

After lunch, most of the adults, having retired to the sitting room, which was the only really warm room in the whole house, indulged unwittingly in forty winks. First to go was uncle Phil slumped down in his winged chair with his legs and feet stretched out before him. Then one after another, depending on the comfort of the chair, they all allowed slumber to take over. Whilst they were dozing, the children played with their new toys, and by accident, Geoffrey tripped over uncle Phil's feet which abruptly brought him back to wakefulness with a mumble of "hold up, hold up." He soon fell asleep again.

As evening approached, it was time to dress for dinner. After a while, the grown-ups came down from their rooms attired in evening dresses and dinner jackets. When Geoffrey saw his father's dress shirt, he remarked to him that it was "like cardboard Daddy" as he wrapped his little knuckles on it. The front part over his chest was indeed a shiny white hard material. The three young cousins also had changed into smarter clothes, and now it was time for dinner. The dining room table looked terrific with lots of crackers and holly and bowls of tangerines and nuts together with packs of dates. Each place was laid with silver cutlery; rows of knives, forks and spoons in different shapes and sizes to cater for all the dishes. Meanwhile, an aperitif sherry was served in the sitting room accompanied by more 'Happy Christmas', 'Your good health', and much bonhomie. It wasn't long before the gong in the hall boomed to indicate it was time for dinner, which prompted a general movement towards the dining room for the evening's feast.

After everybody had found their places and were seated, the first course, a consommé, was served along with wine for the elders. This was quite soon disposed of, and as the wine started to make its mark, the banter increased. Now it was time for the turkey, and an enormous bird, too heavy for Granny to bear alone, was brought in and placed before Uncle Phil, the designated carver. There was sausage meat stuffing at one end and green stuffing at the other, and the whole bird was surrounded by small chipolatas. There were brussels sprouts and peas and lots of crispy roast potatoes over which was poured delicious rich gravy. Eventually, when Uncle Phil had carved and carved for what seemed like an eternity, everybody had a serving of roast turkey. Second helpings were soon being asked for, even before the poor man had hardly begun to eat his own first helping.

It didn't take Geoffrey long to empty his plate, and he was already looking forward to the Christmas pudding. But the grown-ups, it would seem, were in no rush whatsoever. David, Charles and Geoffrey had to remain at the table on their best behaviour, so they were obliged to wait patiently until their seniors ate and drank at their own pace. Eventually, the dirty plates were replaced by clean bowls for the Christmas pudding and mince pies. Thea, who as a child had been deprived of good food, was quick to help carry away the remains of the turkey. On its voyage down the passage to the scullery, when she thought no one was looking, she quickly raised and tilted the whole dish to her mouth and enjoyed as much of the delicious turkey dripping as she could, knowing that it probably would otherwise be wasted.

At last, in came the Christmas pudding all aflame, as was the tradition. For luck, Granny always mixed in silver charms when she made the puddings, and there were also a few silver sixpences. Eating her delicious pudding had to be done with care to avoid biting one of her charms, or indeed swallowing one; many were already rather deformed from being accidentally champed upon. To be sure that the children each had a sixpence in their pudding, Uncle Phil, who again was serving, had a small reserve in his pocket from which, he not so secretly, extracted one and pushed it into the portion he was serving. Hygiene was not exactly optimal as the sixpences shared space in his pocket with his not so clean handkerchief and were pushed into the pudding with his not so clean fingers; but it didn't seem to matter as the pudding, accompanied by a good dollop of brandy butter, was absolutely delicious.

Even though everyone was beginning to feel quite replete, most had a little space left for the port and stilton cheese. This wasn't anything for the cousins, but they had to maintain their patience and wait until it was time to pull the crackers. They did, however, enjoy the tangerines and dates, and there was also a jar of genuine Turkish delight which did a lot to satisfy a sweet tooth. When the moment for crackers finally arrived, they all took one, crossed their arms and with their free hand took hold of their neighbour's cracker. When the circle was complete, everybody pulled at once and there followed a mass of small explosions accompanied by that special smell of sulphur that comes but once a year. Out of the crackers, various items flew out all over the place and everybody, regardless of their age, grabbed for the contents, mainly paper hats. As a result of the wine, all inhibitions were lost, and paper hats became 'de rigueur'. Every cracker contained some sort of plastic charm, a paper hat and a weak joke such as: 'Q. When is a fountain not a fountain? A. When it's a square tin (squirting)'. There were always a few crackers extra, and these the boys were quick to pull with their favourite person; top of the list, of course, was their mother and father.

Eventually, it was time for bed and tomorrow, they would make the homeward journey.

Chapter 8

It was always nice to be home again, and this time was no exception, although a homecoming from school was always by far the best. Now that Christmas was over, subtle reminders occasionally popped up that the days were once again counting down to the beginning of term. At least now, he wasn't so desperately behind in class which made the return a little easier. His school report had arrived, and apart from history and geography, his father was quite pleased. Even the headmaster's report from Mr Pont rounded off with '…and what a P.A. (Personal Assistant)!'

Geoffrey's lack of knowledge in history made itself known when he was using his Christmas money to buy an Airfix plastic model. Having already made and carefully painted such historical figures as Henry VIII, whilst looking around in the model shop for a new character, he spotted The Black Prince. The name meant nothing to him, but it looked like a nice model, so he decided to buy it. On the packaging, the last letters of Prince were a little obscured, so when he went to the counter and the shopkeeper asked, "And how can I help you?" Geoffrey replied, "I'd like the Black Pringe, please."

"Oh, you mean the Black Prince," said the assistant.

"No, the Black Pringe," he protested.

Then the man took down the model and showed Geoffrey the packet properly so that he saw his mistake, but thanks to his historical ignorance, he still didn't know who The Black Prince was, but neither did the shop assistant.

As the days ticked away one by one, the weather became colder and colder. Soon the routine of trying on clothing started again, which as always set in motion the butterflies in his tummy. Once again, they made their usual visit to Miss Mott's sweet shop to stock up for the term but now that David no longer took sweets back to school, it was only necessary to buy for Geoffrey. Things started to look more and more grim as the day of departure loomed nearer and nearer. Then, on his last full day at home, Geoffrey heard the telephone ring. Thea answered it, and Geoffrey could overhear small pieces of the conversation, enough to realise that it was something to do with school. When his mother rang off, she told Geoffrey the news. He had been right, it was indeed the school ringing and what a piece of luck, they had rung to say that due to the cold weather some pipes had frozen and the heating had broken down, so, unfortunately, Geoffrey must stay at home at least another day. 'Unfortunately' was not how he would have described it, as nothing could have been better. They would be informed when Geoffrey could return. During the conversation, they told Thea that if Geoffrey had any ice skates and even a hockey stick, he should also bring them back to school. Having already learned to skate when the 'fens' froze over, he was a fairly accomplished skater. His father had previously acquired some skates for the boys but no boots. To solve this, he screwed the skates onto their cricket boots. This worked quite well and actually taught them to skate better since the cricket boots provided no ankle support whatsoever, having only thin canvas uppers; thus, they were forced to skate without relying on the support of leather lace-ups.

Sure enough, after two extra days' holiday, the telephone call came and back to school it was. Now he was in the 'top dorms', which meant that sometimes he would be sent down to the floor below to be in charge of one of the junior dormitories. Luckily it didn't happen directly as it was bad enough trying to overcome his own homesickness without coping with other small boy's misery. Soon they found out why they had their ice skates; the school lake was frozen, and instead of playing rugby, they were to play ice hockey on the lake. This was fun, and Geoffrey was far more enthusiastic about this than playing rugby. He was also one of the best skaters, so just for once, he was in his element. But all good things come to an end; the weather became warmer, the ice melted, and it was back to the rugby pitch.

Up in the top dorms, Geoffrey became friends with a boy called Ambrose. Unlike Geoffrey, Ambrose's stage of puberty was well advanced, and he was already developing quite a substantial growth of hair on his upper lip, albeit rather soft. Combined with this, although nothing to do with his puberty, his hair was a little unusual in that his fringe, instead of falling down onto his forehead, stuck straight out like a sun-shade. None of this mattered to Geoffrey as they were just good friends, and in their free time on Sundays, they built a hut together in the woods situated in the school grounds. This was quite a popular pastime for the senior boys who gathered together bits of plank and all sorts of debris that could be found. Using these, they constructed rather primitive huts. Often with the help of a few bricks and mud, a little fireplace with a chimney was made, and after gaining permission from the duty master, it was allowed to make a fire in these fireplaces. Geoffrey and Ambrose had built such a hut which was much like all the rest with walls made from old pieces of hardboard and a tin roof held up by some dead branches found in the woods. The floor was just dry earth covered by an old sack with another sack hanging over the entrance in place of a door. Small boys could enter by doubling forward, but for adults, it was definitely a hands and knees operation. One Sunday afternoon, the two boys had gathered some twigs and made a small fire in their fireplace. They lay there on their tummies watching the fire and chattering away when suddenly the entrance sack was whisked away, and the space was filled by Mr Pont's moustached face. He rapidly cast an eye over the two boys and then just asked if everything was alright, reminding them it was not long until the bell for tea, before disappearing again. Geoffrey didn't understand why he had crept upon them, as if he expected to catch them breaking a rule or doing something they shouldn't. Later he understood why; due to Ambrose's advanced state of puberty, he was afraid that something out of order might be taking place. The only happening of this sort involved Mr Pont himself.

In the school grounds, there was a considerable amount of deciduous woods providing a home to a multitude of grey squirrels. These little animals had become used to being in the neighbourhood of mankind, and many were relatively tame, indeed brave enough to rush around the school buildings. The headmaster's mother, Mrs Pont, a rather fragile, grey-haired old lady, liked to feed the squirrels if she had some tit-bits. Geoffrey was watching one day when she endeavoured to offer an old bread crust to one of these creatures that scampered around on the low roof of the covered way to the yard. Her age and fragility meant that she couldn't quite hold the bread crust high enough so that the poor creature needed to stretch down towards her to grasp it. Unable to quite reach it, he lost his grip and fell onto her head. Giving a shriek, she dropped the crust, and the squirrel missed his lunch. Geoffrey thought the whole episode was quite funny, but anyway, after that episode, the poor old lady gave up feeding them. It wasn't long after when a commotion in the kitchens caught Geoffrey's interest, and he just had to go and see what it was all about. The Spanish kitchen staff had captured one of these poor squirrels in a sack after it they had found it stealing food. Two men walked out across the yard carrying the sack, which now and again changed shape as the squirrel moved around, seeking an escape from its captivity. They left the yard, and the Spaniard bearing the hessian sack approached a tree just outside the entrance. Geoffrey followed, expecting to see him release the little animal, but instead, the man lifted the sack backwards over his shoulder and with full force swung it against the tree. Geoffrey's mouth fell open with shock, and he was filled with revulsion as he saw the sack jumping around madly with traces of blood seeping through. One more swing, one more thwack against the tree and all movement stopped. Geoffrey, who loved nature, was horrified, and the image of what happened scarred his innocent mind.

The weeks passed slowly, and in the fifth form, they were now working towards the following term's Common Entrance exam, causing the tempo in the classroom to increase all the time. Common Entrance was the entrance exam to public school, so it was very important for the school to be able to boast as many passes as possible. It was also very important for the boys, as a failure could seriously affect their future. Luckily, now that Geoffrey was in with his own year, he was able to keep up rather well and didn't suffer too much. There were no more 'satis' reports, but he still feared the Monday evening scripture test. Outside, now that the ice was gone and the rugby pitch could be used again, it was time for the rugby teams to be selected. Geoffrey was rather small and light, but he could run quite fast, so he was usually chosen to play on the wing. It was not very often that he got his hands on the ball, and mostly he was just running backwards and forwards in hope. During one 'away' match, it rained throughout; the ball was as slippery as an eel, and the pitch was a quagmire. Geoffrey had learned that when the ball was loose, it was good to fall on it, putting the player's body between the ball and the feet of the opposition, so, armed with this knowledge, time after time, he fell on the ball and waited for a rough scrummage to form over him. Sometimes it seemed that having fallen perhaps a little too early, lying there in the mud, he had to wait for ages before all the boots started hacking away around him. Anyway, he received much praise from both Mr Pont and the sports master. This was probably why he was awarded his half colours, of which he was very proud.

With only a few more weeks to go, everybody started looking forward to Easter. By now, Geoffrey had learned that to help survive boarding school, he needed to always have something to which he could look forward. The last day of term arrived, and after singing 'There is a green hill far away…' they were released for the Easter break, albeit a rather short holiday. Thea had made hot cross buns to eat on Good Friday, and on Easter Sunday, at breakfast time, he, David and now Clare each found a big chocolate egg standing in their place at the table. Geoffrey's egg was always milk chocolate, and David's was dark chocolate but inside, both were filled with delicious pralines. It did not take many days to devour first the chocolates and then the egg, but somehow David always managed to make his last longer.

It also always happened that during the Easter holiday, David and Clare and later Williams all celebrated their birthdays in April, with David and Clare's falling on consecutive days. These three were lucky to be able to enjoy their birthdays at home, whereas Geoffrey was always obliged to celebrate his at school on his own. His mother and father realised that apart from this, with the other three all having birthdays, Geoffrey was rather left out, so usually, they gave him a little present as a kind of consolation prize. Thea usually organised a party for Clare, inviting all Clare's friends from school together with the children of their own friends. The party always involved hiding small chocolate eggs and bunnies in the bushes and trees all around the garden. When given the signal, the children rushed around, grabbing every chocolate they could find. It was always the greediest children who found the most and came back first with their hands and pockets full.

Once again, the holiday was drawing to an end, and it was time to start his last term at preparatory school. His father unscrewed the ice skates from his cricket boots and replaced them with studs. His trunk was packed, now including his cricket bat, and it was off to school again. It was drummed into him that this term, he had to work especially hard so that he passed his entrance exam to Haileybury.

On his return to school, Geoffrey found that he had been appointed as squad leader of Stanton squad. In addition, he was occasional dormitory captain and was soon to be chosen as captain of the second X1 cricket team. In the classroom, he was still much nearer the top than the bottom, especially in mathematics. He was thankful for this, for Mr Pont was finding it more and more effective to beat information into his boys with his cane and didn't waste any time in administering a few strokes here and there to the non-performers. The only drawback to being good at mathematics was that it allowed Mr Pratt endless chances to fondle Geoffrey's posterior, whereas other boys received strokes of his cane. Up until now, Thea had dressed her boys in rather old-fashioned underwear; baggy, shapeless items. Not wanting to be different from the rest, Geoffrey reported to Thea that all the other boys sported Jockey 'Y' fronts or something similar, so he persuaded her that he must have the same. For some reason, he couldn't explain when Thea helped him to try them on, his little manhood stood embarrassingly to attention. "Oh, Geoffrey," she exclaimed as she stroked his front to see if it really was so.

"It does that sometimes, Mummy," said Geoffrey, feeling rather awkward. However, back in the maths lessons, the snugger fitting underwear helped hinder Mr Pont's roaming fingers under his short trousers.

As the build-up to the Common Entrance (CE) exams became greater and greater, the boys underwent more and more trial exams using old common entrance papers. Latin, arithmetic, algebra and geometry were no problem for Geoffrey, and when standing beside Mr Pont while he corrected his answers, it gave the headmaster plenty of opportunities to slide his hand up Geoffrey's trouser leg and stroke and squeeze his cheeks even though his new underwear made it slightly less straightforward. It seemed that the headmaster felt more justified in his actions when Geoffrey's exercise book had all the right answers. For

Geoffrey, having his posterior fumbled was eminently better than being persecuted and having it beaten for getting everything wrong. However, as usual, history and geography were appalling. Time after time, it was made quite clear to Geoffrey by both the teachers and his parents that if he wanted to go to Haileybury, he must pass the CE. It never crossed Geoffrey's mind that he would not pass anyway, and the irony was that, exams or not, he was somewhat indifferent about going to Haileybury, it was really only for his father's sake. It just seemed to be his destiny according to his father's wish.

The Sunday night preceding the exam week was full of anticipation. The chatter in the dormitory was rather subdued, and Geoffrey, probably not alone, when kneeling by his bed to say his prayers, asked the Lord to help him. Monday morning arrived after a rather sleepless night thinking about Latin participles and French tenses. The gym had been arranged as an exam hall, and all the CE students were assigned a place to sit. Day by day and one by one, they worked their way through all the exams; some were easier than others, or it could be said less difficult, and for Geoffrey, only history was a catastrophe. The master invigilating kept a careful eye out for any cheating or whispering, and some boys could be seen resting their foreheads on their hands and running fingers through their hair as panic set in when they realised that they did not know how to answer a difficult question. When at last, the ordeal was over, it was not long before results started filtering through from the various schools. Most of Geoffrey's were good, especially algebra, for which he scored 99%. This made him Mr Pont's favourite, but it was short-lived as quite soon his history marks came through; a dreadful 18%, and it was only thanks to Mr Pont's persuasive telephone call to the headmaster of Haileybury that he was accepted.

With the exams out of the way, school life became far more relaxed. Sporting activities were coming to the fore with the swimming sports day fast approaching, closely followed by the athletics sports day combined with the parents' open day. As far as swimming was concerned, Geoffrey was fairly mediocre, breaststroke being his best. The swimming pool was an outside pool, and every afternoon, boys had to take a dip regardless of the weather or temperature. This was in addition to the early morning swim, which provided Mr Pont with his daily excitement, watching all the little boys running around naked. The swimming pool, surrounded by a wall approximately chest high, was of no great size but adequate for the school. The procedure was to leave your towel on the grass and queue along the wall until it was time to go in. At the entrance, every boy had to step into a galvanised tub of water to wash his feet. Often while waiting at the wall, it was not uncommon to be bullied by some bigger boys who had found a new trick. When a boy was least expecting it, they would grab him by the nipples and twist and pull quite painfully so. Invariably they picked on Geoffrey to inflict this nasty trick, so he always had to be on his guard, but still, they managed to give him a twist of the nipple when he wasn't looking. His poor nipples never really recovered from this ill-treatment and thereafter remained just slightly more prominent than he felt they should have been.

The swimming competition was not a major attraction for many parents, and only a few turned up to watch their darling boys perform. Even without his mother and father to cheer him on, Geoffrey managed to achieve a medal in the final of the breaststroke. In the meantime, they were being prepared for the athletic sports day and gymnastic display. Although being rather skinny and small, he was perhaps a little better than most when it came to running, to the extent that he ended up in the final of the 440 yards, 220 yards and the hurdles, and of course, a quarter part of the squad relay race. Prior to the running heats, all these events had to be practised, the high jump included, which was not Geoffrey's forte. During one practice session, a boy, who, as it happened, was also going to Haileybury, prepared for his jump using the scissors style. He half ran a few paces towards the jump, and just at the moment he approached the bar for take-off, something went awry and instead of his right leg lifting high in the air, he crumpled into the sand, screaming and crying. Even though he was slim in stature, the force of his lift-off split his kneecap. He was soon whisked away to hospital, not to be seen again until at Haileybury the next term.

The school caretaker had cut the grass short and carefully marked out the running track with white lines, so everything was ready for the big day. In addition to all the athletics, a group of boys who were best at gymnastics had been practising endlessly under the instructions of Mr Dorsey in preparation for performing a gymnastics display for the parents. Because gymnastics was the one thing that Geoffrey enjoyed, he had become perhaps the best of all, and for this reason, he was chosen to be the display leader, which gave him his first taste of responsibility. If he took a wrong turn, then the whole show went haywire. Whereas the athletics took place on the main playing field, the gymnastics display was to be performed on a big lawn close to the main house with rows of chairs arranged for a large audience of parents, teachers, and all and sundry. The house was quite a walk from the playing fields, so in between these two events, tea for the parents was served in close proximity to the gymnastics lawn. During the tea break, the boys had a chance to recover in between running their little legs off and then performing gymnastics. The last practice session had been the day before sports day, and the grand finale was for five boys to stand on their heads with their legs apart directly in front of the parents, with Geoffrey as the centrepiece. As this was also a type of dress rehearsal, they were all kitted out in their white shorts and vests. Underwear was never worn under sports clothes, and the majority of boys were still too underdeveloped to even know about, let alone need, 'jock straps'. Geoffrey's legs were rather skinny, and the cotton shorts were rather baggy, so when standing on his head, the legs of his shorts fell aside, exposing his private parts for the entire audience to admire. This, of course, was quickly spotted by Mr Pont, who ordered Matron to take in a stitch or two on Geoffrey's shorts so there would be no embarrassment.

The following day was the big day, and as they were finishing their lunch, the sound of crunching gravel could be heard as parents started arriving in their Jaguars and Rovers, parking in front of and behind Mr Pont's pride and joy, a pre-war Bentley which stood there for all to see with its shiny black paint and polished chrome gleaming in the sun. Slowly but surely, all the parents trudged their way, this time on foot, back down the driveway again to the sports field in preparation for watching their sons compete on the running track. Those boys who had made it to the final and were competing, Geoffrey included, donned their sports clothes and gym shoes and made their way to the track ready to run.

'Crack' went the starting pistol, fired by the Latin master, and off they charged for the 440 yards race. Geoffrey seemed to be going nicely up at the front until about halfway, when he realised he had no chance to maintain the same pace for much longer, let alone enough energy for a sprint finish. Flap, flap, flap went his gym shoes on the short dry grass. His feet seemed to be made of lead and were becoming heavier and heavier, while his legs felt weaker and weaker with every stride. Right behind him, he could hear other shoes similarly beating on the turf, getting closer and closer. Inevitably, first, one boy passed him and then another, but gasping for breath, he managed to hold his place all the way to the finish, running down the home straight to the cheers and clapping of proud parents. Eventually, after all the races had been run, Geoffrey was only able to boast a second place for his squad, Stanton. But his little bit of glory was still to come.

Now the races were over, quite a procession of teachers, parents and boys made their way back to the school for tea. Mrs Webster was busy serving the parents as they arrived for the afternoon's refreshments. Pouring cup after cup of tea from a giant aluminium teapot, she handed them out one after another. The time neared for Geoffrey's big moment, and parents were ushered to the seating arrangements made ready for the gymnastics display.

Every move was at the command of Mr Dorsey's whistle. The team was all lined up 'in the wings', waiting and ready to go. 'Peep', there was the first command, and Geoffrey proudly trotted out onto the grass leading the entourage round a circuit in front of the parents before they began a series of somersaults and handsprings on the mat. With the mat work out of the way, the boys reassembled while the box horse and springboard were arranged, ready for the next display. To begin with, the springboard was placed at the end of the horse so that the performers could make a leapfrog action over its length. This was one of the easier moves, but only as long as the leaping boy placed his hands far enough forward, otherwise there was touchdown with his backside before it cleared the end of the horse. After the horse had been turned from lengthways to sideways, there followed more exciting head flips and hand flips over the horse, finishing up with Geoffrey leading his team with an impressive angel jump. This required the gymnast to make an extra high jump from the springboard so that no hands or feet touched the horse at all, and with arms outstretched on either side, he flew over the horse like an angel. Mr Dorsey was, of course, always there, ready to receive and catch any boy who didn't quite clear the horse. Now it was time for the finale, with some of the boys making a human pyramid while Geoffrey and four others performed their headstands. This time his genitals remained unseen. A final ‘peep’ from Mr Darcy’s whistle, and in unison, they all stood on their feet once again before Geoffrey led his troupe off the grass and back into the school accompanied by much clapping. Geoffrey’s proud moment was over.

After quickly changing back into their school uniforms, the boys reunited with their parents in the gym, now being used as an exhibition hall to show off all the boy’s accomplishments of the term. There was a display of their paintings and various artwork, a display of their carpentry achievements comprising mostly ‘mortise and tenon’ and ‘dovetail’ joints, and the entries for the writing competition. Amongst the throng of parents, Geoffrey located his mother and father admiring his paintings; he liked to think they were admiring them anyway. Finally, this busy, parents' open day was rounded off with prize giving. Mr Pont took his place on the stage, immaculate as usual in a grey double-breasted suit and his black shoes shining like his Bentley. He spoke briefly about the Common Entrance and scholarship achievements before the long-winded process of awarding all the prizes. These included not only the awards for the athletics but also for the art, the handwriting, the carpentry and the model cup. Following in David's footsteps, Geoffrey won the model cup. He was also awarded second prize for art. Every year he was pipped to the post for the art prize by a boy called Newton, who was just that much better than Geoffrey. George made a thorough inspection of Geoffrey's carpentry efforts and gave his mark of approval. For once, Geoffrey actually received a little praise from him, probably because he himself had also learnt carpentry and was well accomplished in his meticulous way. Geoffrey also suspected he wanted to be sure that the extra money for carpentry lessons had not been wasted.

Finally, the long and exciting day drew to an end; his mother and father said goodbye, and he waved them off down the drive. He didn't feel like crying this time as he knew it was only a few more days before he would be going home, this time for good!

Part II: Haileybury

Chapter 9

The summer holiday that followed seemed to be one of the best. Geoffrey was free from all his prep school bullying, beatings and classroom abuse, and as yet, he didn't know what it was going to be like at Haileybury. Just now, it was a case of 'better the devil you don't know!' Summer holidays were always long, and it was some weeks before the dread started to creep in again with the occasional thought about going back to school. In the meantime, Geoffrey and his brother David always found something interesting to do, whether it be a bicycle ride or some other exciting pastime.

During one of their bike rides, they hadn't decided where they were going, but they just cycled anyway to see where it would take them. About a mile from home, they passed over a railway crossing on their way to the next village. Just on the other side of the railway track, David spotted an old farm trailer bearing a very large round metal tank. Attached to an outlet at one end of the tank was a big, fat, black hosepipe. The trailer appeared to have been there, unmoved, for a long while. The wooden frame had become green with moss, and grass had grown high round the half-deflated tyres with their time-hardened, cracked rubber. The pipe itself was a good deal overgrown, which prompted David to announce that it was derelict and unwanted. For some inexplicable reason, in his mechanically minded way, he decided that this big hose pipe was something that he needed and would be very useful. He was already busy planning how to remove it and transport it home without drawing too much attention. Both the boys knew that it was not really theirs to take, so it was best not to be seen. Just across the railway track on the other side of the road was a little house where the railway gatekeeper sat when he wasn't opening and closing the gates. Lying on his tummy so that he would be, as he thought, out of sight of the watchman, David set about removing the hose. After he had managed to detach the pipe, the two boys dragged it into a ditch leading away from the trailer and away from the railway, all the while believing they had not been seen. Then together with their two bicycles, they battled their way through the bushes and scrub overgrowing the ditch, until they thought they were out of sight and it was safe to reappear on the road.

The quickest way home was, of course, the way they had come, but that would mean passing by the gatekeeper again, so they decided they must go on to Harston, the next village, and then traverse along a muddy track they called Donkey Lane. This route would lead them back over the railway line to where the track joined up with a proper road. A left turn at the bottom of the bridge on the other side would eventually take them back to Little Shelford and home. This detour added an extra three miles to their journey, but this meant nothing to the intrepid brothers.

On their eventual arrival home, David and Geoffrey sneaked in through the gate and hid the pipe behind a mound of earth George had left while preparing a large herbaceous border at the front. Their plan had not extended far enough as to what they should do with the hosepipe, but the need to hide it only underlined the fact that they knew it was wrong. They hardly had time to take off their muddy shoes before the front doorbell rang. "I'll go, Mummy," said Geoffrey while Thea was busy taking off her apron that she always referred to as her 'pinny'. On opening the door, Geoffrey was startled to be confronted by the daunting sight of a large policeman filling the doorway. "Is your mother in?" he asked, as at that moment, she appeared behind Geoffrey. "Oh good, Mrs Finch?" he asked, and already assuming that it was, he continued, "I have had reports that two small boys have taken a water pipe from a farm tank near the railway crossing belonging to Howards Farm." The policeman had barely finished his sentence before Thea immediately turned to Geoffrey and asked, "Geoffrey, did you take it?"

"Yes," he admitted, "we thought it wasn't wanted anymore!"

"Where is it now, and where is David?" she demanded, feeling very small and wrong-footed under the watchful eye of the policeman.

"It's over there, by the earth," said Geoffrey pointing to where the end of the wretched pipe could be seen. At this point, David appeared, wondering what was going on. He soon realised and wished he had stayed away.

"What *have* you boys been up to?" she demanded, not really expecting an answer as the whole situation was quite clear. "Wait until Daddy hears about this. Now you must take it back at once, and this evening you will go to Mr Howard and apologise. I can't imagine what you thought you were doing!" she said angrily and continued to the policeman, "I'm so sorry, they have never done anything like this before or taken anything in their lives, but they will put it back immediately." The policeman pondered for a moment and then said, "The gatekeeper saw everything, Mrs Finch; he had watched the whole procedure and rang us directly. But, if they return it to where it belongs, then we will say no more about it, and we'll leave it up to you to reprimand them." and with that, he trudged off down the drive again.

Thea was furious with the boys and at the same time terrified that the neighbours would see the police at their door; the spying eyes of Mrs Brundle, who lived over the road, missed nothing, and the danger of full speed gossip was imminent. However, the moment passed, and now it was only David and Geoffrey's punishment waiting. Directly, they were sent back with the hosepipe to reinstall it where it rightfully belonged. On their return, they both wondered what was going to happen next. "After tea, you will go to the farm and apologise to Mr Howard." instructed their mother. She was particularly upset by the whole affair as, apart from having the police at her door, she regularly bought eggs from Mrs Howard who, over and above the statutory dozen, always put in an extra one or two brown eggs for the boys, proclaiming that "Frankie like a white egg" as if that was a good reason to give an extra egg or two, because Frankie, her son, preferred white eggs. Every time they bought eggs, she made this statement with her arms folded across her ample bosom, bouncing them up and down. But now, after the boys had had their tea, they walked round to the farm which lay just round the corner about half a mile away. They knocked on the door of the farmhouse they knew so well. Mrs Howard opened it and this time, not smiling, she said, "What 'ave you boys been up to? You'd better come in. I think it's Mr Howard you want to see, 'e's in the front room 'aving his tea." She ushered them into a room leading from the kitchen, and there sat Mr Howard.

"Come in, boys, what can I do for you?" he said rather than asked, knowing full well why they were there.

"Mummy said we must come and say sorry," said David. Geoffrey, being even more shy than David, always left the talking and the lead role to his brother. And after all, the whole thing was his idea.

"Sorry for what?" asked Mr Howard.

"We took a pipe from your water tank," said David looking at the floor rather than at Mr Howard. Geoffrey was squirming, thinking to himself that this ignominious episode must soon be over.

"Oh yes, I heard something about that. Is it back where it should be now?" he asked.

"Yes," said David meekly.

"And are you sorry too?" he suddenly turned and directed this question to Geoffrey.

"Yes," he replied barely audibly.

"Good. Then you better go on home, and I'll forget this ever happened." Mr Howard did not really know how to handle the situation and was also glad to be over with it.

"Thank you, Mr Howard." David said as he half pushed Geoffrey back out of the door, and with a 'Good-bye' to Mrs Howard, they rushed out of the house into the farmyard and beat a hasty retreat home. In the meantime, their father had returned from work and having heard the whole story from Thea, he wasted no time admonishing them and putting them both over his knee for a good walloping. At last, the whole episode was closed, but the boys had something to whisper about in bed that night.

It wasn't long before the nights started drawing in, and there was dew on the lawn in the morning; the summer holiday was over, and once again, George could take both his sons back to the same school. Geoffrey was now thirteen, and after all the years in short trousers at prep school, he, at last, sported long grey flannels. Preparing for Haileybury, apart from anything else, he had to learn how to put the collar on his shirt. All shirts were white with detachable collars, which were extremely stiff with an edge that rubbed unmercifully on small boy's necks. The shirt cuffs also required cufflinks. Just to master donning a shirt at a good pace required some practice. A short stud at the back held the collar onto the shirt, and a longer one at the front passed first through both layers of the shirt neck and then both layers of the collar. When the tie was in place, no studs were visible. The supposed advantage of all this was that collars could be changed frequently, avoiding the need to change the whole shirt.

Everything was new to Geoffrey; detachable collars were just a minor hurdle. Now his whole wardrobe was more grown-up, and he had proper lace-up shoes, brown for every day and black for Sundays, and there was no one but himself to polish them. The contents of his tuck box also changed enormously. Gone were the toys and sweets, replaced by a mug and a plate, coffee, sugar and a few basic items of food to supplement the school food. Geoffrey, not wanting to be different, was keen that all his clothing was right and conformed to the rules. Thus there were quite a few discussions with Thea before eventually, everything was packed and loaded into the car. As their departure became more and more imminent, David became less and less talkative, and Geoffrey became more and more nervous as his fear of starting at Haileybury began to get the better of him. On the occasions he had previously accompanied George, when leaving or picking up David, he was always in awe of the size of the school compared to his own. Now it was his turn to be left alone in that oppressive establishment.

The journey to school was endured almost all the way in silence as the two brothers were stuck in their own thoughts. Geoffrey's were half in dread as to how it was going to be and the other half thinking about home. All the while, their father puffed away contentedly on his pipe, probably remembering his days at Haileybury. It did not seem to worry him that he was leaving his two sons to suffer through the 'man-making' public school system. Geoffrey still could not understand how they could send him away from the bosom of the family if they really loved him. But, as Polly bounced off potholes, on reflection, he realised that they never actually *said* they did love him. Up Hailey Lane and just a few hundred yards more before George swung the dormobile through the entrance onto the school road, passing the science block that later would be Geoffrey's undoing.

George parked Polly behind the old study block, which was as near as one could get to the quadrangle. Two trunks, two tuck-boxes and two overnight cases had to be unloaded and carried to the boy's 'House'. Following in their father's footsteps, and indeed their grandfathers' and great grandfathers', they were placed in 'Bartle Frere' house. David, having already been at Haileybury for a couple of years, knew all the ropes and led the way. To make their way to their house, they must cross the quadrangle, this being mainly grass traversed by asphalt paths splitting it into segments. David informed Geoffrey that only masters were allowed to walk on the grass, and on no account should he set foot on it. They climbed the steps up to 'Bartle Frere' house, where a noticeboard hung in the entrance hall showing the compartment numbers for each boy. As they entered 'House' to which it was normally referred, Geoffrey was taken aback at its length. There were fifty compartments, each with a bed, a chest of drawers, a chair, and on the wall at the end of each was a mirror and a shelf with a row of pegs on which to hang clothes. Each compartment was separated from the next by a waist-high, panelled, dividing wall. There were twenty-five compartments down each side of the one big long room. At exactly halfway, there was a wide opening that led past shoe lockers to the washroom. The most junior boys started down at one end, and as the years passed, they gradually worked their way up to the other end, where the 'head of house' and dormitory prefects had their compartments. Bartle Frere's inmates were some of the luckier ones since one or two houses of which there were eleven had no dividing walls between the beds, thereby diminishing any privacy even further.

As they stood there in the middle of House, Geoffrey turned to the left to find his bed down at the end while David found his just above the halfway mark. Geoffrey's was next to last on one side, where there were a couple of other new boys starting to unpack. After dumping his case on his bed, they all returned to the car to fetch the rest of their belongings. Their father knew which way to go turning this way and that without hesitation since nothing much had changed since he attended the school, but as they trudged back and forth, Geoffrey wondered how on earth he could ever find his way around alone and already experienced a terrible sense of foreboding. Passing by other various entrances, the voices and shouts of boys could be heard with a ring of echo. In his warm little home, there was no echo;

here, everything seemed so big and overwhelming. When all their belongings were unloaded and deposited in their compartments, there was nothing more to be done except for their father to depart. The last thread attached to home was about to be severed. They accompanied him back to the dormobile to say goodbye, but there were no hugs; the boys were young men now, and young men shake hands when they say farewell. If George felt any emotions, he did not show them. He shook their hands with no more than a 'good-bye' to each, climbed onto the driver's seat and left. The boys stood there for a second, Geoffrey feeling totally out of his depth, before returning to House to unpack their clothes, David to his compartment and Geoffrey down to the other end. At prep school, crying was frowned upon, but here and now, it was absolutely out of the question.

Geoffrey found his neighbours also unpacking and, after an exchange of names, discovered that on one side was a boy called Oboloski and on the other was Brandon. Oboloski, or Obbo, as he soon became known, claimed to have some heritage of a Russian prince, but if there was any truth in this, it would never be known. He was treated no differently either by the masters or by the other boys. Some of the new boys already knew each other, having attended Haileybury Junior School, which fed a large percentage to Haileybury proper, so already, not being part of their gang, Geoffrey felt at a disadvantage. It didn't take long, however, before the Junior school entity disintegrated, and they all found out who they wanted as friends.

New boys were known as 'new guvnors' whereas junior boys were just 'guvnors' and were accommodated along with second and sometimes third term boys in the dormitory classroom, otherwise referred to as the DC. Here each boy had a locker where he could keep his books and other belongings. This was where Geoffrey's tuck box waited to be unpacked into his locker, but in the meantime, while busy sorting out the contents of his trunk in his compartment, Williams, the head of the DC, approached the new guvnors and informed them that soon a bell would ring, and they must go to the dining hall where a cup of tea and a snack could be found. He explained that nearly always, there were two bells, the first one, which rang five minutes before an event, was aptly known as the 'fiver'. It was like a warning that now there were only five minutes to be at some specific destination such as the dining hall for a meal. If a boy was later than the second bell, he would be punished. After their snack, they must return to the DC, where he would tell them what to prepare for this evening and what to expect the following morning.

Sure enough, a bell, a rather nasty electric variety, soon sounded, and Geoffrey and the other boys found their way to the dining hall. One of the boys seemed to know the way, so Geoffrey just followed along. Once again, he was dumbfounded by the sheer size of the hall; large enough to accommodate six hundred boys and a large number of staff. Evenly placed throughout the hall, there stood table after table after table, and every single table and bench had been hand made with an adze. Each piece of furniture bore the maker's trademark, a tiny mouse carved near the foot of every item. But just at this moment, Geoffrey was more involved with his 'lost' feeling and, as usual, his sense of abandonment. Was this what leaders and other men of importance had also suffered, he asked himself. Even now, 'stiff upper lip' prevailed.

Back in the DC, Williams soon appeared and told them what the procedures were for the next few days. As captain of the DC, it was his duty to teach them everything about the school. They must learn the names of all the houses, and all their different colours, the names of their housemasters and the names of all the buildings. The list was endless. They must get up half an hour before everybody else, and before breakfast he would take them round the school, teaching them everything they needed to know. After two weeks, they would be tested, and to achieve a pass, they must have at least ninety per cent correct. During these two weeks, they had to endure a cold bath every morning before going out on their educational promenade. When going to the bathroom for a shower or indeed a cold bath, all boys must walk, not run, naked from their compartment with their towel over their shoulder; round the waist was forbidden. This was a permanent feature for the junior half of the house. Already trying to remember all these rules, which were only the tip of the iceberg, Geoffrey felt on the verge of panic and wondered how on earth he would be able to survive.

After finding the locker bearing the same number as his compartment, he unpacked his tuck box. It was not long before the bell rang again, this time signalling bedtime for the junior boys. Back in his compartment, Geoffrey changed into his pyjamas and made his way to the bathroom. Greeted by rows of basins, two baths and a number of showers, Geoffrey shyly found a free basin, washed his face and hands, and cleaned his teeth. After spending a penny, he made his way back to his compartment and climbed into bed. Never wanting to look out of place, he kept an eye on what the other boys were doing to make sure he wasn't the only one already in bed. This bed was of the same standard as at his prep school; hard, squeaky and thin. After a little chit chat as the boys got to know each other, the lights went out, and it was time to sleep, but sleep did not come quickly to Geoffrey. In his head, he went through again and again what was going to happen in the morning, dreading the idea of a cold bath. As these thoughts eventually subsided, they were replaced by thoughts of home. Silently he wished he was there in his own bed, and as often before, he wondered what the rest of his family was doing. As much as he hated it, he knew his only option was just to survive. He listened to the squeaks and rustlings as the other boys turned in their beds, also trying to fall asleep. Curled up under the thin bedclothes, sleep finally overcame him.

He woke before any bells rang, listening and waiting to see what was going to happen. Then his first day began. Signalled by the bell, the new guvnors scrambled out of bed, some less willing than others. With pyjamas off and towels over their shoulders, they walked naked to the cold baths awaiting them. Although they all wanted to get it over with as quickly as possible, running was not allowed. Not many seconds were spent in the water, so it did not take long for all the boys to undergo the rude awakening followed by a quick brushing of the teeth and then the naked walk back down the dormitory. Geoffrey was glad he had practised putting on his shirt and sorting out the collar because now, when time was of the essence, he quite soon was fully dressed and ready to go.

They were allowed five minutes from the moment the 'fiver' rang to assemble in the entrance hall. Bartle Frere was next to Clock House, which, mid-placed at the head of the quadrangle, faced the chapel standing in its glory with its green copper dome. Aptly named, Clock House proudly kept the whole school aware of the time, chiming every quarter of an hour. Being so close to Bartle Frere, its chimes could not be missed, so when it rang the hour, and a few of the new guvnors had not yet appeared, Williams wasted no time in ticking them off.

There were only six new guvnors in Bartle Frere, but this first morning it took some time before they were all assembled. Eventually, they all followed Williams outside, down the steps and into the quadrangle. Similar small groups could also be seen appearing from other houses, and so began their early morning educational tour.

Chapter 10

Geoffrey's first day at Haileybury was underway. Almost before they began their tour, Williams admonished one of his gang for having his hands in his pockets and his jacket unbuttoned. They were quick to learn that jackets must always be buttoned, and hands in pockets was strictly forbidden. Williams then led them to the centre of Quad, where the paths dissecting the grass crossed in the middle. From here he could teach the new guvnors the names of all the buildings surrounding them. Standing there, Geoffrey felt totally intimidated by the sheer enormity of the school. Originally it was the East India College, founded in 1806 as a training institution. Eventually, after the college was closed, it was restarted a few years later in 1862, as a public school which became Haileybury. Thereafter, Imperial Service College was added, having been the training hub of personnel for the British Empire. Thus, there were many new names to be learnt, not only of the buildings enclosing Quad, but of many more outside.

Bartle Frere house with Trevelyan below stood on one side of Clock House, and on the other Colvin and Thomason. There were two more houses facing onto Quad, namely Lawrence and Edmonstone. Geoffrey learned the different colours of all the houses, including those outside Quad, and he learned the names of all the housemasters. Everything had to be committed to memory. If this was just the beginning, he wondered how would he ever be able to remember all the information that was still to come over the next two weeks. Forming one side of Quad was the Old study block, and the two houses Lawrence and Edmonstone, with Big School squeezed in between. As its name described, Big School was a large building whose main function was primarily the venue for plays, concerts and other major events. Just as Geoffrey and the gang of new guvnors had worked their way round as far as Chapel, which was the easiest to remember, the 'fiver' for breakfast rang, so directly Williams led the gang to the dining hall, ready to experience their first meal in the gigantic eating room, commonly known as just 'Hall'.

The roof of this building was actually a dome, claiming to be one of Europe's largest unsupported domes. It led to some very special acoustics inside; if a person talked quietly in one corner, the sound travelled up the corner, followed the inner curvature of the dome and down again at the opposite corner so that whatever had been said could be clearly heard at the other side. However, when the entire school was eating and talking at the same time, the sound level was raised by so many decibels that any normal conversation was almost out of the question. Hall was primarily a square building with a rounded protrusion at one end, housing a horseshoe-shaped table for the prefects. Inside, the oak-panelled walls bearing portraits of historical figures linked to the school surrounded the vast dining area. The Bartle Frere tables were nearest the entrance doors on one side, and after following the others into Hall, Geoffrey found his place, last but one, at the end of the junior table, the seating positions following the same order as the compartments. Everybody remained standing as more and more bleary-eyed boys made their way in, whilst the chattering alone raised the noise level to an ear-splitting degree.

Suddenly the noise came to an abrupt halt, silenced by the resonance of a gong constructed from a massive, brass, World War I shell captured from the Germans. As the sound of the gong subsided, the head boy said grace, a string of latin, "Benedic domine, nobis et donis tuis" ending with 'Dominum Nostrum' all of which was a trifle unclear to Geoffrey. But grace was barely over before the silence rapidly disappeared again as six hundred boys simultaneously sat down and continued their chattering. At the serving end of each table, a large tray of scrambled egg arrived together with some off-white slices of something described as toast. The scrambled egg, made en masse, had a watery consistency that soaked unappetisingly into the 'toast'. This morning, Geoffrey's nervousness did nothing to help his appetite; but when hungry, most of the boys were not too fussy about what they ate. Tea, known as 'orink', came from a large metal urn, one for each table. Its only resemblance to tea being that it was a warm brown liquid, but with a spoonful of sugar, it was however quite drinkable. In the middle of each table was some sliced bread, a bowl of marmalade, and another bowl containing 'groise', that being the school's answer to butter. Apart from the names of places and masters and such, Geoffrey began to learn all the other slang references used throughout the school. It wasn't long before the gong sounded again announcing the closing grace 'benedicto benedicatur'. All these sounds, bells and gongs, were for Geoffrey always a signal that it was one step nearer to something he feared. Sometimes, of course, it was the opposite, when a bell might signal the end of some torment, but just now it meant his first lesson loomed closer.

Breakfast over, the boys had half an hour before Chapel, so they made their way back to the DC. More information was drummed into Geoffrey and the rest of the new guvnors during this short break, so they at least knew where to find their form rooms. Importantly they learnt that masters were known as 'beaks' and whenever a boy passed even near to a beak he must always 'tip' him. To tip a beak required a subtle raising of a finger as a type of acknowledgement; failure to do so could be well punished, especially if the beak was strict. As they all endeavoured to absorb this latest information their instruction time was halted by the ringing of the fiver for Chapel. Out of the DC, down the stairs and across Quad to Chapel where Geoffrey and his new companions were shown in which pews they could sit. The service was not unlike that at his prep school, but with far more pomp and everything was so enormously large. Looking upwards, the dome, with its gold inscription all the way round, towered above him, whilst the organ, whose massive pipes could be seen hiding behind grilled screens, droned a melancholy recital. Exactly on time, the service began, and it wasn't long before Geoffrey knew this daily routine like the back of his hand. The lesson was always read by a college prefect (CP). CP's sat at the back of Chapel making it a long walk for the lesson reader when making his way to the elevated lectern standing at the fore. On the left was the pulpit for the priest and on the right was the lectern for the lessons. When the lesson was over, the ensuing silence was only broken by the reader's steps clicking on the polished stone floor all the way back to his pew. Apart from Bartle Frere's head of House, none of the CP's were familiar to Geoffrey, but he had learned that they could be identified by their tie, that being black with white spots. He also learned that if their paths were crossed, they didn't hesitate to dish out punishments.

Chapel service was soon over, and Geoffrey's first obstacle was to find his way to the form room block and then to his classroom. The most junior boys started in the 'removes' and graduated through the 'middles' to the 'fifths', 'upper fifths' and for some to the 'sixths'. This term Geoffrey was in Remove C which was the first step on the way to his GCE 'O' levels. Another new boy in Bartle Frere was also in Remove C and seemed to know where they had to be, so Geoffrey tagged along with him. The corridors were crowded with a tangle of boys going this way and that but eventually having battled through the hustle and bustle they found the right door. There were already a few other boys there, sitting at the desks and Geoffrey found a place to sit more or less in the middle. He was not at all comfortable to sit at the front but neither did he want to sit at the back; as was his character at this time, he had no desire to draw attention to himself. The desks, with benches attached, appeared to be very old and Geoffrey felt sure that George had probably sat on exactly the same bench during his time there. Designed for two boys to sit at each, they were well worn and over the years, pupils had carved their initials into the surface of the desk leaving it no longer smooth. Geoffrey always kept an eye open for the initials of one of his forefathers but never found any that fitted the bill.

It wasn't long before nearly all the places were taken, and Geoffrey sat nervously waiting to see what was going to happen next. As he sat there wondering, in walked a beak, clad in a black gown creating the perfect image of a typical school teacher, looking exactly as a teacher should, and as they had for so many years. After introducing himself as the form master, he continued by making a roll call, quickly establishing that no one was missing, and all names were now known. After what seemed like an endless amount of information, which Geoffrey struggled to remember, they were despatched to the 'book room' where they collected all the textbooks and exercise books they needed. Unlike his last school, boys kept all their learning attributes in their lockers and only took the books they needed for the appropriate lessons. Just as the last boy came back from the book room clutching all his books, the bell rang to signal the end of the first lesson. Directly, throughout the whole form room block, the sound of chatter could be heard as boys moved around to their next lesson. So the procedure repeated itself during the morning with a half-hour break, aptly named 'the half', between the first two lessons and the second two.

Geoffrey made his way back to the DC and unloaded his books into his locker. On earlier advice from David, he had packed a few edibles in his tuck box which were now stashed in his locker, so he grabbed a biscuit to keep his hunger at bay and see him through until lunchtime. The half was already nearing its end, so Geoffrey made his way back towards the form rooms for the second two lessons and just to remind him, the fiver rang, warning of the imminent start of these. He began to realise that for the next five years a very large part of his life was going to be controlled by a combination of bells and noticeboards. It also soon became clear that the whole school revolved around a repetitive routine governed by rules that were not to be broken. On his way to lunch, he passed a beak walking towards him and it was only luck that, at the very last minute he remembered to raise his finger to tip him. Lunch was a very similar episode to breakfast and Geoffrey had already begun to know the procedure. He also discovered that it was quite an advantage to be able to eat quickly. If the food was nice it was always devoured in no time at all, with nothing left when the slow eaters were ready for more, so it was vital to eat fast to have a chance of a second helping. The food also followed a set pattern, invariably the same dishes on the same day each week. Even though a menu was posted outside the entrance to Hall it was quite easy to know what would be served purely by the day of the week. Wednesday evening was always the highlight of the week when beef burgers and chips were served for supper; the popularity of the chips often causing the unlucky servers to have to battle to obtain more. Sometimes it was like feeding meat to a gang of starving hyenas.

Following lunch, another break spent in the DC allowed food to be digested before the afternoon's sport. Williams used this time to give more information to the new guvnors. They learned that when they had passed the guvnors test at the end of the first two weeks, they were eligible for 'fagging'. Geoffrey was just wondering what fagging entailed when a dormitory prefect, a DP, entered the DC and called for a fag. One of the second term boys volunteered and was sent to buy some goods from the school shop, alias the 'Grubber'. If the 'fag' performed his task well, he could expect a small tip which made the job worthwhile, but not all the prefects were so generous, so it wasn't to be taken for granted that a tip would be forthcoming. Guvnors could also be chosen by their house prefects to be private fags. This meant they were dedicated to fag throughout the term for that one person, namely their fagmaster. The role of a private fag was onerous; every morning the fagmaster's bed had to be made and his shoes polished, in addition to any other tasks he may wish. The hardest job of all was preparing his uniform for the cadet force. The uniform had to be pressed with knife-like creases in the trousers, the boots must have their toe caps gleaming with a mirror finish, the belt needed to be 'blanco'd' and the brasses polished along with the cap badge. Every Wednesday afternoon all those in the CCF (combined cadet force) had to go on parade. Luckily it wasn't a dress parade every week, meaning that often the dress code was ‘denims’ or ‘mufti’, these being a more relaxed attire.

According to the noticeboard, this first afternoon Geoffrey and his new companions must assemble out on Twenty Acre. Duly named because of its size, Twenty Acre provided a significant number of rugby pitches that catered for all levels of rugby. In the drying room, Geoffrey found his rugby shorts and shirt, and rather self-consciously, dressed ready for games. Out in the entrance hall, he donned his rugby boots and made his way to the playing fields. The afternoon was spent running this way and that, passing and catching a rugby ball, and various other manoeuvres designed for the boys to demonstrate their rugby skills. Geoffrey’s abilities soon made it clear that he was not built for the scrum but was quite adequate for one of the outside positions. When it came to tackling competence, he gritted his teeth, plucked up all his courage and threw himself at the boy charging towards him. At the last moment, he closed his eyes and hoped for the best. It proved quite successful and he gained some credit with the master in charge. At last, they all returned to House to shower and get ready for the afternoon’s lessons. Off came the games clothes and now, completely naked, he slung his towel over his shoulder and without running, that being forbidden, he made his way as fast as possible to the washroom for his shower; but still, he had to make the return journey back to his compartment with his undeveloped and not so manly credentials on display. It took him quite a while to become used to walking around without a stitch of clothing and without embarrassment.

Back in the DC, another short spell of free time before the evening lessons allowed boys to make themselves something to eat or drink. Geoffrey still only had his biscuits to nibble on, so he made do with these, while he hoped he would soon find out where the Grubber was. While crunching on his custard cream, he thought about tea at home with Thea's homemade cake, but all this achieved was enhancement of his loneliness. By now he had started to get to know his fellow chums and whom he liked more than others. Brandon, who soon became known as just 'Brad', was the son of a banker and seemed quite a decent sort of chap, whereas Geoffrey considered Obbo to be a bit of a show-off. Having come from the Junior school he thought he was somebody special; somebody of greater status than the rest of his fellow guvnors. The DC was furnished with wooden tables and chairs, with a single gas ring in one corner which was sufficient to boil a kettle. The room was kept warm by an open fire which was fuelled with coal and Geoffrey soon discovered that making toast in front of it was a popular pastime.

Yet again the fiver rang for the evening lessons, so once more it was time to head back to the form room block. Geoffrey had now mastered finding his way around the form rooms and where he should be for each lesson. His earlier embarrassment at prep school, when made an example of by Mr Pont for not reading the noticeboard had not been totally in vain, as he now spent ample time standing in front of noticeboards trying to make sure he wasn't going to go wrong or miss anything. The two evening lessons passed uneventfully, and Geoffrey had started to get to know his classmates from other houses. With the day's lessons over, there was just enough time for Geoffrey to dump his books back in his locker before going directly to Hall for his first supper which followed the same pattern as the other meals. Mr Mann, his housemaster, made an entrance to check that everything and everybody was in order. He was not a big man and his posture was such that he carried himself with his head pushed forward. He had wire-framed glasses which he wore sometimes on top of his head and if crossed he became like an enraged bull with anger written all over his face. Simultaneously, his neck reddened and appeared to swell, making his head protrude even further forward. At this moment, he had nothing to be angry about and soon disappeared again before the gong signalled the end of supper.

In the DC, the boys had begun to know each other quite well so the chatter level had escalated considerably with a combination of broken and unbroken voices, the highest treble of them all belonging to Jolyon, a boy claiming to be a distant relative of the Admiral of the Fleet. It was not long before the bell signalled the start of 'prep', the equivalent of homework, so the boys sat quietly and endeavoured to fulfil the tasks they had been set before the next day's lessons. Geoffrey found it hard to concentrate, often thinking about home, but in the end, he completed his prep just in time for house prayers. Everybody gathered in House and stood there waiting as if something was about to happen which indeed it did. Walking with his short little stride Mr Mann reappeared and clutching a prayer book, he made his way to where all 'his' boys had assembled. Encircled by the boys, Mr Mann read a prayer, followed by everybody reciting the Lord's prayer. A final 'amen' and it was bedtime for the junior half of House.

When in bed, Geoffrey felt the most alone, just as he had during his time at prep school. He thought about life at home, and jealously, he thought about his sister Clare tucked up in her own cosy bed. He was thirteen now and homesickness had taken on a different form. He was no longer missing the love of his parents; any demonstrative love had disappeared long ago. But he was missing the security of home and now he felt trapped in a situation in which he had no wish to be. He thought about his first full day at Haileybury that he had survived, but how were the next days and months going to be? So far he had endured one day, just one day. What lay in store for him tomorrow, he wondered.

Chapter 11

Dreading his cold bath, Geoffrey woke before any bells rang. This morning though, he was woken by the clanging of a bucket and some cheerful but tuneless and monotonous whistling. He lay there listening but had no desire to stick his head up to see over the compartment wall. It had been made clear to him that there should be no noise in House early in the morning before the fiver for breakfast rang, so he wondered what was going on. Then he heard a hushed voice say "Good morning Charlie," to which came a loud reply "Mornin', Sir," accompanied by what seemed to be extra clanking. This was Geoffrey's first encounter with Charlie. Charlie, who called everyone 'Sir', was the house 'Toby' whose job it was to keep the house clean, help serve at meals and generally look after the boys. Every house had a Toby, but Charlie had been Bartle Frere's Toby for many years, long enough to clearly remember George when he was also an inmate of the house. On a daily basis, he washed out the bathroom and toilets and kept the house floor highly polished. Some houses had only rough wooden floors, but Charlie was particularly proud of his floor, which was one of the best. Every single morning before all the boys arose, Charlie performed his cleaning duties, and the daily clanking of his bucket was an accepted part of the morning ritual. No matter how quietly he was addressed, Charlie's standard reply, "Mornin', Sir," came at full volume.

Geoffrey's listening was interrupted by the bell to waken the new guvnors for their morning educational tour. In and out of the cold bath, a wrestle with his collar studs and then out into the cold morning air; Geoffrey's second day was underway. Williams led the new guvnors round the school, pointing out and naming all the buildings whilst reminding them that they must remember everything if they wanted to pass the guvnor's test. What was the name of the housemaster's wife? What were the colours of the Thomason house? What was the building next to the Grubber? The list was endless. Because the term started in the middle of the week, the weekend was almost upon them, which gave Geoffrey something to which he could look forward, even though there were four lessons on Saturday morning to soldier through before they were free. After another lonely night thinking about home, Saturday arrived, which cheered him up; only the four lessons to get through. On the way out of Hall after breakfast, he bumped into David. Even though they were in the same house, this was the first time he had had any contact with David. Geoffrey thought it strange that at home, they did everything together, but at school, they lived two separate lives. However, on most Saturday evenings there was usually a film being shown in Big

School, and David said they should go together. At last, some close family contact pleased Geoffrey no end even though David never talked about home. But anyway, now he really had something to which he could look forward. He always needed something on the horizon which would make him glad.

That afternoon, Geoffrey found himself alone in the DC with Williams. Although he took his role seriously as captain of the DC, he was actually quite a decent chap. In this respect, he decided to warn Geoffrey that at the end of term, when everybody had gathered in House, each new guvnor must stand on the table at the senior end and sing a song to all and sundry. He advised Geoffrey to choose a song he thought he could sing, and when he was confident that he could remember all the words, he could practise in front of Williams. This alarmed Geoffrey somewhat, and every now and again, Williams asked him if he had a song ready, which only served to remind him of what lay ahead. He mentioned this to the other new guvnors, but they were loath to believe him until Williams backed up his story.

In the evening, he met up with David in Big School. David was with a couple of his friends, but although they were far more senior to Geoffrey, they did not object to his presence. Still with the singing performance on his mind, he asked David if he really had to sing at the end of term. David didn't deny it, so Geoffrey slumped even deeper into the fear of making a fool of himself. In the meantime, while boys were slowly filling the hall and the projectionist was busy loading the reels, Big School was filled with the beat of 'The Dave Clark Five' and other popular bands. The boys around him talked about the latest groups and 'releases' and Geoffrey found this banter rather interesting. Being with the more senior boys and with the loud music playing, Geoffrey liked the atmosphere. It was something new to him, and he found it quite exciting. Although at his prep school he had been told he couldn't sing, he liked music, especially such as they played now, with a lively beat. He began to get a taste for 'pop' music and soon picked up the group names and other jargon. At home, George and Thea had not yet got used to the idea of 'pop'. George's taste was Glen Miller and jazz, whereas Thea's was more along the Porgy and Bess line. Thea liked to sing, so Geoffrey became familiar with various songs from Thea's singing repertoire, but George never really showed much musical enthusiasm at all. Only occasionally, he could be seen tapping his foot if some jazz came on the radio. He always claimed that he wanted to be a priest, but he was let down by his dreadful, out of tune growl, that being his answer to singing.

The film came to an end, and although David and his friends still had an hour before bedtime, for Geoffrey, it was already time for him to report back to House and prepare for bed. On Sunday mornings, there was an extra half hour in bed before the day began, but for the new guvnors, this first Sunday's extra half hour only provided for an extended learning session, with no extra time in bed. There were two Chapel services on Sundays, a compulsory long service, usually in the morning and a short service in the evening, which, just like before, had a serious impact on exeat times. Apart from Chapel, there was plenty of free time, and after breakfast, Geoffrey wrote his letter to 'Mummy and Daddy'. He only wrote about what had happened during the first few days; he no longer wrote that he wanted to come home. That was now a thing of the past, as was crying. Regardless of any mental or physical pain, he had learnt to hold back any tears and never, ever cried again.

He needed to give his letter to David so that his and David's letter could go in the same envelope. David shared a study with three other boys in the 'Old' study block, and with his newly gained knowledge of the buildings, he managed to find his way there. Timidly he knocked on the door and poked his head into the room. He spotted David sitting in his armchair, also writing his letter. His study mates were busy hanging posters of fast cars and pin-up girls, trying to create an atmosphere in the room and escape from the four, drab, cream coloured walls. "Come in Finch, Dave is over there," said one of them as he gestured towards David. He had never heard anyone call his brother 'Dave' before; Geoffrey thought it sounded a little common. He delivered his letter and feeling out of place, he quickly left and returned to the DC.

Back in the DC, the other boys were playing table tennis with well-worn bats and a rather tired net, but it worked sufficiently enough. So far, all the boys in the DC seemed to get along, but as yet no firm friendships had formed. All had their different backgrounds, but there still remained the established bond between the boys from the Junior School. Later on, the occasional fight occurred but prefects soon put a stop to them and dished out punishments to the offenders, regardless of who was to blame. Geoffrey began to learn that most importantly, he must look after himself and do whatever it takes to save his own skin.

Before he knew it, it was time for lunch. School Sunday lunch was actually not too awful, the most common being the kitchen's answer to roast meat of one sort or another, which was served ready-sliced in large metal baking dishes. Even for Geoffrey, the meat was mostly edible, but unlike his prep school, there was no punishment for leaving fat or gristle. The meat was accompanied by roast potatoes served in rather beaten up aluminium dishes that were extremely misshapen and definitely past their best. Their contents, however, made the whole lunch worthwhile, the majority being nice and crunchy. Along with the potatoes came a seasonal vegetable. Peas, which had taken on a more pastel shade of green, were the most common. Sometimes it was Brussels sprouts which could be better named as just sprout since their individuality had long since disappeared. With plenty of gravy poured over the potatoes and peas, Geoffrey considered it far more to his liking than the lunches at his prep school.

Williams had instructed Geoffrey to light the fire in the DC after lunch, so while the other boys looked on, he struggled with some kindling and newspaper and endless matches. After a couple of failed attempts and a large amount of smoke filling the room, he finally succeeded, but not until Williams had pronounced that he must suffer 'guvnor's fire torture' for using too many matches. Geoffrey wondered what 'fire torture' entailed, but whatever it was, it made him rather nervous; just the word torture filled him with trepidation. With a shovelful of coal, the open fire started to burn merrily and throw out some warmth. Soon the coals were glowing nicely, and Williams summoned Geoffrey.

"Finch, come here!" he ordered, and Geoffrey, not wanting to disobey, came forward to where Williams stood next to the fire.

“Stand there with your back to the fire,” he said, pointing to a spot directly in front of the fire, “and don’t move away,” he added. Geoffrey obliged, and it was only a few seconds before he felt the heat through his trousers. After a few minutes, it felt as if they were on fire and there was a definite smell of singeing.

“Now stand still, and don’t move,” he stressed again as he bent down and grasping the front of both trouser legs, he pulled them hard against the backs of Geoffrey’s legs.

“Ow, ow, ow!” cried Geoffrey as the material burned the more delicate skin of his legs. The pain from the burning was quite substantial for a long while, but apart from some red stripes down the backs of his legs, there was no further physical damage. As Williams released the hot material, Geoffrey hopped around, trying to keep his trousers away from his legs. The other boys laughed while Geoffrey held back his tears.

The afternoon was interspersed with roll calls, again shortened to just ‘call’, the first being at four o’clock, the second at six o’clock just before Chapel. Calls were not to be missed. If permission to miss call had not earlier been granted, typically for an exeat, failure to stand and be counted was a guarantee for punishment. The most common form of punishment was lines to write. These were not ordinary lines such as ‘I must not run in the corridor’; they were far more complicated. The lines were named ‘dates’ and had to be written neatly on special paper. Geoffrey had heard some talk about ‘dates’ and ‘date paper’ and wondered what it was, but now, Spratt, another member of the DC had earned himself a punishment of ‘3x’, that being three times dates. Through Spratt’s misdemeanour, all the other new guvnors found out what a ‘dates’ punishment involved. First, the special paper had to be purchased from the Bookroom at the cost of one penny a sheet, and then a list of dates which could be borrowed or bought was also needed. The list comprised of around ten different dates, each being approximately one line long. These had to be written out with the script fitting neatly between the lines on the paper. Added to this, since there were ten different lines, it was difficult to commit them to memory, so each had to be copied in turn. The end result was very time consuming, that being the meaning of the punishment. Geoffrey soon discovered that 3x was really quite a light punishment, the most common was 5x, but sometimes 10x, with the worst of all being ‘10x and a ticket’. The ‘ticket’ being a note to take to the offender’s housemaster, who would then further admonish the boy. If a boy was unfortunate enough to accumulate three tickets, it automatically dictated a beating. Beatings were quite a common occurrence and could be administered by either the housemaster or the head of House. If the latter considered it necessary to beat a boy, he had first to gain permission from the housemaster. When such an occasion arose, all the house prefects were obliged to witness the event which took place in the DC after the guvnors and new guvnors had been sent away.

One day after lunch, when Geoffrey was on his way back to the DC, he wondered why other guvnors were hanging around outside. "What's going on?" he asked. "Someone's getting a beating, so we are not allowed in there," came the answer. Almost immediately, Geoffrey heard the thwack of a cane striking a backside, again and again, four strokes, followed by a slight pause before the victim came rushing out rubbing his posterior. Fortunately, house beatings were not a common occurrence during Geoffrey's time in the DC. Most canings were carried out by Housemasters, or even the headmaster for particularly serious offences.

On Sundays, though, there were no beatings, and after a short evening service in Chapel, it was supper time, and Geoffrey's first Sunday was drawing to a close. With a whole week of early rising, cold baths, and lessons lying ahead of him, Geoffrey felt as if he was drowning in misery, and it was with a dreadful sinking feeling that he crept into bed again, wondering how he was going to survive. One more week and still lots to learn about the school; he must not fail the test. What were the colours of Edmonstone and who lived at the top of Big School? He tried to remember all the information he had learnt as he lay in his bed, going over it again and again, until he eventually fell asleep.

There it was, the bell telling him it was time to face the day and indeed face the week. He crept out of bed, as did the other guvnors, took off his pyjamas and made his naked way to the bathroom where the two baths were already filled with ice-cold water. Quickly in and out, he returned to his compartment, dressed, made his bed and went out to the hall. He had already fallen into the morning routine, which, apart from the cold baths, wasn't going to change much for a few years. As Williams led the group around the school, Geoffrey tried hard to take in all the names and places, telling himself that he must pass the test, otherwise, apart from the ignominy of failing, it prolonged the cold bath treatment another week. He ticked the days off as, at last, the weekend neared. When Friday arrived, Geoffrey was just preparing to go to Chapel when he heard that Fridays were different, so instead of Chapel, there was 'lists' in Big School. Wondering what 'lists' was, he followed the others into Big School. After a hymn, Mr Seward, the headmaster, stepped onto the stage to address the school. He was quite a large man with a booming voice, and when clad in his black gown, his whole being was enough to strike fear into most boys, especially Geoffrey. This Friday, his announcements were short and soon over, but at least Geoffrey now knew the meaning of lists. Saturday evening was again spent with David and his friends watching the film in Big School, but for Geoffrey, it was rather overshadowed by the knowledge that the next morning the guvnor's test lay in wait for him.

The time for Geoffrey to clear the first hurdle of his duration at Haileybury arrived in the form of the guvnor's test. Even though he was really nervous, the test wasn't as bad as he had expected. He was more nervous about failing than about the test itself, but by the skin of his teeth, he managed to pass it, much to his relief. This made his Sunday a much brighter prospect. At a loose end in the afternoon, he found himself alone in the DC with only Williams as company. Williams was doing his 'prep', but after a while, he closed his books and suggested to Geoffrey that it would be a good idea if he practised singing his song while he judged Geoffrey's performance. Geoffrey didn't think it was a good idea at all but didn't feel in a position to object, so obeying Williams' instructions, he stood on a chair, "To make it more like the real thing," said Williams, while Geoffrey struggled to prepare himself mentally. "What are you going to sing?" he asked. Geoffrey hadn't really made up his mind, but since his repertoire was somewhat limited and it would be just before Christmas, he replied, "Once in royal." He had considered singing Molly Malone again, but after the previous performance, he didn't feel it brought him a great deal of luck. "Alright, let's hear you then," said Williams. So Geoffrey, who was not one to make an exhibition of himself and feeling desperately awkward, started singing, "Once in royal David's city" in his high pitched, unbroken, treble voice. Standing there, elevated on the chair, was totally against his inner wishes and he just wanted it to stop, but at least there was only Williams to embarrass him. After all, at the end of the term, the whole house, fifty boys, were going to boo and shout at him; how will he feel then? At the end of the first verse, Williams interrupted and said, "Not bad, you were mostly in tune, but you will need to sing louder when you do it at the end of term. Just saying 'the end of term' sounded nice, but Geoffrey knew it was a million miles away, and a lot would happen before then.

After another go at the first verse, Williams let Geoffrey off the hook, so he climbed down from the chair just as Brad and Jolyon came into the DC. They started playing ping-pong when suddenly Jolyon stopped and in his squeaky voice, asked Williams, "What's a guvnor's brew?"

"Why do you ask that?" he replied.

"I heard some Trevelyan guvnors saying that Gosford was going to get guvnors brew if he didn't watch out, what is it?" he asked again.

“It’s not something you would like, but I dare say you will find out soon enough,” said Williams. That left them all wondering what on earth it could be. If it was going to be worse than guvnor’s fire torture, then Geoffrey didn’t want to know, but it wouldn’t be long before he found out.

Chapter 12

Monday morning came around again, and it was a subdued group of boys who made their way to Hall for breakfast. Two DP's had chosen Oboloski and Spratt to be their private fags. It was both good and bad to be a private fag. It meant many routine daily tasks in addition to always being on call for any extra errands, but on the plus side, if the fag had performed his duties well, he was usually rewarded with a reasonable tip at the end of term. Now, for these two, with their fag duties waiting, they both left quickly after breakfast to make the beds and polish the shoes of their fagmasters. Geoffrey was just on his way into the DC to prepare for his first two Monday morning lessons when he was accosted by Cartier, one of Bartle Frere's prefects, who also had the higher rank of college prefect.

As soon as new guvnors had passed their test, the race was on for the prefects to pick the guvnor they liked best or considered would perform best as their private fag. So now it was Geoffrey's turn when Cartier asked Geoffrey to be his fag. In some respects, it was considered an honour to be asked, so it was taken for granted that the guvnor would accept such a request. Geoffrey was no exception, and since the Cartier emporium was known to be rather wealthy, Geoffrey didn't hesitate to accept in anticipation of a handsome tip at the end of term. When Cartier started showing Geoffrey what he had to do, he soon realised it was not going to be all plain sailing. The more mundane tasks such as making his bed and cleaning his shoes were easy, but it happened that Cartier held quite a high rank in the naval section of the CCF. The army uniforms were bad enough, but those of the navy section were the worst. The belts and gaiters were white, thus requiring white blanco, which was much more difficult than the khaki to apply evenly, and any marks were far more visible. It was a must to remove the belt brasses for polishing, it being virtually impossible to shine them once installed on the belt as the slightest slip with the Brasso showed directly on the newly blanco'd webbing. The gaiters were almost more of a problem with white webbing and small black leather straps and buckles that had to be blacked with boot polish requiring extremely careful application. As if this wasn't bad enough, having shown Geoffrey how to take care of all the accessories, Cartier then produced the trousers which needed to be pressed. Unlike ordinary trousers, they were well flared and instead of pressing the creases lengthways, the creases had to be in the opposite direction, across the legs in equal distances from the bottom to the top. Geoffrey realised that his term of fagging for Cartier was going to be quite tough, and he wasn't looking forward to the day when Cartier had his first dress parade.

Geoffrey was not afraid of the tasks that had now been bestowed upon him, but as was his usual problem, he was afraid of making a mess of it and the consequent ignominy of a ticking off. All went well to start with, and Geoffrey's bed making received a thumbs up from Cartier, as did his shoe polishing. Wednesday afternoons were reserved for Combined Cadet Force activities which replaced rugby, cricket and all other sports. Luckily for Geoffrey, on this first Wednesday, there were no dress parades, but nevertheless, he had to polish Cartier's boots until they shone with a mirror finish. New guvnors did not participate in the CCF during their first term, but preparing the uniform for their fagmaster was bad enough, although they did learn how it all went together when their time came to do their turn of duty. Later, when Geoffrey himself had to serve his statutory three years, he found out that the worst scenario was to be sent on the assault course when in full uniform directly after a dress parade, causing the polished boots to be scuffed to bits and the uniform to become covered in mud and dirt. Often the commanding officer, out of meanness, ordered another dress parade the following week to see how well his squad had cleaned up their uniforms. When the end of term arrived and the fagmasters paid their tips to their fags Geoffrey awaited eagerly in the hope of a few pounds for his term's work. His disappointment must have shown when he received the least of all from the richest of all. He could only be thankful for everything he had learnt.

But now it was Monday morning, and having survived the first two lessons, in the half, Geoffrey went to the Grubber to treat himself to a snack and a fizzy drink. The Grubber, a solid building of red bricks, had not changed much since George attended the school. In his day, there was often a queue of boys outside waiting for it to open and for want of anything better to do while they waited, they scored hemispherical holes in the brickwork with the coins they were soon going to spend. By twisting them back and forth against the relatively soft bricks, they made round indentations in the wall. Eventually, a large part of the wall became just a mass of holes of different sizes according to the size of the coin. Times changed, and there was seldom a queue anymore, so there was very little increase in the number of holes.

Between lunch and games, Geoffrey and the other members of the DC were killing time before it was time to change for rugby when Williams came in and announced that Jolyon, having failed to clean up properly, had earned himself a guvnor's brew. Williams instructed him to sit on a chair whilst two others held him fast. He then showed Geoffrey and the rest how to make a concoction that the offender, in this case Jolyon, must drink. Using a base of cold coffee with some sour milk, a dash of ink was then added. The pickings from Brad's nose and a gob of saliva from Spratt were thrown in. Geoffrey, feeling rather disgusted by the proceedings, was somewhat unwilling to participate but to save face, thought he better do something, so he found a stale biscuit that he crumbled into the mixture. The dishcloth was then squeezed out into the mug, and the brew was ready. All this took place under Jolyon's nose so he could see exactly what he was about to be forced to drink. Now he was told that to make it a little easier for him, he would be blindfolded so he couldn't see what was on its way into his mouth. During the whole process, the other boys held him down in the chair. Once blindfolded, unknown to Jolyon, the mug of 'brew' was replaced by a mug of plain water, which he was then forced to drink. How he struggled and spat and swore. He twisted and wriggled, trying everything possible to avoid any of the foul liquid passing his lips, but in spite of his protestations, an amount of the water entered his mouth. His shirtfront became quite wet from the spillage, thanks to his struggles. Even though it was only water, in his mind, it was the revolting mixture which was enough to make him retch almost to the point of vomiting. At last, the blindfold was removed, and the poor boy realised how he had been fooled. He bravely tried to see the funny side and keep smiling, but the laughter from everyone was a trifle half-hearted as most were glad that they had not been the victim.

Geoffrey soldiered on, becoming more and more familiar with the workings and nuances of the school. The days came and went, each one much like the last, only interspersed with weekends. He was learning fast how to survive but still was afraid of authority. This fear seemed to have become instilled in his character. To help him survive, he still relied on always having something to which he could look forward. Through the week, he could look forward to the weekend, which mostly sufficed, but when he knew there was an exeat coming, that was best of all. Eventually, it was time for his first day out of public school. Saturday had been chosen, and Geoffrey had great difficulty concentrating on his morning lessons. Eventually, the bell rang, bringing the last one to a close. These were the occasions when the bell was Geoffrey's friend and sometimes even his saviour. He wasted no time in packing up his books and rushing back to the DC to cast them into his locker. He hurried back to meet with David behind the Old study block, and as he panted round the corner, he could see, through the austere black railings, the faithful Polly with George sitting behind the wheel puffing away on his pipe as usual. His heart leapt at the sight that he had missed for what seemed an eternity but was actually only a few weeks. Now he was going home, and although he had to be back later that evening, he shut that out of his mind and just enjoyed the moment to its full.

"Hello boys," greeted his father as they hopped in. He engaged first gear and they drove off.

He was, of course, glad to see his father, but home was what he longed for most. The journey home was just a little shorter than that from his last school, but it still seemed to take much too long. At last, the landmarks became more and more familiar and eventually, George swung Polly into the drive. Both David and Geoffrey rushed inside, where they surprised Thea, who was busy preparing lunch in the kitchen. As before, when he came home from prep school, everything seemed so small, but now it seemed even smaller, compared to the enormity of Haileybury. Up the stairs, two at a time, along the landing and into his room where everything was just as he had left it. He stood there for a minute, looking around at all his familiar things, quietly savouring the moment and being thankful he was back home, albeit briefly. His dreaming was broken by Thea calling that lunch was ready. He made his way down again and sat in his usual place. Whilst George carved the roast joint, Thea brought the vegetables to the table; nothing had changed, but then why should it, thought Geoffrey. After all, he had only been away for a few weeks, but what he did know was that home was where he wanted to be; about this there was no doubt. There was still tea and an early supper to enjoy before it was time for the unwelcome return journey back to hard benches and hard masters.

More weeks passed as the nights drew in, and the weather became colder and wetter. Geoffrey had become quite adept at fulfilling all his fag duties both for Cartier and other fag requests, mostly running to the Grubber to buy a loaf of bread or some other forgotten item.

At regular intervals, Williams made Geoffrey stand on a chair and sing his end of term song. One day, Williams introduced a further torment for the new guvnors; the mountain railway. This involved climbing round the DC without putting a foot on the floor. Luckily for Geoffrey, he was quite agile and light, but for the heavier boys, it was a trifle troublesome. Many feet touched the floor, gaining the owners a kick on the backside. By clinging on to the lockers and using the door to swing across to the next block, it was possible to clatter round the whole room. Geoffrey was now familiar with all the variations of new guvnors harassment apart from ordinary bullying that was a daily ongoing feature. Sometimes he wondered why all this was necessary; was it making him stronger or just more afraid? Must he go through all this just because it was what his parents wanted? Most often, he struggled just trying to think of a way out of it.

Christmas was approaching and Jack Hindley, the music master, had started congregational carol practice for the forthcoming carol service. At last, Geoffrey sensed that his release was not a million miles away and although there were school exams to battle through first, the end of term was fast becoming actual. However, still lurking in the back of his mind was singing to the whole of Bartle Frere house on the last night of term. The nearer it came, the more the butterflies grew in his stomach and the more he dreaded it, but on the other hand, he couldn't wait for the end of term to arrive. He felt trapped in the horns of a dilemma, and he desperately tried to find a way to escape the singing; one way or another he must 'get out of it', as his already developed instinct told him. But he just couldn't think of how, feigning illness on the last night of term was not a sensible option; perhaps he wouldn't be allowed home. The other boys who were meant to sing didn't seem concerned about it at all and just carried on more and more excitedly as the end drew nearer. Having been unable to think of any avoiding tactic, Geoffrey decided that he had no option but to 'bite the bullet' and do it, telling himself that it wouldn't be too bad and would be quickly over; after all, he had performed similarly at his prep school.

Charlie had opened the boxroom and everybody found their trunks and tuck boxes which they carried back to their compartment. During carpentry classes at prep school,

Geoffrey had made his own tuck box, but the dimensions he had been given were a slightly non-standard size, so when all the tuck boxes were stacked together, Geoffrey's didn't quite fit with the rest. Strangely, this non-conformity was somewhat similar to Geoffrey himself. In the DC, Geoffrey carefully packed his books and belongings into his tuck box until eventually, his locker was empty, the remains of nearly empty biscuit packets and some crusts of bread boasting a green mould were discarded into the rubbish bin. In his compartment, he packed his clothes into his trunk, topped off with a pile of dirty rugby shirts and shorts. All that remained were just his overnight things that could quickly be thrown into his little brown suitcase on which George had stencilled his name.

Although he kept his emotions hidden, Geoffrey's excitement grew and grew as the moment when he would be driving towards home with these foreboding structures behind him, became nearer and nearer. Only one more night, and now it seemed to matter not that it was chilly in bed. Only the idea of his impending singing performance marred his moments of elation. Soon the bell rang for call, after which everybody filed into Hall for the term's last supper. It occurred to Geoffrey that call was a trifle unnecessary, after all, who was going to abscond on the last evening when everyone was going home the next day. But rules and routines must be followed regardless. After supper, when everyone was back in House, the atmosphere was becoming increasingly electric. Geoffrey did not know what was going to happen, only that he had to stand on the table at the head of House and perform. Amongst the second termers, there seemed to be much whispering going on, and at the same time, Geoffrey couldn't help but notice glances being thrown in his direction. Suddenly everybody started moving up towards the senior end of House, where the performance table stood. The gathering there grew, and someone gave Geoffrey a push as he was hustled along to join the melee. His nerves were in shreds as he thought to himself that now the time had finally arrived. Performing on a stage to an unseen audience was one thing, but to stand up there in front of all these boys, every one of which knew him, was a far more daunting matter.

Amongst all the pushing and shoving, Williams suddenly appeared beside him and said, "Finch, are you ready to sing? There's something I must tell you first."

Chapter 13

Williams drew closer to Geoffrey so that he could be heard above the cacophony. Geoffrey wondered what he could possibly be going to say but decided that anyway, nothing could make it any worse. His legs were already all atremble and had the light been better it could be seen how ashen his face was. Speaking directly into Geoffrey's ear, he said, "You don't have to sing, it was just a trick. We've been fooling you all the time. It's a tradition and next term, you must do the same to the other new guvnors."

Geoffrey didn't know whether to laugh or cry, but he felt an enormous load lifted from his shoulders, and the sense of relief was indescribable. Now he could enjoy the end of term celebrations to their full, although he had no idea what was involved. But first, he squeezed through all the boys and found David to tell him that he didn't have to sing. He was so happy he could hardly contain himself and get the words out. David of course, knew all along, having been through the ordeal himself, so Geoffrey felt rather disappointed that David had also kept the secret, even from his own brother, which was of course why he wasn't excited about it.

Suddenly one of the prefects, whose last school day was coming to an end and thus had completed his 'sentence', jumped up onto the table and started making a speech. Geoffrey thought how lucky the boy was, never needing to come back, whilst he himself had only just begun. Before the prefect had properly finished his farewell speech, he was manhandled off the table, and borne on the shoulders of a gang of boys, he was propelled at full speed the whole way to the junior end of House and back again with his bearers slipping and sliding on Charlie's polished floor. Careering back to the senior end, the possibility of stopping was minimal, and the whole entourage crashed into the table and wall. Directly, the next leaver was hoisted onto the table to say his farewells amidst much shouting and whistling before being dragged again onto the shoulders of all his friends and the mobile gaggle of boys charged up and down House once more. This term there were only a few boys leaving the school, so this excitement was soon over, but directly everybody spread out and started singing the Hokey Cokey. Geoffrey had never heard of the song and had no idea what was going on but endeavoured to join in as best as he could. To begin with, he watched as the other boys put their 'left arm in' and 'shake it all about', and then their right arm, interspersed with leaping up and down crying, "Oooh Hokey Cokey Cokey." He soon picked it up and was in time to put his 'left leg in', his 'right leg in', and finally his 'whole self in' at which point he was bumped, pushed and squashed as everybody 'shook themselves about'. Being of small stature, he was almost trampled underfoot, but at last, it came to an end.

Had anyone been looking, they might have spotted a pair of eyes hiding behind spectacles that reflected the lights; those of Mr Mann, the housemaster, who was lurking in the hallway keeping an eye on proceedings to make sure nothing got out of hand. As the Hokey Cokey came to an end, he made his presence known and advised everyone to calm down and the junior boys to make themselves ready for bed. In spite of the excitement of going home in the morning, Geoffrey had no trouble falling asleep and slept soundly until the wake-up bell rang in the morning. A few years later, the end of term celebrations became out of hand, and someone unknown locked the door to prevent Mr Mann from entering. Whilst he battered at the door demanding to be let in, boys shouted obscenities at him from the windows. The end result was a very subdued end of term, and the following term was very tightly controlled.

Unlike other mornings, he happily jumped out of bed and was ready for breakfast in no time at all, even after having folded up all his bedclothes. He wouldn't be sleeping in that bed again; next term, he would be a few rungs further up the ladder. Unlike ordinary days when time passed at a steady pace, to Geoffrey, it now felt as if everything took twice as long as normal. He could barely sit still throughout the chapel service, but finally, it came to an end, and he rushed back to House to take first his trunk, and then his tuck box and overnight case to the back of Big School where George was going to collect the brothers Finch. David was also busy conveying his bits and pieces to the same place, so there was soon quite a pile of their belongings. They had hardly finished bearing forth everything when they saw the friendly sight of their father driving towards them in Polly, the cream and blue dormobile. It didn't take long to load the trunks and boxes into the back of Polly and the boys were quick to climb in and sit in the front on the bench seat beside George. Polly set off with a row of three male Finchs looking out of the windscreen, two of whom were smiling happily and not looking back.

On the way home, David chatted to his father about the latest happenings at school and what he needed for his study the next term. Geoffrey was happy to remain quiet and dream about being home and what he was going to do. George told them that after Christmas he had arranged a trip for just the two of them, to go skiing in Austria. Geoffrey didn't know much about skiing, but it sounded like fun. Thea had arranged for them to borrow some ski boots from a friend in the village. These they must go and try on for size, and she had bought some ski pants for them both. They already had anoraks which were considered adequate for skiing. The boys remembered that their mother and father had also been on a skiing trip, for the duration of which they had been packed off to stay with Granny, so for the rest of the journey home, they pestered George with questions about skiing.

When at last they swung in through the always open gates, Thea rushed out to greet them. Geoffrey thought how wonderful it was to be home again; it had seemed like an eternity since he was here last. At prep school, the boys were almost constantly kept occupied, so time disappeared quite fast, but at Haileybury boys had far more time to themselves, which seemed to make terms drag out much longer.

After lunch, George left to go back to his office, and Thea took the boys to her friends to try on their ski boots. Luckily, neither David nor Geoffrey knew anything about ski attire, because the leather boots that were produced were by no means modern. There was a type of inner and outer part where first the inner part was laced, and then the outer part could be closed and laced up over the top. The result was that just putting on these boots was extremely time consuming and not something to be done in a hurry. But since the boys were going to wear them almost constantly, including for travelling, they were not going to be taken on and off very often.

Christmas passed, and the day arrived when the intrepid brothers set off on their journey to Sölden in the Tyrolean mountains of Austria. With their ski boots on their feet and woolly hats and gloves in their suitcase, George and Thea put them on a train to London from Cambridge station where they embarked on the first stage of their long journey. This train took them to Liverpool Street, where they changed to another more comfortable train that in principal would take them all the way to Austria, interrupted only by the ferry crossing to France. Once they had boarded the ferry and stowed their suitcase in a special luggage room, they explored the ship. After a while, they found a place to sit where they could pass the time watching all the other passengers. They were situated not far from the boat's shop, and quite soon a gang of 'hooray Henrys' were making themselves known nearby the entrance. The boys couldn't help but notice their unnecessarily loud exclamations in very upper-class accents. The 'gang' comprised two boisterous young couples, one of whom sported a fine head of red hair and was known as Willy. His name was not difficult to miss as the others were constantly remarking "Oh Willy!" It wasn't long before both David and Geoffrey were mimicking and accentuating their accents repeating over and over, "Oh Willy."

Luckily for Geoffrey, the crossing was quite calm because he was by no means a good sea sailor, feeling nauseous at the slightest swell. Eventually, they disembarked and found their way onto the train bound for

Austria. By now it was evening, and the boys were already beginning to feel rather tired, but they knew that their train was a 'sleeper' and this leg of the journey would be overnight. With Geoffrey tagging along behind, David, the leader of the two, found the right compartment. The compartment was for six, and although the bunks were still in the 'seat' position, after checking their tickets, they discovered that they were going to sleep at the top. Just as they were figuring out how the seats converted to bunks, the door slid open and their other four fellow members of the compartment squeezed their way in and slumped onto the seats with all sorts of cases and bags of duty-free beverages. The first person that entered sporting his fine head of red hair couldn't be mistaken, and Geoffrey and David were simultaneously shocked as they realised it was the "Oh Willy" gang. As they exchanged glances of recognition of the situation, they were hustled and bustled out of the way as the now six people, four adults, two young boys, and a lot of baggage jostled for position in the small space between the seats.

After much discussion and persuasion, David agreed to let one couple exchange their top bunks for the middle pair and finally, the six members settled down in their seats. Since David did most of the talking, Geoffrey did not have much to say about the bunk swap and anyway, neither of them was in a position to protest too much as they were soon overpowered by the quick-talking couple who wanted to change places. Geoffrey discovered later why they wanted to sleep at the top. Almost disappearing in their seats, engulfed by the other four, the boys sat quietly, slightly entranced by the hoity-toity talk that mostly washed over their heads, while the train clickety-clacked its way towards Austria. The members of the gang were actually quite friendly, asking the brothers where they came from, where they were going and where they went to school, but the boys, being rather shy, were not ones to indulge in deep conversation, so the general chit chat soon resumed amongst themselves. After a while, the door slid open, and a uniformed man appeared in the doorway; speaking only French, it transpired he wanted to check all their passports. Willy and his friends tried to converse with the man, but their French was hardly better than David and Geoffrey's. When the poor man didn't immediately understand what they were trying to say, the hooray Henrys seemed to think that by increasing the volume, he would be able to understand better, so by the time he had finished going through all the passports, dutifully looking at each person in turn, the foursome were practically shouting at him. Eventually, when he was at last satisfied, he just shrugged his shoulders as if to say, 'what a bunch' and muttered unwillingly "merci" as he made his exit.

Evening had come and gone, and the general consensus of opinion was that it was time for some sleep. Once again, considerable confusion started as everyone began trying to discover how the seats converted into bunks and how to climb into them. Eventually, each person was lying in their chosen bunk. Strung between the top bunks was a net to prevent an occupant at the top-level from inadvertently falling to the floor. While Geoffrey lay there, he could see through the net and spied the girl and her fiancé begin their amorous antics. They soon realised that they were rather visible, so once again there was more activity and movement while they endeavoured to fill up the net with jackets and bags so that all spy holes were blocked and they could indulge in their canoodling without being seen. For the boys anyway, the rhythmical sound and rocking movement of the train soon closed their eyes.

Morning arrived, and blearily everyone managed to organise themselves and the compartment back to something approaching normality, whilst in the middle of all this activity, they were paid another visit by another passport official. This time however, the gang were rather more subdued and didn't bother to try out their non-existent German on him. It wasn't long before Geoffrey sensed the train beginning to slow and sure enough, it gradually drew into a station and came to a halt. Willy and his friends appeared to know what was happening as they grabbed their bags, ready to disembark, informing David and Geoffrey that now they had to board a bus that would take them up the mountain to Sölden. As they clambered off the train, having gathered their suitcases, Geoffrey noticed that it was considerably colder here and was glad to be wearing his anorak. Between the train and the busses, a young lady representing their travel company greeted them and checked the boys off her list of travellers before showing them which bus they should take for their resort. They climbed on board and found a couple of seats from where they had a good view. Slowly the bus filled with all the other passengers, and Geoffrey was almost disappointed when he didn't see Willy and his gang climb on the same bus. Eventually, the doors slammed shut and the bus moved off to start the last leg of their journey. It soon left the town, and it wasn't long before the roads became smaller and the bus began to climb. Geoffrey found this much more exciting than sitting on a train, as it now felt as though they really were in a different land, and looking out of the window, he could see the change from the drab greys and greens to bright white, where the snow began at the higher altitude. After a while, the bus started slowing at regular intervals, and Geoffrey could hear the engine working harder as the driver navigated a sharp corner. They climbed higher and higher, and the sharp corners became hairpin bends, confidently taken by the driver who swung the bus round. Sometimes it seemed to Geoffrey that the bus was almost hanging over the edge, which only added to the excitement of the moment, but he never felt afraid.

After many turns, left and right with the bus grinding away in low gears, they eventually entered a valley and before them lay Sölden, a typical alpine ski resort. The bus stopped at a couple of hotels, depositing other travellers, before the boys were shown their pension, a small hotel called the 'Almrausch' situated quite near the centre of the village. They checked in and found their room, where they were greatly impressed by the duvets on their beds. Only being used to sheets and blankets, these were something completely new to them, and they decided they were some sort of barrage balloons. Now it was time to find some skis and other paraphernalia required for skiing, so following the instructions of their guide, they made their way to the ski-hire shop where the assistant found them a couple of pairs of suitable skis and showed them how to attach them to their boots and adjust the bindings. After nearly two days of travelling, the boys were feeling somewhat tired, so soon after their typically Austrian dinner they retired to their room and crept under their 'barrage balloons'.

In the morning, with renewed energy, they were excited about their first ski lesson, so armed with their skis and punktekarte lift pass, they found Helmut, their instructor, with a group of other eager to learn students of varying ages. Following the first efforts of snowplough turns, it soon became clear which members of Helmut's group were more adept than others at learning how to ski. The morning soon disappeared practising these turns with Helmut calling "Ziss vay" and "veight on ze uzzer ski, zo!" The return back to the Almrausch for lunch meant using a lift, which in turn meant using their punktekarte. The boys thought this rather a waste to pay to go down, so vowed that as soon as they were proficient enough, they would try to ski down the easiest route. A few more lessons and at the end of the next day, they decided to give it a go. It must have been the slowest descent that season, but after many falls and reattachment of skis, they finally made it to the bottom.

The next day, spurred on by their achievement, they were ready to ski down for lunch after the morning lessons. Geoffrey led the way and, having lost control but keeping his balance, managed to make it past the most difficult section and stopped to wait for David. David however didn't fare so well and just as he was almost through the worst, his skis crossed and he suffered an enormous crash. The bindings on his skis should have released, but to the detriment of his knee and ankle, one ski stayed firmly attached, causing a nasty twist mostly to his ankle. After a visit to the doctor, David was out of action for a couple of days, meaning that Geoffrey was now on his own for the lessons and had to fend for himself. After always following David's leadership, this was a little unnerving for him, but now he was in this position and having no choice but to make the best of it, he overcame his shyness and managed rather well. Staying in the same hotel was an Australian girl, and each time she met David, she enquired after his well being with a "How's ye inkle?" It didn't take many times for this to happen before David and Geoffrey, the mimic specialists, were asking each other, "How's ye inkle?"

After the first week, the boys had become quite adept at skiing, albeit singularly lacking in style and Helmut's class had dwindled to just the two of them plus a girl who had also become quite accomplished. This made the lessons much more fun for everybody including Helmut, since he could take his three pupils on some of the easier runs whilst instructing them at the same time. Often, after lunch, the girl decided not to join the boys, so then they were taken on even more daring runs. The boys used up most of their punktekarts using the T-bar lift to go up and down on the lower piste. Mostly they rode together, but occasionally Geoffrey found himself alone, which made the balance a little uneven. Added to this, halfway up, the piste sloped slightly down and Geoffrey's weight was not enough to pull the T-bar cable all the way out, resulting in him being lifted off the snow and dangling in mid-air for a few yards. This happened more than once, and he discovered that by trying to keep the tips of his skis in the ruts, he could stay facing in the right direction but once or twice, hanging there on the end of the wire, he revolved all the way round so that he was pointing back down the slope. When he didn't manage to turn far enough round again, the inevitable result was a crash landing, and he had to start again. As the days turned into evenings, the temperature dropped considerably against which the boy's anoraks, gloves and boots were no match. Their anoraks were pitifully thin, barely adequate for English weather, and their gloves were not much better so almost every evening, back in their room, they had to thaw out their fingers. Not knowing any better, they plunged their hands into warm water to speed up the process, and as the blood started to circulate the cries of "ow, ow, ow" increased in volume. A quick rest on their beds, and it was soon time for dinner.

The dishes served for dinner were always a surprise; the boys never quite knew what to expect. Often when there was a soup, the waitress served it in such a way that the person being served could not see what was coming, whereas the person sitting opposite could. Invariably the soup contained large knödel alias Tyrolean dumplings, which landed in the bowl of soup with a 'splosh'. Geoffrey was quick to discover that it was best to watch the expression on his brother's face when he himself was being served. If he started trying not to laugh, Geoffrey knew there was something out of the ordinary waiting in his bowl. The menu was always fixed so it was a case of take it or leave it and indeed, one evening when they were served tongue, it was a 'leave it' situation. At home, tongue was always pressed and then thinly sliced, but here, both David and Geoffrey were shocked when the waitress placed, in the middle of their table, a long plate on which lay a whole tongue exactly as if it had just been removed from a cow, complete with the rough skin on the upper surface. Her departing "Guten appetit" was wishful thinking. It had been sliced into thick slices, but neither of the boys had any appetite for such a dish, so made up for it with extra desert. After dinner, David and Geoffrey usually went across the street to a bar where a small band, clad in traditional lederhosen, played out their repertoire of thigh-slapping, Tyrolean music. They nearly always found themselves sharing a corner table with a middle-aged group who were quick to inform the boys, "We're from 'Uddersfield. We run a a pub called 'The bunch of Carrots' and went on laughingly, "Eeee, it's not quite like this 'ere, but this is nice, 'cept ye can't get a nice pint 'ere!" They were a friendly lot, welcoming them into their group, plying the boys with numerous rum and coke drinks, even though

Geoffrey had only just turned fourteen. Neither he nor David ever felt the least bit 'tipsy' from these drinks suggesting that the bartender did no more than show their glasses to the rum bottle.

From their village, Sölden, there was a chair lift up to Hochsölden, which lay another seven hundred metres higher up the mountain. There was also a road weaving its way up, but in winter, it was a treacherous climb for many vehicles. If a car came to a halt for any reason, it was very difficult to move off again. With snow banks on either side, the road was also very narrow, so for this reason, to avoid vehicles meeting each other, ascents were made on even hours and descents were made on uneven hours. Helmut had told the boys that the road down made a fabulous toboggan run and toboggans could be hired at the bottom of the chair lift which took them up to Hochsölden. To make this run down in the dark made it even more exciting. Armed with this information, they decided they must have a go. So the following evening, clutching their toboggans and with blankets wrapped around them, the lift assistant helped them each in turn onto a chair as it swung around the enormous pulley wheel. Quite soon, it felt rather cold sitting still on the chair dangling in mid-air, and Geoffrey was extremely glad for his blanket. Rumour had it that somebody froze to death when the lift was shut down for the night while there remained a passenger still sitting on it halfway up. But on this occasion, David and Geoffrey arrived safely at the top with their toboggans. Dragging them along the road, they soon found where the road entered the village and it was only a short distance further, before the downward incline began.

They wasted no time in getting started; each sitting on his mount, they made a couple of helping pushes with their feet, and the toboggans started to gather momentum. Faster and faster they went, with spurts of icy snow coming from the heels of their boots as they tried to control both their speed and direction. The two brothers liked the excitement of speed, so slowing their steeds was kept to a minimum, and quite soon, it began to resemble a race. Like every mountain road, it meandered back and forth all the way down with hairpin bends following one after the other. The faster the boys went, the more difficult it was to steer round each corner, with each one seeming to be sharper than the last. It didn't take long before they were leaving the village and the street lighting had come to an end, so now they were obliged to navigate their way by moonlight which only added to the excitement. As they became more adept at manoeuvring their toboggans, they slid with even greater velocity down the ice-clad road, sometimes relying on the snowbank to bump their way round a bend. On and on, they bumped and scrabbled their way down, sometimes almost tipping over and sometimes finding it necessary to extricate themselves from piles of snow, all accompanied by much laughter, until the lights from the village below drew nearer and nearer. The final run-in was rather an anti-climax as the incline was very slight, and the road was straight, requiring them to walk the last few hundred yards dragging their toboggans behind them, but that evening was one they would never forget.

Their daily ski lesson routine was interrupted by a day's outing to Obergurgl, a village further up the valley. Pack lunches were made ready by the Almrausch pension and early in the morning, they found the coach that would take them up to Obergurgl. After the driver had loaded their skis onto the back of the coach the boys climbed up the steps and sat themselves in the seats furthest forward next to the door, providing them with the best view of all and David hung the plastic bag containing their lunches on a hook by the window. When it was established that no one was missing, the coach set off. Although their ski class was now much bigger after being regrouped, it was fun to ski down unfamiliar pistes and runs. Being more daring and adventurous than most, the two brothers were invariably first to arrive everywhere. Today was no exception when they returned to the coach for their lunch. As they opened the door, they were hit by an overpowering smell of egg and salami. It didn't take long to discover that the odours emanated from their own lunch packs, which had been hanging in the sun in the window of the coach. As the boys sat there by the door, they couldn't help laughing. Every time someone else climbed aboard, they reeled backwards from the smell with much grimacing and exclamations of "ooof" and "pheew" and even "Oh good Lord!" After eating the contents of their offensive lunch packs, the smell subsided. On their return journey, it thankfully had disappeared altogether.

The days flew by and suddenly, it was time to return the skis to the hire shop after their last descent down the nursery slope. Together they searched every souvenir shop in the village for something to take back to George and Thea. Knowing that they were not particularly fond of tasteless nick-nacks, it took the boys quite some time, but in the end, Geoffrey plumped for a small bottle of cherry brandy for George and a carved wooden Tyrolean gnome for Thea. The gnome stayed in Thea's cabinet full of miniatures for evermore, and similarly, the cherry brandy remained unopened for a very, very long time.

The morning arrived to board the bus for the start of their homeward journey. Both David and Geoffrey were rather subdued but inwardly, Geoffrey felt a little gladness to be going home; after all, there was only one day at home before the awful return to school. Everything went uneventfully until they boarded the ferry to take them back to Dover. As the ship left the harbour, the wind seemed to increase accordingly, and it wasn't long before the vessel was heaving up and down on a very heavy sea, accompanied by intermittent crashing as it hit yet another large wave. Geoffrey very soon began to feel dreadfully seasick, and only by sitting very still with his head in his hands did he manage to avoid vomiting. Sitting in close proximity at a little table, two middle-aged women were occupied with their picnic lunch and thermos of coffee. Their main topic of conversation was how they liked their eggs cooked for breakfast. All this did little to help Geoffrey keep his breakfast down, and just as he was preparing to tell them to please talk about something else and put away their picnic, the ship made an enormous roll to one side, causing everything to fly off the table. Not only did their picnic go for a burton, but the chair in which the main talker was sitting, missing its safety attachment to the floor, also capsized and deposited its occupant on the floor. Geoffrey felt a sense of divine retribution mixed with feeling slightly sorry as her precious thermos was smashed to pieces.

As the ship approached the harbour, Geoffrey began to feel a sense of relief, although the heaving of the ship didn't seem to abate at all. While still holding his head in his hands, to his dismay, he heard it announced that due to the stormy weather, it was too rough for the ship to dock, so they must wait outside the harbour for a while longer until the rough seas subsided a little. An hour passed, and just when he began to think he could not keep the contents of his stomach down any longer, the captain announced that at last they were allowed to enter the harbour and would be docking shortly. How relieved Geoffrey felt as he made his way over the covered gangway and had his feet firmly planted on terra firma without the horizon moving menacingly before his eyes. The brothers boarded the train for London, and it wasn't long before, slowly but surely, it squeaked and clanked its way into Liverpool Street station. Their train to Cambridge wasn't leaving until over an hour later, so together, they wandered around the station to kill time. Apart from the usual newsagent and photo booth, tucked away in a corner, they found a cubicle where they could make their own two-minute recording on a 45 rpm disc. Together they decided this would be fun, so they scrabbled together the two shillings and sixpence required and pushed the coins into the slot. Following some whirring and clicking, the machine was ready and David started relating where they were and where they had been. Geoffrey soon chipped in with his half-broken voice fluctuating between treble and bass, describing the dish served in Austria as "tongue straight out from the cow" in not altogether correct English. Whilst they related about "Oh Willy" and other happenings with David in his grown-up way interspersing Geoffrey with "stupid boy," the two minutes soon came to an end and the machine spat out a rather primitive looking disc. But now, it was time to embark on the last leg of their homeward journey.

As the train pulled in at Cambridge station, the boys, peering through the dirty windows of the carriage, spotted George and Thea waiting on the platform to meet them. They jumped off the train with their bags and rushed to their parents. There were plenty of smiles, especially from Thea, but no enormous hugs; it seemed to Geoffrey that the time spent at boarding school had already made its impact on shows of affection which appeared to no longer exist. Affection from the heart probably did but was never shown and as time moved on, Geoffrey began to forget how it felt, although subconsciously, he knew he was missing something.

In the car, they told all their tales of the trip and were still holding forth as they arrived in front of Griffins. Quickly, they rushed to the record player to see if their recording had come to anything. After a little difficulty starting it off, David's dark brown voice and Geoffrey's squeaky tones could be heard through the loudspeaker, making their report of the skiing holiday. Their moment of gladness was cut short by their being reminded that tomorrow was their last day of holiday and there was much to do, so it was straight to bed after supper. Geoffrey felt rather tired anyway, so was happy to be able to climb into his own bed again, but thinking about school once more sent a surge of dread through him, and his stomach turned over and over. There were no more 'barrage balloons' on his bed, just his old faithful, typically English, sheet, blanket and eiderdown under which Geoffrey snuggled. He was dreaming almost before the light was out.

The next day was the usual 'back to school' type, spent trying on clothes and packing, all the while the knot in Geoffrey's stomach grew bigger and tighter; such a contrast after the slopes of Sölden. But back to school it was, and the next day, George deposited his two sons behind the study block as usual. Geoffrey had developed a defence mechanism to cope with the return to school, and although his outside showed little emotions, inside, he was in a turmoil, not knowing how he was going to cope with it and come through once again. He went to the noticeboard and discovered what his dreaded first lesson was going to be the following morning.

Chapter 14

To his horror, he discovered it was to be history. Even though history was one of Geoffrey's worst subjects, it wasn't so much the subject that he feared, but in this case, it was the master. And it was indeed The Master, the headmaster, Mr Seward, who went by the not so nice nickname of the 'booming turd' due to his powerful booming voice. The combination of this and the whole stature of the man made Geoffrey extremely nervous, but there was nothing to be done and he knew there was no way out of it. He didn't know it then, but he was going to come up before the 'booming turd' in more difficult times later, but now, just being back at school was bad enough and the thought of starting off the whole term with this, only set him deeper into the depths of despair on his first night back at the establishment.

However, once the routines were going again and Geoffrey had re-established friendships, school life became bearable, helped along by always having an exeat somewhere on the horizon. The Saturday film in Big School was still the highlight of the week when he could meet with David and hear some of the latest pop songs which were played before the film started. Geoffrey began to be quite familiar with the various groups, and it was at this time that the Beatles and Rolling Stones started to gain their reputations.

Life in the DC had become a little wilder now that Geoffrey and his fellow inmates had become fully familiar with the workings of the school and were not so afraid to break rules. The attitude of some of the boys was that rules were there to be broken, and illegal games and activities were both invented and played. One such popular game was 'bog roll bingo', which actually was not played in the DC but in the house toilets or 'bogs'. Just inside the entrance to the bogs, stood the urinals, which headed up a row of seven cubicles. These were not for the faint-hearted as they offered very little privacy to the user. The doors, being more akin to bar doors, started at knee level and stopped at chest level, so anybody passing could look over the door and see if that particular toilet was occupied and what the occupant was doing. For this reason, the first two or three were avoided, and number seven was reserved for anyone smitten with TC. Better known by the boys as 'testicle corrosion', TC was a rash on the inside of the legs next to the scrotum. Those who suffered from this were obliged to wear special underpants supplied by the sanitorium. The wearing of these of course announced to everyone that they had the disease and were subsequently outcast until the rash was gone. However, the cubicle walls were a little more substantial, but still with a sizeable gap between the floor and the bottom of the wall and similarly between the top of the wall and the ceiling. The game was to hurl toilet rolls between the top of the dividing walls and the ceiling, trying to make it land in number seven. The thrower needed to stand with his back to the urinals and, with all his might cast a roll very hard and very straight and see in which cubicle its trajectory came to an end. The further the roll flew, the higher the score, causing a good deal of excitement and shouting, which echoed round the bathroom, but this game was not good for toilet roll economy as many rolls landed in the bowl itself resulting in a substantial mess of soggy toilet paper.

At regular intervals, every boy was summoned to the sanitorium or 'san' for a check-up by the school doctor, for both TC and a puberty check. In the examination room, each boy was told to "drop your bags," and now naked from the waist down, the order came to "look at the bottles" lined up on a shelf nearby, and finally "cough." If the boy's testicles didn't hop up and down when coughing, then he had a problem, but Geoffrey's performed exactly as they should, bouncing around merrily.

There were no new boys in the DC this term, so there were no 'guvnor's brews' and very little 'torturing', but a rather dangerous new 'game' was discovered, which caused participants to lose consciousness. Luckily it was entirely at the individuals' own discretion or even bravery as to how far to go. Geoffrey happened to be looking on when Brandon showed how it was done. He squatted on his haunches and breathed very hard and deeply for a short period. He then quickly stood up, put his finger in his mouth and with his lips tight round his finger, he blew as hard as he could. Geoffrey could see his eyes start to roll, and just when it seemed he was about to crumple to the floor, he stopped blowing and just managed to remain conscious although extremely dizzy and wobbly on his feet, clutching at furniture to hold himself upright. A few days later, when Geoffrey and a few inmates were at a loose end in the DC, Jolyon decided to have a go at the dizzy game. He squatted down and panted away, stood up quickly and blew. Almost directly, he blacked out and luckily, Obbo was at hand to catch him as he fell to the floor. He fell in such a way that it was easy for Obbo to lay him directly on his back, but something in his unconscious state caused him to repeatedly bang his head up and down on the floor. Just as Geoffrey and everyone was looking on, wondering what was happening, they were all startled as the door opened and in walked Mr Mann; his timing was perfect! There lay Jolyon on the floor banging his head while Mr Mann looked on. "What's going on here?" he asked, and just at that moment, Jolyon rejoined the world and stopped his head banging. Poor boy had to pull himself together and act as if he was only playing the fool. "Oh nothing, sir," he was quick to reply as he tried to stand up in a perfectly normal manner.

"Well I don't think the floor is a good place for a lie down," he grunted, as he turned on his heel and left. When talking about Mr Mann, the boys just dropped the Mr and referred to him as Mann. Mann made a special sort of noise when he spoke, usually just as he started a sentence or when most people might say 'er'. He produced a sound best described as a cross between a throat clearance and a piglet grunting which Geoffrey, like most of the boys, found easy to impersonate. Mann was not a large man and sometimes used a walking stick with which he gesticulated at boys while he walked slightly bowed with his head pushed forward. He was an easy target for everyone to emulate.

Geoffrey's voice was just about fully broken, and he was aware of changes to his body taking place. Apart from Jolyon, who still had a rather squeaky voice, his fellow inmates had all started to develop pubic hair and 'bum fluff' on their upper lips. There were often sexual oriented jokes and talk of 'wanking' and other words, the meaning of which Geoffrey had no idea. The gang from the Junior School seemed to be more advanced in these matters, and he did not want to appear stupid by asking, but he was quick to discover that 'wanking' was a slang word for masturbation. But there again, he did not really know what masturbation was and when they talked about 'shag spots', neither did he know what 'shag' meant. What he did know was that sometimes his little penis became stiff as a ramrod, as embarrassingly it had in front of Thea when she had him try on his new underpants. But he still didn't really know why this happened, although he was starting to gain some idea. Unable to make his own contributions, he listened in to all the talk and picked up a little knowledge about the workings of sex and what to do with his apparatus. After lights out, it was not unusual to see the blankets on a boy's bed jumping up and down as he enjoyed his own private moment of fantasy. Having learned enough, Geoffrey decided to give it a go himself, so one evening, when the junior end of the house was finally quiet, Geoffrey started playing with himself. He rubbed away at his little cock for what seemed like ages and tried to fantasise about sex, but he didn't really know what to fantasise about and although once or twice he experienced a nice feeling, nothing else happened, and he fell asleep. He knew something more should happen and a few nights later, he thought he would have another go, so with both hands under the blankets he worked away on his member. After a good deal of stroking and rubbing, he suddenly felt a sensation passing through his body, the likes of which he had never ever experienced before. At the same moment, a kind of buzz went through him and just as he felt he had no control over anything, uncontrollable spasms attacked his loins, and a strange fluid erupted into his pyjamas. Geoffrey had achieved his first orgasm and wanted to tell everybody that at last, he had made it, but of course, it was something he must keep to himself. But now he knew what it was all about; wonderful, he thought, as he directly fell asleep.

Days passed, mostly boring for Geoffrey, playing ping-pong and reading books, interspersed with running fag errands for DP's. When an errand involved a trip to the Grubber, Geoffrey often bought himself a Joly Roll, which he ate from one end to the other. A Joly Roll was a Swiss roll which under normal circumstances, would be cut into slices and suffice for a whole family. But as a supplement to the school food, the way to eat a Joly Roll was to open it at one end and just eat away to the other. Geoffrey also soon learnt that another popular supplement was Fussels sweetened condensed milk. This sickly concoction came in cans which were opened with a can opener piercing a triangular hole, one at each side, from which the sticky sweet liquid could be sucked. It took more than a few days to consume all the contents and after each sucking session, the residue surrounding the hole dried, causing a rather unpleasant yellow crust to build up around the edge.

At his prep school, Geoffrey had enjoyed carpentry, even with the limited equipment and tools provided, but here at

Haileybury, the carpentry shop was far more advanced, even equipped with lathes. In spite of the slightly frightening experience of a large lump of wood revolving at high speed directly under his nose, he wasted no time in selecting a piece of beech and attaching it to a lathe. With some guidance from the carpentry master, after just a few sessions in the workshop, he had turned quite a respectable fruit bowl which he now only needed to polish. The end result was well received by George and Thea and remained on their sideboard for a great many years. Geoffrey always felt happier being creative with his hands, as opposed to sitting on a classroom bench, and time passed all too quickly when he was absorbed in his woodwork or painting in the art school. But attending an expensive public school was the first step to gaining a degree at university, not to becoming a carpenter. Geoffrey's artistic tendencies never came into his academic picture, not even later when his disappointing reports arrived. For the moment, he followed the rules, being too afraid of the consequences of breaking them, but this was to change, and the change came soon after completing his 'O' levels when he started to go off the school rails.

This term, Geoffrey's new fag master was Stokes, who luckily was far less demanding than Cartier mainly because he had completed his service in the Combined Cadet Force, which meant no uniform to be pressed or boots to polish. In addition, Stokes often stayed in bed until after breakfast, lying there with just his wavy-haired head sticking out from under the blankets. Geoffrey was always glad when these mornings occurred because they avoided having to make his bed. Generally speaking, Stokes's easy-going ways made Geoffrey feel far more at ease, which in turn made school life much less of a nightmare, but nothing ever took away the pain of missing home, which Geoffrey now kept buried somewhere in his inner self. Days came and went, tests and essays interrupted daily lessons, and the weeks turned into months. Exeats were always over too quickly, and although Geoffrey longed for them, he sometimes wondered if it was worth the suffering each time when leaving home to return to school. Mostly Geoffrey just accepted his situation and thought that if that's what David has been through, then so must he, but occasionally he questioned what his goal was and why must he go through all this hardship and misery. Following after David, it was clear to him that he must first pass his 'O' levels to reach the fifth forms, where he would then study for his 'A' levels with the aim of reaching university. And what then, he wondered? Did he soon have to decide what he wanted to be for the rest of his life? He didn't know; just now his main ambition, and all he cared about, was making it through each term. Occasionally, he stopped to consider what the school was making of him; he felt his only achievement was survival. Surviving by the methods he had developed to do so, he did not realise that his methods were not good for his self-esteem or leadership qualities.

And so, the terms passed one by one. Geoffrey graduated from the 'removes' forms to the 'middles' where he studied for his 'O' levels. Trigonometry had entered his mathematics curricula, and history and geography continued to haunt him, although knowing that he would probably fail these two anyway, he didn't care too much. He found the lessons rather boring, but it was both fun and easy to lead the geography master, nicknamed Loopy, onto red herrings. Just a mention of somewhere he had spent a holiday, and he was off on a tangent for most of the lesson. Geoffrey had noticed that Loopy would invariably let it slip that he was going to give the class a test, so when this happened, it could be avoided by starting him off on one of his favourite subjects until it was far too late for the test to take place. Loopy did have his limits, though. During one of his ramblings about France and his holiday in Provence, Geoffrey, Woolley and another boy were otherwise engaged, causing Woolley to let out a rather unstifled laugh. This prompted Loopy to become angry and ask who was responsible. It was easy to know when he was becoming angry because he jingled the loose change he had in his pocket. Nobody owned up, which only served to increase his anger causing enormous jingle jangling while he threatened the whole class with detention. Geoffrey, not being impressed by this change of events, decided something must be done. One more time, and with a final jangle, Loopy asked, “Last chance, own up, who was laughing?”

“It was me, sir,” said Geoffrey as he put up his hand.

“Come and see me after the lesson,” puffed Loopy. Geoffrey had to think quickly, the lesson was nearly over, and he did not want to take the punishment for Woolley. So when the bell signalled the end of the lesson, he dutifully reported to Loopy.

“Well, Finch, what was that all about? Why were you laughing?”

“Actually, sir, it wasn’t me, but I could see you were rather angry, so I thought someone better own up, so I said it was me,” lied Geoffrey.

“You shouldn’t really do that. The culprit should own up and I’m sure you know who it was!”

“Yes, sir”

“Well, don’t do it again and now go away,” said Loopy.

Geoffrey wasted no time in exiting the form room and quickly caught up with Woolley, who anyway was not one of his favourite friends and said, “I got you off that one and saved you three times dates! You can buy me a hot dog in the Grubber.”

"Yeah, alright, thanks, Finch. It was a laugh, though, wasn't it?"

So, in the 'half', Woolley bought a hot dog for Geoffrey, and that little episode was closed. Having both been turned through the same prep school mill, they had that much in common and were, therefore, friends but never 'best friends'.

There were two 'O' levels which had to be passed, namely English Language and Elementary Maths and these were taken in the winter term allowing a retake, if necessary, in the summer together with all the other 'O' levels. For some boys, Elementary Maths was not so elementary, but fortunately for Geoffrey, it was indeed elementary, and he passed without a problem, although he only scraped through the English by the skin of his teeth. The rest of these exams waited for him towards the end of the next term, which arrived all too soon.

It wasn't long into the summer term when Flynn, a boy two terms Geoffrey's senior, landed himself into trouble. There were a few boys in the school who found it hard to follow the rules, resulting in many punishments, mostly detention and writing 'dates'. If a boy made a serious misdemeanour, his most likely punishment was ten times dates and a ticket. The ticket meant he had to report to his housemaster, and in the event of this happening three times, it automatically dictated a beating, the number of strokes decided by the housemaster. Flynn was a big, tough chap but not a bully, although many boys were slightly afraid of him; it turned out later that Geoffrey would share a study with him. But just now, he was in trouble with both the house prefects and masters for different violations. The college prefect, who was head of House, was also allowed to perform a beating after gaining permission from the housemaster. These were quite rare, but when they did happen, they were carried out in the DC under the eyes of all the other house prefects. On this occasion, during lunch, Flynn was told to report to the DC afterwards. Lunchtimes were also Mr Mann's favourite time to find anyone he wanted to see or have report to him. Geoffrey already knew the dreaded feeling of Mr Mann's hand on his shoulder when he stood behind the bench on which the boys were seated. When he passed on the opposite side, Geoffrey knew he was safe. Today though, it was Flynn who felt his hand pressing on his shoulder where it remained while he was instructed to come to his study after lunch.

"But Sir, I have to go to the DC after lunch…" but before he could finish, he was interrupted by Mr Mann "when they have finished with you, come to me!" he ordered. Flynn didn't appear to show much emotion and just replied with a resigned, "Yes, Sir."

Lunch was soon over, and the boys from DC were told to wait in House. One by one, the prefects filed into the DC to witness the beating. It wasn't long before it began, and even from House, the swish and then the thwack could be heard as Flynn received his caning. After just two or three strokes, however, prefect Oldham appeared back in House since, although obliged to watch, he found it so disturbing that he just couldn't see it through and came out of the DC in tears. When the sounds stopped, Flynn soon came through House on his way to directly receive his second beating from Mr Mann. Still, he showed no emotion, but later on that evening, he flinched as he sat in his bath and Geoffrey could see his backside revealed a mass of slightly bleeding weals from his double beating. Geoffrey just accepted that beatings were a part of school life and were best avoided. It was almost a game to see to what extent rules could be broken without being caught. Up until now, Geoffrey had been rather a 'good boy' albeit perhaps not the most industrious in the classroom, but this was soon to change when he discovered that existence at school could become quite exciting by not always following the rules.

For the time being, though, knowing he must pass his 'O' levels, he tried to do his best at his school work. Having left the DC long behind him for more new guvnors to fill, Geoffrey had graduated to the houserooms, which he found to be rather more relaxed. Situated at the top of a flight of stone stairs, there were two houserooms with only a handful of boys in each, and each inmate had his own desk with a combined bookshelf and locker, allowing for more concentration and less distraction from others. Talking was forbidden during prep, but of course, this didn't mean that it didn't happen, and it was not uncommon for Mr Mann or indeed Mr Chark, Bartle Frere's second housemaster, to creep silently up the stairway and listen outside the doors with the aim of catching someone talking. Suddenly the door would burst open, and there stood Mr Mann or whoever was on duty ready to dish out dates to anyone who had been talking or was perhaps studying a magazine instead of writing an essay. This only happened a few times before Brad came up with the idea of sprinkling sugar on the steps so that it was impossible to sneak up the stairs without making a crunching sound loud enough to warn the boys of someone's approach. This only worked a few times before Mr Mann admonished the boys in his grunting tones, with "Someone has spilt sugar on the stairs; I hope there is no more spilt after it has been cleared it up!" He knew full well the real reason.

Most evenings, the whole of House, except for the juniors who went to bed at nine o'clock, congregated in one of the houserooms for house prayers, which more often than not were held by Mr Mann. He would read a passage from the bible, say a prayer and then together, everyone recited the Lord's prayer. The whole performance took place with everyone standing, shuffling about until a crowded circle around Mr Munn was formed. For many, this was just another part of the daily curriculum, and to the relief of most was soon over, but one evening while Geoffrey stood there in his own world, not listening to Mr Mann's banter, and without thinking, he rather audibly broke wind. To make matters worse, the unmistakable rasping sound occurred with perfect timing in the short silence following the bible reading. The room was filled with stifled giggles, and when it came to the Lord's prayer, there were many unable to utter a sound. Luckily for Geoffrey, the situation allowed him to escape punishment as Mr Mann was obliged just to continue as if nothing had happened. Neither could any of the prefects pinpoint the culprit and were not loath to anyway as they also had found it hard to keep a straight face.

As the 'O' level examinations approached, more and more time was assigned to revising. Geoffrey was always glad when the class was told to revise because it meant a free period from the form room when all the pupils could sit in their houserooms and revise. Most boys were dutiful and tried to 'swat up' on the weaker parts of their different subjects. In the main, Geoffrey also studied his books but was easily distracted and didn't always make the most of his time. He had been spending more and more time in the art school where he liked painting, experimenting with oil paints, but unfortunately for Geoffrey, art, the one thing he enjoyed, was not an 'O' level in the curriculum.

On the Monday morning that signalled the start of the official GCE examinations, Geoffrey awoke with much more dread than on a normal Monday. At breakfast, when the post was handed round, there was a good luck card for him from home. He realised it was as important for his parents as it was for him to pass his exams. Big school, rearranged into an examination hall, was laid out in such a way that nobody sat too near another, minimising the opportunity to cheat. Each desk had special examination foolscap, and the invigilator handed out the question papers, face down, to each student. Checking the clock, which was for all to see, precisely as it struck the hour, the invigilator announced, "You may begin!" and with that, everyone turned over the question paper and scanned through the questions. Like most boys, Geoffrey hated exams, but these important ones made him extra nervous, and as he looked through the questions, he was quick to realise what he could or could not answer. When it came to his weaker subjects, his stomach turned over, and he felt a wave of panic pass through him as sweat broke out on his noble brow when he discovered there was hardly a question that he was able to answer. Why couldn't he be like the Medlock twins, "I bet they can answer everything," he thought to himself. On the other hand, for his better subjects, he was equally relieved to see that it was plain sailing, and he could knuckle down and answer everything without any big problem.

But eventually, like all things good or bad, this terrible week came to an end. Geoffrey found it hard to admit to himself that he had failed, but he knew full well which subjects would not make a pass, although he secretly hoped that by some miracle, he might scrape through. For now, the pressure was off, and Geoffrey just had to stay out of trouble for the rest of the term, but all the time, hanging over him like the sword of Damocles, was the knowledge that the exam results which could have a major impact on his future were still to come and come they would, but not until he had started his summer holiday, which was about to begin.

Chapter 15

As always, it was wonderful to be home again and for the first day or two, school and exams didn't enter Geoffrey's mind. But it wasn't long before subtle and not-so-subtle reminders popped up that made his stomach turn over. "I wonder when your 'O' level results will come Geoff," mused George at breakfast one morning, making Geoffrey wince at the thought that any day now, the tell-tale envelope bearing the news would arrive. If it was not in the morning's post, it will surely be there tomorrow. Sure enough, the next morning, just as breakfast was underway and Geoffrey was tucking into his cornflakes, albeit with little appetite, the sound of the postman's bicycle against the house was heard, followed by the unmistakable 'plop' as letters fell to the floor in the hall. "I'll go," said Geoffrey as he rushed to the hall to retrieve the post. Shuffling through the letters, he quickly found the envelope over which he had been so apprehensive. Handing it to George, he held his breath as his father opened it and extracted the enclosed document, which he studied for a moment whilst still crunching away on his cornflakes. Unemotionally he reported, "History and geography weren't up to much, but at least you managed to pass the rest." None of them were top scores, but apart from history and geography, all the others that mattered were good enough to avoid a fail which made

Geoffrey so happy he could hardly finish his breakfast. Now he could enjoy the rest of the school holiday.

Having made the step from 'O' levels to 'A' levels, the pressure was on to decide what he wanted to do in life, which meant that as a fifteen-year-old, he had to choose what route to take that would steer his future. This was where the trouble started; in short, Geoffrey didn't know. He had always been interested in animals and nature, so with some subtle suggestions from his parents, he thought, maybe, he wanted to be a vet. Whatever was decided at this time dictated which 'A' level subjects he must study for entry to university. Having more or less settled for the veterinary line, George was quick to arrange, via a friend of a friend, for Geoffrey to visit the veterinary school just outside Cambridge. Geoffrey wondered if this was to see how he reacted to blood and operations and other macabre sights. In one room, he was shown a monkey's head with the top of the skull opened to expose the brain. The colour of the monkey's face was the same shade of grey as the colour of its brain, but none of this upset Geoffrey, although he felt the people around him watching to see if he had paled or looked ready to vomit. If this was some sort of test, then he passed admirably. What he did discover, however, which to him was even more frightening, was that it took six years to complete the education and qualify as a veterinarian.

Directly, this dampened any ideas he had of becoming a vet, but he refrained from saying anything at this stage, and it was soon decided he should study physics, chemistry and biology. Physics and chemistry were the lowest pass grades of all his 'O' levels, so he was not entirely inspired to pursue these subjects further, but it had been decided for him that that was the course to take, so he said nothing.

More information from Mr Mann, the housemaster, came through a little later confirming that Geoffrey would now be in the fifth forms with science as his main subject. Also, he would leave the houserooms and move into a study. His study would be number eleven, situated in the Old study block. Known as O11, this study was for four boys. It was normal to start in a four-man study, later graduating to a double and finally, if desired, to a single. Many preferred to share a study, and single studies were mostly occupied by less popular boys or boys without many friends. It was considered a privilege to be in a study, as the occupants were now considered adult enough to be trusted and therefore had much more freedom. The inmates could bring their own furniture and decorate the small room with posters varying from pin-up girls to exotic motor cars. Other drapes to cover the walls were used to make the rooms more friendly. Most boys scrounged an old armchair from home, across the arms of which a board was laid to form a type of desk allowing the owner to sit in comfort while studying. Now that David had left Haileybury and was on his way to university, he no longer needed his chair, so Geoffrey was lucky enough to inherit his furniture. Rumour had it that the occupants of a four-man study were having a race to see who could ejaculate quickest with a frying pan as the receptacle. The four contestants were kneeling on the floor, busy with themselves, when their housemaster walked in unannounced. All he said was, “What’s this? Communal masturbation?” and walked out again.

The summer holiday came to an end, and the usual return to school process was underway at home, but now that David had left the school, Geoffrey was going back on his own. He had hardened to the process so wasn’t so bothered by being alone this time, but it was still a mixture of fear, hate and loneliness that possessed him. Subconsciously, he had closed the door on love, although that was what he wanted most but without knowing it. Nevertheless, back to school it was, and once again, the gloom struck as they drove towards the grey buildings and green copper dome of the chapel. George was able to park quite near Geoffrey’s study, much nearer than when he had been in the houserooms, so the unloading was done quite quickly. As usual, there were no hugs when the final moment arrived for his father to say goodbye, just a formal handshake. Even though a huge lump had formed in his throat, he was fifteen now and definitely too big to cry, but why did he still feel this way, he wondered.

The term was soon underway, and Geoffrey and his three study comrades had organised their study so that it was more homely and inviting. One boy, who during the holidays, was the drummer for a band, provided a record player since he liked to listen to the latest pop music, and each inmate had some item that could be shared by all. Amongst the four boys, decisions were reached fairly amicably, and there weren't too many arguments. This suited Geoffrey as he had already discovered that he disliked conflicts and liked to be liked. Geoffrey had led a somewhat sheltered life at home in his village and was still rather naïve, so it wasn't long before his eyes were opened and he started to wander off the straight and narrow. Two of Geoffrey's colleagues had already embarked on a tobacco addiction and had brought back to school with them a couple of packets of cigarettes. Geoffrey was impressed by this and thought it was rather tough to smoke, so it wasn't long, of course, before he also wanted to be one of the boys. Needless to say, he soon tried his first cigarette. Nowhere was safe to smoke as there was always the chance of being spotted by a master, but some places were safer than others. One day when they had some free time, Geoffrey followed along with his study mates to the back of the swimming pool for a smoke. He was loaned a cigarette which he lit whilst concentrating on holding it correctly and trying to look the part. After a few coughs and splutters, he became used to inhaling the smoke. Although it made him feel slightly peculiar, and he wasn't sure that he really enjoyed it, he played along anyway. This was the start of Geoffrey's addiction for many years to come, although at this stage, the addiction was more the excitement of breaking the rules, knowing that to get caught meant a beating.

None of the subjects Geoffrey was meant to be studying were to his liking. He expected to like biology, but Geoffrey found the master exceptionally boring, which left him totally uninspired; similarly with physics, although slightly less so. The physics master, Mr Wardle, didn't seem to care if boys were there or not. One boy tested his interest by sitting under the desk for a double lesson. Not once during the two forty-minute sessions did Mr Wardle tell him to sit up properly. As far as Geoffrey was concerned, lessons were there to be attended, and 'prep' was to be done, just as much as was needed to stay unpunished. Geoffrey's main aim now was keeping out of trouble and making a game of not getting caught whilst breaking the rules. It didn't take long before Mr Mann felt fairly sure that Geoffrey was up to no good regarding tobacco, but his inability to catch him made him extremely angry.

In spite of smoking a few cigarettes, Geoffrey was above average at running, both cross country and the longer track distances. He played rugby for the house but was much too light to play in any of the school teams, so he ended up running the mile for the school in the summer term and cross country, also for the school, in the winter term. One damp, grey Saturday when Geoffrey was playing rugby for Bartle Frere in a house match, George, being rather keen on rugby, turned up to watch his son play. Geoffrey was playing on the wing and did not see much of the ball, but when finally, running at full speed, he received a pass from the centre, the only thing he thought to do was dash as fast as possible towards the line in a brave effort to score a try. He hadn't made many paces before a flying tackle from a boy twice his size knocked both the ball and the life out of him. He barely knew what hit him; George was not so impressed.

Geoffrey still had a year to go in the army section of the Combined Cadet Force. This was another of his major dislikes. He disliked having to polish his boots until he could see his face in the toe caps, and he disliked having to march up and down and round and about at minus temperatures with his finger frozen numb, stuck through a rifle. Every Wednesday afternoon, the entire cadet force was obliged to go on parade either in uniform or 'mufti' and play at soldiers for the duration of the afternoon. Geoffrey was one of a group that found it hard to take it seriously. On one of these Wednesday afternoons, Geoffrey's platoon was required to go on a dress parade for inspection. After the inspection, out of spite, the sergeant major sent them on the assault course, which meant the shine on their boots was destroyed, and their uniforms became unrecognisable after the occupants had to crawl through mud. The following week was again a dress parade, so everything had to be cleaned, blanco'd and polished from scratch. Private Taupin had the guts to rebel and went on parade with his uniform still in precisely the same mess it had become following the assault course. When the inspecting sergeant arrived at Taupin, his expression showed first shock and disbelief, followed by anger such that he shouted directly in Taupin's ear, "Private Taupin, one step forward."

Turpin duly obliged with the obligatory stamp of his foot to attention.

Half an inch from his face, the sergeant shouted, "What's this?" indicating the mess on his uniform.

"Shit, Sir," replied Taupin with just a hint of a grin, because he didn't care.

"What did you say?" he screamed, his face now puce with anger.

"Shit, Sir," he repeated.

"You're on a charge! Report to the armoury immediately, and you're on dress parade again next week – clean."

Taupin didn't care and trotted off to the armoury, leaving the rest of the platoon to suffer the now bad mood of the sergeant. The only good thing about these afternoons was that almost every Wednesday evening, the most popular meal of the week, beefburgers and chips, was served, which for Geoffrey was something to look forward to, something that still kept him going.

Once a term, the army, navy and air-force sections all had to spend a whole day performing various exercises in the field. Geoffrey never enjoyed these field days, although they were at least a change from the daily routine. On one such day, Geoffrey's platoon, often referred to as the shags platoon because it was both sloppy and none of its members cared, was split into groups, with Geoffrey's group required to transport a wounded soldier on a stretcher across a swamp. Geoffrey was quick to volunteer to play the part of the wounded as he reckoned all he had to do was lie there and be carried. His team decided it was best to tie Geoffrey onto the stretcher so he couldn't fall off and that he should be face down. Geoffrey didn't quite understand the logic in this, but for them, the whole exercise was anything but serious, so face down it was. All went well until the stretcher-bearers started to sink into the boggy terrain, which more resembled a swamp. As it became increasingly difficult to take any steps in the marsh whilst carrying the weight of the stretcher, the bearers, thinking only about their own well-being, wasted no time in just dumping the stretcher into the quagmire with Geoffrey strapped to it. Slowly, the cold, muddy water seeped through Geoffrey's army denims, and he could feel it penetrating through to his skin. He could cope with this discomfort, but his main concern was his cigarettes hidden in his breast pocket, which had also become soaked, rendering them worthless. His half-empty pack of ten Players No.6 was now only fit for the dustbin. "Oh my fags!" shouted Geoffrey as the wet penetrated his clothing, but being tied down, there was nothing he could do, and luckily there was no master within earshot.

The choice of cigarettes varied amongst the smokers; the majority plumped for Players No.6, these being the cheapest, whereas those with more pocket money chose Embassy. When out on a smoking truancy, the most popular hiding place adopted by the boys was to stuff them down into their Y fronts. When stopped and searched by a suspicious master, matches or a lighter were found, but they never went so far as to check in their underwear, so they never found any cigarettes, thereby frustrating them enormously.

The fearless foursome in study Old 11, when laying out a rather threadbare mat to cover the floorboards, they discovered what appeared to be a hatch in the corner. Outside, the ground sloped noticeably downhill, whereas inside the floor remained level, creating a space under it about three feet deep. After extracting the few nails that fastened it, they soon had the hatch open, enabling them to quickly go under the floor. They rearranged the furniture so that the hatch was covered first by the mat and then by their table, which stood over it. With an extra-long table cloth hanging to the ground, the opening in the floor was invisible. Under the floor, previous occupants had also made a hole in the wall allowing access to a small area under the single study next door. This cubby hole became the perfect den for illicit smoking, except that it wasn't quite perfect because the smell of smoke penetrated the single study above, and the occupant began to complain that he had been accused of smoking by his housemaster. To solve this, they rigged up an extractor fan by attaching blades to an old tape recorder motor. This Heath Robinson affair blew the smoke out through a small vent in the wall to the outside world. It improved the situation, but still, they had to avoid too much use of the den.

One morning, when Geoffrey was very much a novice smoker, he had a free period, so thinking, "Now is my chance," he dived under the table, down through the hatch and into the den. He wasted no time in pulling out his packet of ten cigarettes and quickly lit one. They were rather small cigarettes and were soon consumed. Thinking he better make the most of the opportunity, he promptly lit another and smoked that as well, which turned out to be his undoing. Quite suddenly, he felt rather nauseous and realised that with his inexperience to inhale two cigarettes in quick succession the second cigarette had been a big mistake. He climbed back through the hatch and sat under the table for a moment. Hearing there was no one else in the study, he came out of hiding and went to his chair. There he sat, trying to fend off the feeling of throwing up. Eventually, it passed, luckily in time for the next lesson, but still, it wasn't enough to deter him from having another puff later.

Although they tried to keep their den a secret, it wasn't long before other smokers wanted to use it and its popularity became dangerous. One boy had just emerged from down under and was still under the table when the duty master entered the study. The boy had to stay squatting under the table as quiet as a mouse for what seemed like an eternity until eventually the master left the room and he could crawl out from his hiding place.

Through his newly gained habit, Geoffrey had gathered a set of smoker friends who were perhaps not the best sort for him. He was easily led astray, and it did not help him concentrate on his academic studies either. There were also one or two boys who had interests of another nature, but Geoffrey was still naïve enough not to realise this, although so far nothing untoward occurred.

There remained a few more terms to suffer in the cadet force, but once again, he had found a way to make the whole farce easier for himself. Although his singing left much to be desired, Geoffrey had always been interested in music, and when Mr Causer, the music master, was looking for some bugle players for the Corps band, it turned out that he was quite competent at achieving an acceptable sound from this instrument. To be part of the Corps band was absolutely the easiest way through the CCF. No one inspected the band too closely, and there was very little marching to be done. Geoffrey's abilities with his bugle improved a little to begin with, but as practising was not his favourite pastime, he was never really competent, but for Geoffrey, this didn't matter; if he couldn't hit the right note, he just puffed his cheeks a bit, acting the part, lost amongst all the other bugle players, and nobody knew there wasn't a sound coming from his bugle. Life in the band was easy. Apart from the weekly irritation of having to don his army kit and go on parade, there was another major factor he had to reckon with; that was camp. At least once during their term of service, boys were expected to attend camp. This being a week spent living in tents, surviving on 'rations' and running around the countryside fulfilling military exercises. Hygiene was almost nonexistent, with toilet facilities being more communal rather than private and washing barely came into the picture. Most parents complained about the state and odour emanating from their son when he arrived home, banishing him directly to the bath. Urinals were provided for by nature, and for 'number twos', a plank with a row of large holes erected over a ditch sufficed. Geoffrey heard of stories about boys drinking ice cold water from a mountain stream in Scotland only to find a little further up a dead sheep stuck in the very same brook. None of this appealed to Geoffrey one little bit, and apart from all the discomfort, camp always took place during the first week of the summer holidays. Geoffrey could think of far better ways to spend that holiday time and vowed to himself that camp needed to be avoided at all costs. As far as he was concerned, there was so much against it that he had to work out a way to avoid going, but how, he asked himself.

Chapter 16

Terms came and went, and with each end of term, Geoffrey enjoyed the wonderful relief and feeling of freedom from the shackles of the institution. After all his years away at boarding school, his sublime gladness now was just to be home and had no reflection on George and Thea. Indeed it was not uncommon for Geoffrey to answer his father with 'Sir'. This was, of course, by mistake and a trifle embarrassing, but to Geoffrey, his own father held the same authority as the schoolmasters. Unknowingly, the one ingredient Geoffrey wanted was affection, but sadly, even the little that may have been shown in the past, now never came into the picture.

Every holiday, after a couple of weeks, Geoffrey knew that the arrival of his school report was imminent. It was never a happy day, as he inwardly knew he hadn't really been an achiever, fulfilling just enough to get by. The postman had started to deliver a little later and usually made his delivery after George had gone to work, so Geoffrey, knowing his report had arrived, had to wait until his father was home again for tea in the late afternoon before he was summoned for a 'ticking off' session with Geoffrey promising to try harder next term. Nothing really ever changed, though, and Geoffrey veered even further from the straight and narrow, especially without David to keep a check on him at school.

Meanwhile, back at school, Geoffrey, in spite of his dislike for the place and in spite of his continued nipping out for a surreptitious puff whenever possible, had started to make a positive contribution to the institution, mostly on the running track but also in the school cross country team. He ran for the first eight and managed never to finish lower than sixth place throughout the season, for which he was awarded his colours. It also happened that the year Geoffrey was in the team, after all the interschool matches were over, Haileybury remained unbeaten. Academically though, it was a steady downward slide.

The chemistry master, Mr Harrison, better known as 'Harry Hotplate', often showed his despair by saying to Geoffrey, "Oooh John," (he called everybody John), "why can't you be like Sumner?" Sumner was good at chemistry and was Harry Hotplate's favourite. A few years later, when teaching Geoffrey's younger brother Williams, who was very bright at this subject, he would say, "Oooh John, *don't* be like your brother!" He also came to learn that both David and Geoffrey owned Austin Minis, which they used for rallies and other competitions, so when Harry Hotplate was demonstrating a chemical reaction where the chemicals became 'mobile', he would say to Williams, "Like your brothers John, 'mobile'!" The first time this happened, Williams did not at first understand what he meant, but soon the penny dropped. Harry Hotplate was actually a kind-hearted man but very slightly eccentric. Of no great stature, he wore his thinning grey hair centrally parted, and he had a habit of shooting his eyebrows up and down. Coquelle was the only day boy in the whole school who also happened to be studying chemistry in Geoffrey's class. Studying was perhaps rather optimistic as he only occasionally attended the lessons and sat alone on the front bench. He was somewhat of a rebel refusing to cut his hair and preferring to fraternise with the local motorbike gang in Hertford. He was the only pupil for whom Harry Hotplate had no time, and it took only a few lessons for him to give up totally on the boy. From that point on, it made no difference whether Coquelle was present or not. Harry Hotplate just ignored him. Harry Hotplate's nickname was so commonly used that his real name was easily forgotten. On one occasion, Mr Mann asked Geoffrey who taught him for chemistry, to which Geoffrey quickly replied, "Mr Hotplate, Sir."

"I think you mean Mr Harrison," corrected Mr Mann.

Chemistry practical sessions usually took place during a double lesson. They involved carrying out various experiments, the theory of which Harry Hotplate had taught during a previous lesson. Each workplace had a sink and a

Bunsen burner connected to a gas tap. The boys always worked in pairs, and as the practical session progressed, the boys wrote up what they had done and what the results were – if any. Geoffrey's partner in crime was a chap called Massey, who was a music scholar and had about as much interest in chemistry as Geoffrey did, which meant that their practical lessons were, more often than not, a fiasco. The flame of a Bunsen burner could be adjusted by controlling the flow of air through a hole towards the bottom of the burner pipe. However, it sometimes happened that the gas became ignited at the bottom where it would normally draw in air, causing a roaring noise and the end of the burner to become extremely hot. Geoffrey and Massey were in the habit of purposely making this happen to see how hot the burner became. During these practical lessons, Harry Hotplate toured the class to see how each pair was proceeding. As he approached the duo's workplace, they were quick to extinguish the burner, but having been roaring away for quite some time, it was almost red hot. Harry Hotplate, sensing everything was not quite in order with their experiment, decided to show them how it should be done. As he was about to take the scalding burner with his bare fingers, the boys had to act very quickly, so Geoffrey grabbed a soaking dishcloth and slung it over the offending article creating an enormous hiss and a mass of steam.

“Oooh John, I don’t think that is quite right, you better start again!” and with that, he left them to it.

Massey became a good friend and rekindled Geoffrey’s interest in music. Geoffrey had already learned some basic chords on his guitar with some rather horrendous renderings of ‘The house of the rising sun’. In addition, lying in bed one Sunday morning, he had tortured the rest of the half-sleeping dormitory by practising his harmonica with the introduction to the Beatles song ‘I should have known better’ over and over again. Andrew Massey shared a study with Osman, who, apart from also being a music student, shared the name of Andrew. Geoffrey at this time had moved into a double study together with Flynn, an unlikely study mate, but in practice, it worked rather well, both leaving the other to his own devices. His study was just a few doors further down the corridor from the two Andrews, so Geoffrey was a frequent visitor.

Since Andrew Osman was quite an accomplished trombone player, the three of them decided to form a jazz band with Andrew Massey playing the piano, Andrew Osman the trombone and Geoffrey on the double bass, the basics of which he managed quite admirably. Just the three was not really adequate for a band, so they conscripted a trumpet player, a clarinet player and Richard, the drummer. Andrew Massey found some traditional jazz music, Twelfth

Street Rag, which they used to get started. Their first rendering could only be described as dreadful and even painful to the ears, with Geoffrey's bass thud thudding away and the others sometimes out of time and often out of tune. But after some practising, their sound became quite acceptable. Occasionally, Mr Causer, the music master, joined them with his clarinet and really made it swing. In one or two numbers, there was a bass solo for Geoffrey, which made him nervous each time it approached, but he loved to be playing his part in reproducing traditional jazz, the quality of which might have upset the original artists, but to him, the sound was not so important. Geoffrey revelled in the feeling that, at last, he was achieving something worthwhile. Eventually, the band had come so far as to deserve a name, so by mutual agreement, they called themselves 'The New Dixieland Jazzers'.

After a fair amount of practising, the band reckoned they were good enough to put on a show. They had achieved sufficient repertoire to perform for approximately forty minutes, so with permission from the Master, an appropriate Saturday evening was chosen for the band to demonstrate their merits on the stage in Big School. They made a large poster announcing the 'The New Dixieland Jazzers', which they pinned onto the massive doors in the opening from Quad to the form room block. It happened that just at this time, the song ‘What a day for a daydream’ by The Lovin’ Spoonful had become very popular and could be heard coming from every other study. Jack, the trumpet player, for fun had managed to play quite an acceptable rendering of this, and with a little improvising by the other instruments, the number was to be included in the concert.

The night before performance day, Geoffrey slept very little, and even though he wasn’t going to be on stage until the evening, his appetite at lunch was singularly diminished. At the best of times, he was never very good at concentrating in class, but this Saturday morning, he was totally absent in mind during all four lessons. The afternoon was spent preparing the stage and setting up Richard’s drums, and as the time drew on, not only Geoffrey but all members of the band became more and more nervous. Thea and David had also decided to drive up and watch Geoffrey perform, which made Geoffrey even more anxious to put on a good show.

Slowly but surely, Big School filled until there was quite a sizeable audience, and peeking through the curtains, Geoffrey spotted his mother and brother sitting waiting in apprehension. After a few squeaks and toots from the band warming their instruments, the curtain went up, and The New Dixieland Jazzers launched into a jolly ragtime number. This was a good start, provoking the audience to tap their feet and enjoy the swing. A couple more numbers followed with a very serious looking Geoffrey thumping out the beat on his bass, concentrating for all his worth on the music, which he still found hard to read. Often when practising, Jack would complain that his 'lip was gone', so there was an enforced stop for a while. There was always the fear in the back of everybody's mind that Jack's lip would not last, so when it was time for 'The Daydream' number, featuring Jack, they had a quick discussion as to whether he was still up to it. "Yes, I can do it," said Jack, so following Richard's counting in, clicking his sticks together, they launched into the number. They hadn't accomplished many bars before the notes coming from Jack's trumpet began to sound more and more like an animal in distress. The tune disappeared completely, with just an occasional peep finding its way through the ongoing rhythm. The audience became restless and started whistling the tune for themselves, much to the embarrassment of all. This was a terrible moment for the band, but standing there on the stage, there was no escaping the gaze from all the eyes of the audience. Geoffrey just wanted the floor to swallow him up, but eventually, the 'daydream' better considered as a 'nightmare' came to an end, and they were able to play a better-rehearsed number with significantly more confidence.

It wasn't long before their repertoire was exhausted and the concert came to an end, but an encore for one more number boosted their ego. When the curtain closed, Geoffrey quickly laid down his bass and sprung to meet his mother and brother. Thea greeted him with, "That was lovely darling, I did enjoy it."

"Except for 'Daydream'," said Geoffrey. "That was dreadful."

"Well done, Geoff," said David, and then they fell into rather ordinary banter before Thea decided they must head back home.

Quite often, Andrew Massey and Geoffrey practised alone to try to improve Geoffrey's ability to read music and help him with some of the more difficult parts. Sometimes they practised in Bradby, that being the music hall where most musical concerts took place, and sometimes they practised in the music school situated on the other side of the form room block. This building was divided into a number of sound-proof rooms so boys could practise their different instruments without disturbing each other. One larger room was used as an office for Mr Thomas, a music master who specialised in string instruments, earning him the name of 'Fiddler T'. His room was full of music, and other bric-a-brac amongst which, placed on a shelf behind the piano, was a souvenir from Spain in the form of an ornamental china donkey pulling a cart holding a barrel. Andrew had discovered that this little barrel contained Fiddler T's secret supply of sherry, except it was no longer secret as the two boys were quick to empty it. There was a third music master who was also Andrew's housemaster. All housemasters controlled the pocket money of the boys in their house, so when a boy needed some pocket money, it was necessary to wait his turn outside the housemaster's office before entering and requesting the amount required, which was duly noted in a ledger. During one of their practice sessions, Andrew confided in Geoffrey that sometimes when he went to request some pocket money, his housemaster first asked him to close the door before telling him that there was an extra sixpence for him if he could find it in his trouser pocket. He was quick to realise that this meant rootling around in the man's pocket where his small change nestled close to his private parts. This he knew was absolutely not correct, so sixpence or no sixpence, he wasted no time in declining the offer. But every time he went in for more pocket money, his housemaster became even more forceful that he should look for the sixpence in his pocket. In the end, he only went there when the assistant housemaster was on duty.

Geoffrey had already overheard senior boys describing some junior boys as 'lush', and now he understood what they meant. It was not uncommon, during an argument, to use 'queer' as a means of slander, but as far as Geoffrey knew, it was never used as a meaningful accusation.

During the progression of Geoffrey's puberty, he became more and more aware of what was happening around him. In Bartle Frere, Geoffrey's house, there were no reports of homosexuality, although he heard about some irregularities in one or two other houses, exactly what was going on, he never knew. From the gossip that spread between the boys, it seemed that various masters were the worst offenders, such as Massey's housemaster. A physics master who was also in charge of the swimming teams and frequently, when on duty at the swimming pool, took delight in being excessively ostentatious when drying himself after swimming, standing naked at the head of the pool whilst rubbing himself with his towel for an unnecessarily long time. It wasn't long, however, before Geoffrey fell victim to the advances of other boys.

Occasionally Mr Mann himself took rollcall, usually if he had something to say to his boys. On one such occasion during his address, he read out a list of boys who should assemble in his form room in the science block after lunch the following afternoon. Geoffrey was included in this list, all of whom started in Bartle Frere the same year. They quickly worked out that this wasn't for punishment but for a sex talk, which actually turned out to be more of a biology lesson but was so convoluted that the birds and the bees barely came into it. The handful of boys in the sex-talk gang spread themselves around his classroom to avoid both embarrassment and laughter. Most of the boys reckoned they knew more about sex than Mann himself. When the boys entered the classroom, all the blinds were down so that as soon as the lights were extinguished, the room became darkened. This was primarily to facilitate his slide show, but he had also arranged in such a way that, what little lighting remained, reflected off his glasses, making it impossible to read his face. This was his way of overcoming his own embarrassment when it came to talking about sex. Since Mr Mann had a daughter, the boys laughed amongst themselves that he must have 'done it' at least once, but apart from that once, they just could not envisage the man having sex at all. So, his slide show began, and with his face obscured by his reflecting glasses, he pointed out all the internal bits and pieces of the male and female anatomy but the whole time managed to avoid the fundamentals of the sexual act, although he did touch on the subject of a man's nocturnal emission or 'wet dream' by saying to his audience, "You might wake up to find a sticky mess in your pyjamas." His opinion of masturbation was also made quite clear with his remark, "If you masturbate, you are *weak*!" When eventually the lecture was over, and he dismissed everybody, Geoffrey did not actually feel any the wiser about copulation. He also chose to ignore Mann's comments about masturbation. In the winter, it was often so cold in bed that after climbing between the ice-cold sheets, he directly pulled the sheet and blanket over his head so that his breath helped to warm up the inside of the bed. Eventually, he ran out of air and had to stick his head out to breathe again. Other times he masturbated purely to warm up and help him fall asleep. The sash windows of House were kept open all the year-round, and it wasn't unknown for the occupant of a bed near a window to be woken by rain or wet leaves on his face if the wind was in the wrong direction.

Life in the study block could almost be compared to life in a penitentiary. There was always something going on. Geoffrey was still sharing his double study with Flynn, which seemed to be working out quite well as he had his social circle, and Flynn had his, even though he was a bit of a loner. To liven things up a little, someone had created a short circuit plug, so as soon as it was inserted in a socket, it blew the fuses. When a rather timid master was on duty, the 'special' plug was used, and the fuses blew. As soon as they were replaced downstairs, the same procedure was carried out in the upstairs corridor; and then again downstairs. Of course, it didn't take long for the duty master to blow his own fuse. Often when there was an interval during prep, Geoffrey would nip down the corridor and stick his nose into the study of the two Andrews. Sadly though, sticking his nose in was not advisable as the aroma within was not so pleasant; either they both needed to shower on a more regular basis or change their socks more often. Towards the other end of the corridor was a single study belonging to Thomason house. The occupant of this study, also called George, befriended him, showing him how to make his instant coffee frothy like a cappuccino but without milk and even frequently making it for him. George wore black-framed glasses and was not particularly tall, but for his age was rather well developed. He also had a rather irritating habit of sometimes letting his voice or laugh revert to a high-pitched unbroken variety. He lived overseas, making any exeat out of the question for him, so out of decency, Geoffrey invited him to accompany him to Griffins when he once had a day out. As far as Geoffrey was concerned, his friendship with George was the same as with all his friends, but although George was not queer, the day arrived when Geoffrey was shocked by his intentions.

As Geoffrey was passing his study one day, George beckoned him in and told him to “Close the door, here I’ve made some coffee for us.” So Geoffrey sat down on the only other chair in his study and proceeded to drink the coffee. After chatting for a while, George surprised Geoffrey by asking, “Have you ever kissed a girl?”

“No,” replied Geoffrey, since being locked away in this institution, he hardly knew any girls, let alone kiss one.

“Not just on the lips,” he said, letting out one of his little high pitched laughs, “I mean with your tongue,” said George. Geoffrey didn’t have a clue what he meant.

“Like this,” he said and grabbed Geoffrey thrusting his mouth against Geoffrey’s. A revulsion ran through Geoffrey as he felt George’s scratchy stubble against his face when he tried to force himself on him. Luckily he was strong enough to pull away as George just laughed in his falsetto way. Geoffrey left his study and never went in there again.

After this incident, their friendship was scarred, and Geoffrey kept his distance; although there were no more ill moves from George, there were more unwelcome advances from elsewhere.

Chapter 17

Of those who smoked regularly, there were just a handful of mainstays such as Geoffrey, with always a few 'outsiders' joining now and again. One of these was a rather large, considerably overweight boy nicknamed 'Blob'. He frequently joined the gang for a surreptitious smoke and became a friend, but not a close friend of all the smokers. This friendship also ended abruptly when Blob suggested that just the two of them could enjoy a smoke behind the cricket pitch where they were out of sight. Geoffrey was always open to suggestions for a quick ciggy, so he had no problem going along with it, and off to the hiding place they went. Some secret smoking places were not always ideal for Blob because of his size, but it was no problem on this occasion as there was a sloping grass bank where they could lie without being seen. While they lay there in the grass puffing away, all of a sudden, Blob clumsily tried to slide his free hand into Geoffrey's trouser pocket. Despite the cigarette still smoking in his hand, Geoffrey leapt to his feet in full view of anybody who may have been looking in their direction and demanded, "What the hell are you doing?" Blob had no answer, and Geoffrey left as quickly as possible whilst still trying to remain invisible. He said nothing about the encounter, but Blob was so scared that word might get out that he no longer joined in for a cigarette if Geoffrey was part of the group.

Geoffrey's circle of friends had grown, some of whom would be real, long term friends. But it was with some of the ordinary friends that Geoffrey had the most narrow escapes. Charles Mander started a term after Geoffrey, so his compartment was a few beds further down in the dormitory, but otherwise, the boys were at the same level. Charles and Geoffrey were often to be seen sneaking away for a crafty smoke somewhere, especially when there was just time for a quick one. One such 'quick one' was an evening after dark shortly before bedtime, when they silently crept out of bounds into the bushes behind Mr Mann's garden and quickly lit up. In the dark, there wasn't much to be seen except for two glowing cigarettes, but the smell of smoke was a much greater giveaway. When they were about halfway through their ciggies, they heard footsteps approaching directly towards them. As the steps came closer, the form of the owner could be made out in the darkness. "It's Cooky," whispered Geoffrey. Mr Cook, a mathematics master, was also Bartle Frere's assistant housemaster. "Run," said Charles, and together, whilst pulling their jackets over their heads to hide their faces, they crashed out of the bushes and ran towards the back entrance to House.

Now they had an even bigger problem to avoid being caught. There was only one way back into Quad at this time in the evening, so they knew that Cooky only had to wait by that particular entrance to catch them. “How are we going to get in again?” asked Charles.

“Maybe the grill is still open; let’s try it, come on!” panted Geoffrey. The houses facing Quad had back entrances that were closed off in the evenings by a sliding grill, similar to the safety gate on an elevator. Typically they were locked in the evenings, but very occasionally, this was forgotten, and this was what Geoffrey hoped for. Rushing up the spiral stairs, their hopes were quickly dashed as they faced the locked grill. At exactly the same moment, as they stood there searching each other’s faces for ideas, they heard voices from below where there was a similar entrance to Trevelyan, the house beneath theirs. Together the two boys sprang back down to the other grill and called to the voices they had heard inside. An inmate quickly came forward, and Geoffrey asked, “Who’s on duty?”

“Osman,” replied the boy.

“Get him here quickly,” said Geoffrey. Geoffrey couldn’t believe his luck because he knew that Andrew Osman had made his own key to the grill and all being well would be able to open it for them. Sure enough, Andrew soon appeared and, without hesitating, opened the grill allowing Geoffrey and Charles to creep into Trevelyan's back entrance. However, they still had to make their way through Trevelyan's bathroom, across the dormitory, into Quad, up the stairs and back into their own house. As they passed through the bathroom and dormitory, there were many surprised and quizzical looks, but the two were gone so quickly that no one had time to react. Taking the stairs two at a time, they were into House faster than ever, and by the time Cooky entered to make his check, they were tucked up in bed 'as good as gold'.

But they were not always so lucky. Geoffrey knew that to be outside the quad in the evening was forbidden, and it was always a risk unless permission had been granted or a very good excuse was offered. One evening word came around that there was a fire somewhere near the tennis courts. Geoffrey, Charles and a couple of others reckoned that would be a good enough reason to be out of bounds and set off in that direction, but only with the intention of enjoying a cigarette. As they strode along beside the running track, approaching the science block, suddenly, out of the blue, the headmaster appeared walking towards them. This big man towered over Geoffrey and, with his booming voice, made him feel totally belittled and guiltier than he was already. The boys had their story ready, but the headmaster, quite rightly, didn't believe a word and ordered them to report directly to their housemasters. In addition, he dished out ten times dates and a ticket to each of them. Geoffrey and his gang knew that this time they were in trouble. Some of the masters could be talked round, but there was no chance of that with the 'booming turd'. They made an about-turn, and Geoffrey and Charles slowly made their way back towards the Deanery, Mr Mann's house. The return walk was long and ominous, both knowing they were heading for a heavy punishment, almost like walking to the gallows. It did give them a chance to compare notes so that their stories matched, and at the right moment, when the coast was clear, they sneaked their cigarettes from their jacket pockets into their underpants. Arriving at the front door to the Deanery, they rang the bell and waited.

The door was answered by Mrs Mann, a rather ordinary unattractive housewife, who tried to make herself important on such occasions. She let them in and told them to wait in the hall with an "I'll tell my husband that Finch and Mander are here." She had at least managed to learn the names of all the boys under Mr Mann's command. He kept them waiting an uncomfortably long time and made no bones about showing his irritation at having his evening disturbed. In his office, the boys explained that Mr Seward had ordered them to report to him directly after he found them out of bounds near the science laboratories. Clearly not impressed with their story and neither believing it, he had them empty their pockets which of course only revealed cigarette lighters and some 'Polo' mints, popularly used to cover up the smell of tobacco on the breath. Not wanting to waste any more of his precious evening, he told them to come to his office after lunch the following day. This also gave him a chance to consider what punishment would fit the crime.

Geoffrey was relieved not to be punished directly but knowing that the chances of escaping without a beating were minimal, he had something to keep him awake that night. He and Charles discussed endlessly what they might expect from Mann and, if it was to be a beating, how many strokes. Geoffrey had great difficulty concentrating on his lessons the following morning, and his appetite at lunchtime was somewhat diminished. Finally, when lunch was over, the two of them made their way to the Deanery and waited with other boys whose only errand was to withdraw some money or make a request for an exeat. When Mr Mann came through to his study, he told Geoffrey and Charles to wait until the end. He kept them in suspense as long as he could. As soon as the last boy had left, Geoffrey was summoned by a call from Mr Mann from behind his office door with "Finch, come in." Geoffrey had hardly closed the door before Mr Mann began. "I understand from the Master that he gave you ten times dates."

“Yes, Sir,” replied Geoffrey almost needlessly. In desperation, Geoffrey hoped that Mr Mann might consider that was adequate punishment.

“From what I also hear, I don’t think that’s the first time you’ve been out of bounds after nine o’clock.” He paused for a moment before continuing, “So you’re lucky it's only four,” said Mann as he pulled out his cane from the stand in the corner of his room. Geoffrey knew that the moment he had been dreading had finally arrived.

“Take your jacket off and bend over there.” He said, tapping a chair with his cane. This was a special chair, never used for its proper purpose, over which the victim was obliged to bend. Mann only pulled this forward when there was to be a beating. Geoffrey did as he was told, took up position and fixed his eyes on some books standing on a shelf in front of him. Typical, he thought to himself, they were all physics books. He waited for what seemed an eternity for the first stroke, and then it came. He remembered the sound from his beating at prep school as the cane cut first through the air and then through his trousers. There was a split-second delay before the smart came, but come it did. It felt as if his backside had been branded with a red-hot poker making him want to cry out, but he squeezed his eyes and thought about home. All he wanted to do was rub his bottom, but he must keep his hands on the chair. Then another swish and again the burning as the second stroke was delivered. Oh, oh, oh, how it hurt, and it seemed to Geoffrey that Mann was prolonging the agony by taking his time between each stroke. The third arrived, but with the burning now all over his posterior, he could not tell if it was above or below the previous two. While he waited for the final 'thwack', he realised that Charles could hear each stroke, so the poor boy knew what was soon coming his way. And then swish again the last burning lash; Geoffrey just wanted to stand up and hop about rubbing his bum, but he must wait until the order came from Mann. At last, "Stand up and put your jacket on," Geoffrey heard the words and wasted no time in obeying. Then, as was customary, he said, "Thank you, Sir," while shaking his hand.

"You may leave and send in Mander," ordered Mr Mann. Geoffrey couldn't leave that room fast enough. He wanted to cry, but nobody at his age ever cried; anybody who cried was a wet and open to bullying. Geoffrey rushed out into Quad, thankful that the ordeal was over and was finally able to massage his posterior. He waited until Charles also made his rapid exit, and Geoffrey could see that he was on the edge of tears but said nothing. They compared notes about the caning and then laughed, the relief taking over.

Mr Mann chose to add a further punishment to their beating by gating Geoffrey and Charles for two weeks, thus confining them to college for the assigned duration. It was just a small irritation for Charles, whose home was in Holland, but Geoffrey had to explain to his parents why he could no longer come out for an exeat as planned. Since he wrote a letter home every week, it was not so difficult to write a little white lie in his letter. He had become quite good at it as a means of survival during all these years of imprisonment. Some lies were less white than others, but whatever their colour, it was much easier to write such concocted stories than say them, there being no possibility for interrogation.

The two weeks were soon over, and the next Saturday afternoon, Geoffrey and Charles went on their bikes down to Hertford just to be free from the school for an hour or two. Down was the operative word as the road to the town was indeed downhill almost all the way, which made for an easy and quick journey there, but hard work for the return. After wandering around the shops until it neared time to struggle up the hill again to be back in time for roll call, they thought it would be fun to have a beer. Leaving the shopping area, they found a pub hiding away down a deserted street. Not yet familiar with pubs and opening times, they were disappointed to find that it was closed and there was no sign of life anywhere. However, there was a delivery truck parked next to the pub, and although the light was fading as the evening closed in, Geoffrey thought he could see crates of bottles loaded on the back.

"Charles, look, I'm sure those are bottles there," said Geoffrey.

"I'll bet they are empties," Charles replied pessimistically.

"Wait there and keep guard, I'm going to have a look," and with that, Geoffrey climbed up the side of the lorry, and by stretching his arm over the side rail, he could just reach one or two bottles. While holding on with his left hand, he gripped a bottle with his right and handed it down to Charles.

"Here, grab this while I get another," said Geoffrey and managed to lift out two more bottles before Charles called in a hushed voice. "Quick, I think I heard someone coming," at which point Geoffrey jumped down, and the two boys beat a hasty retreat into the shadows, hiding their ill-gotten gains under their raincoats. They hurried back to their bikes and pedalled their way back up to the Heath, where the school stood in all its glory. When they were finally able to see what they had, they discovered there was a bottle of ginger wine, a bottle of sherry and a bottle of gin. While hiding them away in Charles' study, they decided that since the following day was Sunday, they would go into Goldings wood in the afternoon and have a party.

Sunday arrived, and after lunch, Geoffrey, Charles and two other friends casually strolled into the woods behind the sanatorium. Having found a quiet place, hidden away amongst the trees, the boys sat down on the mossy ground strewn with autumn leaves and opened the bottles. Swigging away straight from the flasks, they passed them round with just a perfunctory wipe of the neck. Very soon, all niceties fell by the wayside as the alcohol began to take effect. The little gathering became increasingly boisterous, and it wasn't long before the two extra friends felt they were adequately inebriated and wisely made their retreat. Charles and Geoffrey, however, were having a whale of a time and weren't giving up so quickly. Nevertheless, time moved on, and it was starting to get dark, so they thought it best to make a move which they endeavoured to do.

Standing up was far more troublesome than they had possibly imagined, not to mention trying to walk straight. At this stage of their drunkenness, everything seemed hilarious as they laughed their way out of the woods back onto the road. Hardly able to stand up, they staggered along towards the school amidst raucous laughter. A figure approached out of the gloom, and Geoffrey, pointing at the person, slurred drunkenly, "It's Laz Newman, look, it's Laz Newman," repeating himself as drunkards do. Luckily for Geoffrey, it wasn't, for Mr Newman, nicknamed Laz, was Trevelyan's housemaster. However, they did realise that they really needed to sober up somewhat before returning for roll call.

"We've got almost half an hour before call; let's go and lie down somewhere," mumbled Charles, who had begun to feel a little under the weather.

"Yeah, but where? Oh, I know, down behind the garages," said Geoffrey, so they wove their way past the entrance to the sanatorium and managed to half scramble and half crawl round the back of the masters' garages. The funny side was rapidly leaving them as nausea began to take over. They flopped down and lay in the damp grass out of sight.

"I think I'm going to puke," said Geoffrey. He had hardly said it before a stream of vomit followed his words and gushed onto the grass beside where they lay. Exactly at the same moment, a master came to take out his car, parked just the other side of the panelled fence forming the back wall of the open garages. Charles' stomach chose to expel the atrocious mixture of alcohol he had cast upon it at the same moment. It was not easy to vomit silently, but Charles managed it quietly enough not to attract attention for fear of discovery. Although they were beginning to sober up slightly, they both felt particularly dreadful, continuing to vomit at regular intervals.

"It's nearly time for call," said Charles.

"I know. We better get back to House," replied Geoffrey as he struggled to his feet. Between them, they managed their return journey without drawing attention to themselves and staggered into House. A few colleagues already in House quickly realised the state they were in and started issuing orders.

"Run the cold baths. We've got to sober them up. Get their clothes off," and with that, the two drunk boys were shoved into cold baths. They sat there shivering for a minute or two before being ordered out and told to get dressed. They just had their clothes on again when Mr Mann entered to take the roll call. Geoffrey and Charles, now able to think a little more clearly, surreptitiously concocted a plan to ask permission to retire early as they were not feeling well. After cleaning their teeth for an extended duration to disguise the horrible odour of alcohol on their breath, one at a time, they approached Mr Mann and requested to be allowed to go to bed early. By the time Geoffrey was ready with his teeth cleaning, Charles had already made his request, so when it was his turn, he found Mr Mann and asked, "Can I go to bed early, Sir? I'm not feeling too good." In his little grizzly voice, Mann's reply was, "What you *and* Mander?"

"Yes, Sir, I think it must have been something we ate for lunch," said Geoffrey. Then after a few of his grunts, Mann said, "that's funny. No one else seems to be ill."

“Yes, Sir, I don’t know what it can have been,” lied Geoffrey.

“Well, alright then,” Mann grudgingly answered. It did not take much to realise they had been up to no good, but what else could he say. They both skipped supper and dived into bed. Geoffrey had never thought that his hard, cold bed could be so welcoming.

Momentarily, during his period of inebriation, he had at least mentally escaped from the prison in which he had been incarcerated for so long, but unknowing to him or anybody else at this stage, it wouldn’t be long before he made his real escape.

Chapter 18

The more Geoffrey shed his boyhood on his way to becoming an adult, the more he became aware of his situation. He hated this institution in which he was kept: to him, it felt more like a prison, but what he disliked most were all the petty rules and standards that had to be obeyed. After so many years, he had learnt what respect was and always showed it when the occasion arose, but inside he felt rebellious against the workings of the school and couldn't wait to leave. His choice to become a vet had long since disappeared, mainly due to the uninspiring teaching, which he actually found rather boring. This did nothing to help his academic achievements. He had already given up chemistry to allow more time for physics and biology, but in practice, he was just glad to have more free time. What he did like was art and spent a considerable amount of time in the art school. Because of this interest, it was suggested that he should try for entry to an art college. Unfortunately, most colleges had already closed their entry books, and the only possibility remaining was the Cambridge College of Arts and Technology, commonly referred to as just the 'tech'. Before the interview, they required some set pieces, including a self-portrait which Geoffrey duly produced and eventually, enjoying an extra day out, went for his interview to show his works of art.

Meanwhile, Geoffrey's choice of friends had varied constantly, with boys drifting in and out of popularity, but two friends who had always been there and remained so were Marko and Irwin, both from Lawrence house. Marko lived not far from Cambridge, so it was relatively easy for them to meet in the holidays. Irwin's home was a little further afield in Essex but still within striking distance, so the three musketeers managed to maintain their friendship even after they had all left school. Irwin was quite a dark horse, mostly a quiet, unassuming chap and not particularly outgoing, but out of school, it was a different story. It transpired that he owned a powerful Triumph motorcycle and when at home in the holidays, he donned a leather jacket and enjoyed the company of the local motorbike gang. During their last term, when the 'A' level examinations started to become a reality, Geoffrey became more and more frustrated at being incarcerated in the establishment and controlled by all its rules and regulations. Although there were some hurdles to overcome, the end was in sight, which only encouraged Geoffrey to want to quit as soon as possible.

Occasionally, on a Saturday after lunch, if they had no other activities to occupy their time, they made their way to a 'safe' pub where they could enjoy a beer before closing time. On one such occasion, when spurred on by their sense of freedom, they started discussing the idea of running away.

Geoffrey latched on to this directly, and Irwin seemed quite taken with the idea, although Marko was not so keen. After this, with the idea of freedom fixated in his mind, Geoffrey could think about nothing else and every time they were alone, he took up the subject. Marko was never really involved, but Geoffrey and Irwin started concocting a plan.

The first stage of their escape was to make their way to where Irwin lived in Chelmsford. Then, when they had made it that far, from just around the corner of his home, they would ring to his mother with some pretext to make her leave the house. Directly she had gone, they would sneak in, grab some clothes, hop on Irwin's motorcycle and drive away as fast as possible. "I've got an extra helmet," added Irwin, thinking about all the details too. Every time they were together, they added to or adjusted the plan. Although Marko had no intention of joining them, he threw in some ideas and added to the conspiracy. "We'll go to the coast," said Irwin. "I've got an old aunt there who can put us up."

"But what are we going to live on?" asked Geoffrey. "I've only got three quid in my Post Office savings."

"We'll get a job," he replied, as if finding a job would be the easiest thing in the world.

The days slipped by, and the exams were coming nearer and nearer. All the 'A' level candidates were 'swatting', trying to catch up on two years' work in a month. Geoffrey sat in his study with his books in front of him, but his mind was elsewhere. When trying to revise, he could read a whole page of physics only to come to the end and realise he hadn't taken in a word. So he read it again and again, but all he could think about was escaping from his prison. They decided that the best day to make their getaway would be when they both had free periods during the first lesson. This would give them a better chance to be far away before they were missed. The nearer the time, the more excited Geoffrey became. The day before they were due to go, Geoffrey met up with Irwin for a secret smoke. As soon as they were in one of their safe places and had lit up, Geoffrey, who was deadly serious about the whole thing, started talking about their trip. After a minute or two of Geoffrey's fantasising about what they could do, Irwin dropped a bombshell when he suddenly announced, "I'm not going anywhere, I'm not running away. We were just having you on to see how far we could go."

"What?" asked Geoffrey disbelievingly "is this a trick?"

"No, really, it's not a trick, just a joke."

"You mean you've been kidding me all this time?" Geoffrey felt his world collapse around him, and now he was becoming angry, "and the trip is off?"

"Yep, I'm afraid so," said Irwin, now starting to feel a little sorry for his friend when he realised how devastated he was. Geoffrey was seething, especially when he realised that Marko was in on it as well. How could he have been so gullible and naïve; he felt like crying, but of course, he didn't.

"Well fuck you, I'm going anyway!" He retorted rather stupidly without thinking what he was saying. All Geoffrey dreamed of was to be away from the institution, no matter what, which only helped his stubbornness get the better of him. He thought to himself, "I'll show them. They think I wouldn't dare." They finished their cigarettes in silence before going their separate ways. Geoffrey was now in a terrible mess; what should he do? They were going to go the following morning, so he thought that if he was going, at least he'd better stick to that part, but the rest of the plan was now meaningless. He spent the remainder of the day in turmoil, and he was mentally absent for all his remaining lessons. Neither did he sleep well that night.

As he tossed and turned in his miserable bed, he weighed up the pros and cons of absconding. His desire just to be away from the place was overwhelming and always seemed to take precedence over everything else. He did not expect to pass his 'A' levels, so what difference did it make? He had nothing to lose. He still did not really know what he was going to do but just hoped that he need never come back again. When the fiver rang in the morning, he was bleary-eyed as he crawled out of bed, but his mind was made up, which gave him renewed strength to get going. He just made it into Hall for breakfast without receiving a punishment for being late, but what the hell, he thought, I'll not be here anyway to write any lines. He ate what he could, but his anticipation and anxiety did little for his appetite. The gong struck, and the head boy said the closing grace, signalling time for everybody to exit the dining hall. There would be no Chapel for Geoffrey today. He reckoned he wouldn't be missed; it was better to be on his way.

After a quick visit to his study to pick up his Post Office savings book, he strolled out of the school as nonchalantly as possible, past the sports field and the science block, through the entrance gate and onto Hailey Lane. Hailey Lane was probably the most dangerous part of his route. At this time in the morning, he absolutely should not be there, and there was no escape if any master should be driving one way or the other. With high hedges on both sides of the lane, there was nowhere to hide, but he had to run the gauntlet as it was the only way to arrive at the main road. It was perhaps just a mile, but even at Geoffrey's brisk pace, it seemed to take forever. Every time he heard a car coming, it sent him into a panic, but nevertheless, luck was on his side, and he arrived safely at the bottom of Hailey Lane without being spotted. Now he was faced with a dilemma; where was he going to go? He still hadn't decided. The only way he knew was the way his father took when he had an exeat, which inevitably led him back to Cambridge, to home. Was that what he wanted? What else could he do? After all the planning, ironically, he was still heading back to where he had sought love and recognition for so many years.

Resigned to the fact that if he didn't turn round and return to school with his tail between his legs, he had no option but to head for Cambridge. So that's what it was going to be, and having made that decision, he removed his tie so that he looked less like a schoolboy on the run and started trying to hitch a lift. He began walking beside the main road with his thumb stuck out in the way he had seen it done by other hitchhikers. It wasn't long before a truck stopped, pulling in a few yards past him. Not wanting to miss his opportunity, Geoffrey ran to catch it up and quickly climbed on the step up to the cab.

"Where do you wanna go, sonny?" asked the driver, seeming quite amiable.

"Cambridge," shouted Geoffrey above the noise of the truck and the traffic.

"I can take you as far as Royston. You'll have to make your own way from there," said the driver.

"That's fine," Geoffrey said as he scrambled into the cab. Sitting high up there, he felt on top of the world as he realised that for the moment, no one could see him, and he was safe from being dragged back to incarceration. Geoffrey hoped the driver wouldn't ask too many questions, but it didn't take long before he piped up with, "What are you gonna do in Cambridge?"

"That's where my parents live," replied Geoffrey

"Oh, but don't you live there too?" he questioned

"Yes, yes, when I'm not at school," he stammered, realising it wasn't such a clever thing to say and that he was already in a tricky situation, so he added, "but I'm just out for the day."

"Oh," said the driver and fortunately left it at that. He pulled out a packet of Embassy cigarettes and offered one to Geoffrey. "Thanks," said Geoffrey and gave the man a light. While they puffed away, filling the cab with smoke, he began to feel rather good; a free ride most of the way and a ciggy to boot. If they could see him now. He looked at his watch and saw that he probably had not been missed as the first period, which he had free, was not yet over. It was rather noisy in the lorry, so there was limited conversation which suited Geoffrey. Soon they were grinding their way through Baldock before embarking on the stretch to Royston, where Geoffrey's truck ride would end.

Shortly after coming into Royston, the driver said, "You'll have to hop out here 'cos this is where I turn off."

Geoffrey thanked the driver as he jumped down from the cab, and almost directly, the truck turned right, leaving the main road. Well, thought Geoffrey, that's a good start, and it's not even ten o'clock yet, so with renewed confidence, he once again stuck out his thumb. The road he was taking, the A10, was a popular way to Cambridge, so it wasn't long before a car stopped, and he was on his way again, this time all the way to the city. The driver was not one for conversation, and eventually, as they neared the end of King's Parade, he asked Geoffrey, "Will this do you?" to which he quickly replied, "Oh yes, thanks," and jumped out. As he watched it drive away, disappearing towards the market square, he wondered, "Now what!" and started to wander aimlessly along Trinity Street, not really aware of where he was going. He had made it this far in no time at all, but now he had no idea what step to take next. He wondered if his absence had been noticed yet. Looking at his watch, he saw that he should be sitting on a wooden bench listening to his physics master trying to drum something into his head. Maybe that would have been a better option, he thought, starting to doubt what he had done. He strolled along to Parker's Piece and smoked a cigarette, all the while trying to decide what to do. In the end, he realised he would have to bite the bullet and go home, so stubbing out his cigarette, he started walking in the direction of Shelford.

He knew it was a good five miles, but he wasn't in any hurry, and anyway, he didn't want to arrive when his father was home for lunch. Luckily for Geoffrey, it was a fine day as he ambled along towards Trumpington, going over and over in his head what he should say to his mother since he would tackle her first before his father came home from work. His father was a man of habit, and it occurred to Geoffrey that he had better take care not to be spotted by him if he drove past on his routine journey home for lunch. As it was, on his way through Trumpington, he saw his father's car parked outside a house that was unknown to him. He knew that his parents did not have any friends in Trumpington, so he wondered what on earth his father was doing there. That gave him something else to think about. He was still naïve enough not to jump to any conclusions that might be wrong. A few minutes later and a little further on, his father drove past him on his way to Shelford. Geoffrey was only about halfway home now, and even though he represented the school for distance running, he felt fatigue setting in, and his feet were beginning to hurt, so he sat at a bus stop to rest. While sitting there watching the traffic, a number 103 bus thundered past, reminding him of his bus journeys home from Islip House when he was just six years old. He had felt loved in those days, before he was sent away, not like now, when he needed it most. He was feeling very alone.

Rising to his feet again, he set off once more towards home, which today had become an unknown quantity. He walked and walked until, at last, he could see the railway bridge that led him into Great Shelford village. At the same moment, he saw his father driving on the other side of the road on his way back to work. Geoffrey quickly turned away, keeping his back to his father to avoid being seen. George sailed past without noticing anything, his thoughts well distant from a chance meeting with his second son walking along the road. Geoffrey resumed his journey, his destination no longer so far away, but at least he was safe in the knowledge that it would only be his mother at home when he arrived. A right turn at the memorial in Great Shelford took him towards Little Shelford and Griffins. Every year, his father fixed a poppy to his lapel and joined many other villagers to lay a wreath at this memorial in memory of those lost in the second war. But that was in November, and now it was summer. On past the church and village school, he followed the meandering road. Past the house where a Jack Russel used to bark at him from an upstairs window frightening him when he was small and on over two bridges, he retraced the steps he had trodden so often a decade earlier. But in those days, his homecoming was a happy one.

A few hundred yards further, his feet crunched on the gravel leading to the front door. He could see his mother sitting in her chair, reading as was her habit in the afternoon. She did not notice him walking up the drive approaching the house, and as he had no key, he was obliged to ring the bell. He didn't know what was going to happen when she opened the front door, but he barely had time to think about it before it swung open. She looked at him slightly bewildered before exclaiming, "Oh darling, what a nice surprise, what are you doing here?" Geoffrey really did not know what he could say except for the truth, so he replied with his voice beginning to break as tears welled in his eyes, "I've run away!" Poor Thea was now the one lost for words, "Oh darling, but why?"

"Because I can't stand it there any longer. I don't want to do my 'A' levels. I just want to start working." He had difficulty making the words come out without a tremor and without breaking down completely. He was saved for the moment as the telephone rang. Typically, the timing was perfect; it was Mr Mann, and Geoffrey could overhear his mother say, "Yes, he's here." He didn't want to listen to anymore.

The ice was broken, but he still had to face his father. He heard her replace the phone before she returned from the hall with a heavy look on her face. "That was Mr Mann," she said, "He says you must return to school as soon as possible with Daddy, and both of you must go and meet with Mr Seward."

“But I don’t want to go back,” protested Geoffrey.

“Don’t be silly darling, you must go back!” she said, “anyway, I must ring Daddy and tell him because he’ll need to come home early in time to take you back.”

In spite of his emotions, Geoffrey was very hungry, having eaten nothing all day, so Thea made a quick sandwich for him, and a little while later, George’s car could be heard pulling into the drive. He did not wear a happy face when he walked in, but to Geoffrey’s relief, he refrained from directly scolding him. He drank his routine cup of tea and announced, “Right Geoff, we’ll take Mummy’s car, so get mini out, and you can drive.” Geoffrey loved driving, so he supposed that driving back to school was a means of lessening any discussion about not returning.

Most of the journey was made in silence, except when his father told him to slow down because he considered sixty miles an hour was fast enough for a learner. Geoffrey felt totally demoralised as he drove through the school entrance, which was actually against the rules as it was forbidden for boys to drive on college grounds. George quickly decided to overlook this rule. As usual, they parked behind the study block, which was much to Geoffrey’s chagrin since there were many eyes watching his return, like a prisoner being brought back by the guards. Together they walked across Quad and rang the Master’s doorbell. He was quick to answer and boomed a "Come in," to them. Even George seemed overpowered by the man who always made Geoffrey feel small and smaller than ever on this occasion. When their discussion started, Geoffrey thought it rather ironic, while Mr Seward was playing a hard line as to whether to allow Geoffrey back, his father was arguing that it was just a misfortune that should be overlooked and that the school should take him back; the latter being completely against what Geoffrey wanted. In the end, it was agreed that Geoffrey could stay to sit his 'A' level examinations, and when completed, it was probably best that he went home. Although this was rather a disgrace to leave early, Geoffrey was actually quite glad because he could start his holiday a week earlier. Once the exams were out of the way, those students sitting them were mostly free for the remaining few days of the term. Geoffrey realised that they wanted him out of the way because they didn't trust him not to cause trouble.

Relieved now that the day was over, he said goodbye to his father rather reservedly before making his way back to House. He felt exhausted, and however hard and uncomfortable his bed might be, at that moment, it seemed rather attractive, but then the questions started, "What happened, Finchy?", "How far did you get?", "What did the Boot (headmaster) say?" and so on and so on. Geoffrey didn't want to talk about it and refrained from saying very much, just concentrating on doing his chores so he could lie in his bed alone with his thoughts, as he had been doing for nigh on ten years. Going over the events of the day, he wasn't proud of what he had done, but there again, neither did he regret it. He realised there would be more questions tomorrow, but tomorrow was another day, and with that, he drifted off to sleep.

Geoffrey's antics were soon forgotten, and the daily routines continued. Both the exams and school athletics were drawing closer. Geoffrey was trying to revise as much as he could, but his heart wasn't in it. The news came through that the Cambridge Tech had not accepted him, so his possible future in the world of art disappeared. He still did not know what he wanted to do or be, but he knew his stay at school could not end soon enough.

In the sports field, Geoffrey was achieving some success running the mile for the school. He had hopes of a good place for this distance on the school sports day, but a skinny boy from Lawrence house ran with apparent ease, and Geoffrey felt fairly sure he would be outrun by him. The school athletics was not only about individual success but also teamwork for the inter-house competition. The running track left much to be desired with large bumps here and there, where tree roots were pushing up the asphalt. When the athletics day finally arrived, the shorter distances were run first, leaving the mile to last. After waiting for what seemed like an eternity, Geoffrey was eventually called to the start, and he lined up with the rest of the entrants.

Bang, the start pistol let off a crack, and they were off. Geoffrey took up second position behind the skinny boy, hoping he could keep pace with him whilst just in front of the rest of the pack. He disliked running the mile, it being such an endurance race, but because he was quite good at it, he persevered, always in the hope of some recognition. Today was no exception, and try as he might, he just could not keep up with the leader who had increased his lead over Geoffrey by a good ten metres by the end of the first lap. While he could hear his own feet smacking down on the asphalt, he could also hear other feet close behind. He knew that most of the other runners were further back, but there was someone else not far behind. He increased his pace a little in the hope of breaking whoever was trying to hang on behind him, but he knew he must hold enough in reserve for the sprint finish. Still, those feet could be heard almost closing in on him as they started the remaining quarter mile. Geoffrey speeded up a little more, almost more than he really wanted, with still four hundred yards to go. It didn't help; whoever it was, was not giving up, but neither was Geoffrey and as they approached the two hundred yard mark, out of the corner of his eye, he could see a large boy, tight on his shoulder, trying to pass him. With the end so close in sight, he was determined not to let that happen. He knew who it was now and knew that Cox, the other boy, was not a runner, but his substantial and strong build, with legs like pistons, meant he could just rely on his strength. As they made the final turn into the last hundred yards, Geoffrey, who was already sprinting, still had him breathing down his neck, but he was not going to give in, and the more Cox endeavoured to pass, the more Geoffrey called on his last reserves of power to hold him off.

At last, they flew over the finishing line, and Geoffrey had managed to stay ahead and hang on to second place, achieving his best time ever. He collapsed onto the grass, gasping for breath, his legs totally finished without an ounce of strength left in them, but proud in the knowledge that he was the second-best out of six hundred boys in the whole school. While he lay there, his chest heaving, he heard Mr Mann addressing him, "Just shows what smoking does for you, doesn't it Finch?" Geoffrey didn't think Mann expected an answer and didn't get one. Geoffrey was anyway not recovered enough to give it. It would have been nice if Mann had congratulated him instead, thought Geoffrey. After all, he had earned valuable points for Bartle Frere house. His attitude only confirmed Geoffrey's reasons for not wanting to be there.

Exam week arrived, causing a degree of panic in many boys who were desperately trying to achieve some last-minute revision. Geoffrey resigned himself to thinking that if he didn't know enough by now, then he never would, and it was too late. So he attended all his exams seated in his assigned place in Big School and did his best to answer the questions. For his practical exams, he adequately dissected a frog for biology and carried out an electrical experiment for physics, but he knew in his heart what the results would be. When his last exam was over, Mr Mann unlocked the boxroom so that Geoffrey could find his trunk and his tuck box. His father was coming to pick him up the next day, Mr Mann informed him.

The following day, he said goodbye to his friends and waited at the back of Big School for his father to arrive. As he stood there beside his few belongings, he felt mixed emotions passing through him. He was elated at being able to go home already, but he would miss the final leaving celebrations, being carried on a gaggle of shoulders the length of house and back, 'for he's a jolly good fellow', the 'hokey cokey' and just making the most of the last night.

Perhaps he wasn't 'a jolly good fellow'. This hurt Geoffrey very much as he needed to be liked, to be loved, which sparked off thoughts deeper inside, making him wonder what had happened to him emotionally over the last ten years shut away at a prison-like boarding school. He had survived, just, so perhaps he was a survivor, but at what price? He no longer knew what love was but knew it was missing. He did not know it, but these wounds were so deep-seated that they would cause him many problems with relationships in the future and indeed for most of his life.

While he dwelled on these thoughts, he saw George driving towards him. He bravely managed a smile, but it was rather shallow. They loaded all his possessions into the back of the car, and his father asked him if that was everything. "Yes, Sir," he replied, and with that 'Sir' to his father, accidental as it was, he knew there really was something missing. Were they so far apart that his own father was like just another master?

During the previous school holiday, with his father's approval, Geoffrey had bought himself a Lambretta scooter which he liked to ride around playing the part of a 'mod'. With his scooter, he gained some independence and freedom, and he decided to ride it back to school for the last evening's concert. He dressed in his most casual clothes in the hope of impressing his friends and set off. He knew the way well enough by now, but still, it was quite a long ride. His speed was somewhat limited, but eventually, he rode through the gates and passed Big School, where the concert would soon start. He swung into a small quadrangle behind the Old studies, where several boys were milling around. It was unusual for a scooter to drive in there, so it produced some quizzical looks, but once Geoffrey had removed his helmet, they recognised who it was. Some of his friends soon gathered around and started chatting. Geoffrey was just discussing the possibility of sneaking in at the back of the concert when the side door to Big School swung open and out stepped Mr Sawtrey, the 'find a sixpence in my pocket' fiend. He strode towards Geoffrey and shouted at him, "Finch, you have left, so get out. Get out now and don't come back. You're not wanted here." Geoffrey started his scooter and drove away, leaving his prison behind him both physically and for the moment mentally.

Chapter 19

Geoffrey wasn't sure if the tears in his eyes were from the wind in his face or the mixture of sadness and anger at being sent away under such a dark cloud. The ride home seemed to take an eternity, and dusk was falling when he arrived home. He parked his Lambretta undercover and went in through the backdoor. In the sitting room, his mother was reading a book, and his father the newspaper. "Did you have a nice time, darling?" called his mother.

"Yes, thanks," lied Geoffrey. He did not feel inclined to tell them how his visit had ended and as he had learnt over the last ten years, he now kept such traumas to himself. He quickly went up to his room and pondered further over the day's events before tuning in to Radio Caroline and going to bed.

Since George had found a position for him at Lloyds bank, Geoffrey soon became a working chap and began to discover the real world. After all those years with only male company, Geoffrey quite naturally had a strong urge to find out about females. The only girls he had anything to do with were those he had met at dancing classes. He hated these classes because of his shyness, making it so traumatic for him to ask one of the fairer sex for a dance. After they had left school, the first girl he kissed properly was Avril, introduced to him by Irwin. Geoffrey found this so exciting it caused direct arousal in his underpants. After a few more clumsy fumbles in the dark and considerable kissing with various girls, Geoffrey embarked on a more serious relationship with Alice, a girl he worked with at the bank. Geoffrey thought he was in love, mainly because Alice was the first female to show any affection for him. This lasted a couple of years, during which she helped him lose his virginity.

At last, after all the boyhood jokes and talks about sex, he had finally experienced the real thing. Geoffrey was over the moon and reckoned there was nothing to beat it, but they seldom had the opportunity for a rerun. Eventually, their romance ended when Alice decided to take up again with a childhood love. Geoffrey was devastated and didn't know how he was going to manage without a girlfriend. When he told his mother, she only said, "Don't worry, darling, there's plenty more fish in the sea." Father George made no comment; secretly, his parents were quite glad since Alice didn't quite meet with their approval – 'not quite top drawer, you know'. This was true, she lived in a council house with an outside loo, and if class distinctions must be made, she was not of the same class as Geoffrey.

By the time their pairing had come to an end, Geoffrey had left the bank. He could see no exciting future there, and to climb the ladder in the banking world, he needed to attend night school and pass endless banking exams. Since his will to study had been well and truly annihilated, this prospect was directly crossed off his list. It so happened that a neighbour in the village offered Geoffrey a job at a computer centre just outside Cambridge. Computers were something new, and Geoffrey thought it could be interesting. It was interesting enough to keep him there for ten years and set him on his way for a top job abroad.

Now with a foot in the door at the government-sponsored computer centre, he was soon able to move from his job in administration to become a computer operator, which he found far more attractive. The computer, Atlas II, was one of only two ever produced by ICL, the other machine, Atlas I, being located at Manchester University. It really was one of a kind with hard discs the size of coffee tables and one-inch magnetic tapes. The director, wisely able to see the future of CAD-CAM, ensured that the computer centre expanded accordingly. The staff was increased manyfold with young programmers and engineers and a whole new wing built to house them. Included in the new building was a large canteen with a modern kitchen. This particular part of the new building proved to be Geoffrey's first major mistake regarding romance.

Every day, regular as clockwork, Geoffrey and his colleagues went to the canteen for coffee in the morning, then lunch and once more for afternoon coffee. The canteen was managed by a girl called Janet with another young girl, Cathy, as her assistant. Both were very much working girls. However, Cathy, not a very tall girl, was a cheeky young lass, who, in spite of some birth deformities, was always cheerful, invariably greeting them with "'allo, what would you handsome fellas like today?" or such like. After a while, Geoffrey found it was often fun to chat and joke with her, and he began to look forward to his coffee breaks just for that reason. Their relationship gathered momentum, and inevitably Geoffrey asked her for a date.

The two were worlds apart in all aspects. Cathy lived with her mother and unemployed father in a council house. In contrast, Geoffrey lived with his mother and professional father in their own house on the upmarket side of Cambridge. Nevertheless, Geoffrey could not help his attraction, probably because, for once, someone showed him interest. He found her fun to be with, and they started going out quite regularly, but at this early stage, he reckoned it was easiest to keep their little romance secret from both home and work. Of course, it didn't take long before the entire computer centre knew what was going on, so no one was surprised when Geoffrey received special service in the canteen. But it remained a secret from his family.

The romance continued unabated, and the longer it went on, the more Geoffrey worried about how he could possibly introduce Cathy to his family. Not only did this colossal class difference exist, but one of her brothers was in prison to boot. He decided for himself to continue keeping Cathy a secret. But as time went by, it bothered him more and more. During all this time, Geoffrey had become increasingly anxious to move out from his parents. He foresaw that as he and Cathy's relationship developed, it could lead to setting up a home together. Eventually, they decided to find a flat where they could live together and even get married.

It wasn't long before Geoffrey was offered a first floor flat in a quiet cul-de-sac by a work colleague who was on the move. So Geoffrey took it without hesitation, and now they were ready. Having decided to marry, there was no question of a church wedding, so they booked in the first available date at the Cambridge registry office, that being the thirteenth of January. This was only ten days away, so now Geoffrey had no choice but to break the news to his parents. He knew he had no option but to 'bite the bullet' and take the plunge, so just one week before the marriage, while drinking coffee with George and Thea, he suddenly announced, "I'm getting married next Saturday!" There was a deathly hush before his mother replied,

"Oh, darling! Goodness! That's a surprise. Who is she? May we meet her?"

"Yes, of course, her name is Cathy; I'll bring her round tomorrow," said Geoffrey at the same time, wishing he hadn't.

"And where is this taking place?" asked his father.

"At the registry office," answered Geoffrey.

"Well, I hope you know what you're doing," was all he said.

The only thing Geoffrey wanted was their blessing, but somehow he didn't really feel he had it; the whole time, he had a nagging feeling in the back of his mind that this wasn't quite right. Was this a repeat of his absconding from school, based on his 'I'll show you anyway' attitude? he asked himself. Now the ice was broken, but he still had to go through the actual introduction, which was also a trifle painful – 'this is my wife to be, a rather short girl from the very lowest class and with a deformity to boot!' But what Geoffrey thought was love helped him through the ordeal. Because someone showed him affection, he was hooked – sadly, he still had a lot to learn. However, the big day arrived, a rather grey winter Saturday morning. The two families met outside the registry office, standing on cold concrete steps in front of a rather uninviting, forlorn building. The whole performance was more than awkward for everybody, both the actual ceremony when Cathy stumbled over some of the more difficult words in the text and the reception afterwards. This was held in their flat with everyone trying to be friendly, but nothing could disguise the enormous difference between the families. Throughout the proceedings, Geoffrey suffered a sense of shame, but his stubbornness to see it through won the day. Eventually, the so-called jollities were over, and he and Cathy escaped for their honeymoon.

After a year, they had scraped enough money together to put a deposit on a semi-detached house being built on a newly developed housing estate outside Cambridge. Situated on top of a hill at the end of a row, they at least only had neighbours on one side. The pocket handkerchief of a garden was in the main only stonehard clay. As soon as their house was finished, they moved in and settled down. There they lived peacefully for another year until Geoffrey succumbed to temptation. At his work, the centre was growing, and the computer was now kept up and running until late in the evening. In turn, this meant that Geoffrey and his fellow operators had to run two shifts; more staff were employed, amongst them a girl who exuded considerable sex appeal. Needless to say, Geoffrey, starting to learn about life, fell for her, hook, line and sinker.

That was the beginning of the end – of his first marriage. The affair could better be described as a sex affair rather than a love affair since Geoffrey soon discovered that this girl, Rosie, had a large appetite for sex. Geoffrey still hadn't worked out how to distinguish between love and sex; another lesson for him. Needless to say, after a few months of clandestine meetings and secret telephone calls, he had discovered that there was much more life to live than he had imagined and once again, believing that this new-found sex was love, he decided to come clean and admit to Cathy what was afoot.

When Geoffrey was working the late shift with his new love Rosie, he always took the opportunity to drive her home afterwards. By coincidence, she lived in the next street to Cathy's parents, where Cathy would often wait for him when he worked late. Geoffrey's car made an unmistakable sound, so she could easily hear when he was coming. One night she heard his car drive in the next street, but it took another ten minutes before she heard it coming back again to her. As she climbed into the car, she asked, "What took you so long round there?" "Oh, I gave one of the operators a lift home," replied Geoffrey, hoping he didn't reek of Rosie's perfume.

"Yeah, but you were there for ages!" she complained as they drove off.

"I know, but she had a question about restarting the computer, and I was explaining to her," lied Geoffrey, knowing he had spent the ten minutes kissing Rosie while she egged him on with "You've got to tell her."

"Oh," Cathy seemed to accept his answer. But then Geoffrey thought to himself, "to hell with this, I can't play these charades any longer," and burst out saying, "actually, I'm seeing someone else."

"No, no, not that bitch Rosie, I knew something was going on!" screamed Cathy as she attempted to jump out of the moving car.

"Stop it," shouted Geoffrey leaning over, pulling her door closed again, "we'll go home and discuss it." And discuss it they did – the whole night.

There followed an exceptionally traumatic period with many tears shed on all sides, and even though she was willing to forgive him, he was emphatic about leaving her. In no time at all, he was caught in the horns of a dilemma. Even his parents were siding with Cathy telling him to stay, while his new 'love' pressured him to leave. Even during a heated discussion, his father threatened to outcast him by telling him, "You're no son of mine." This remark cut very deep, absolutely devastating Geoffrey, but for once, he stuck to his guns and followed his wish, doing what he wanted, not what he thought was expected of him. Needless to say, this destructive relationship with Rosie soon came to an end, and Geoffrey was alone once more.

So much damage had been done during his term of boarding that now the effects were becoming apparent. Geoffrey's search for the love and approval he had missed for so long had only brought more grief. It was quite a few years before he tried again, but with an unhappy ending once more, although this time, the boot was on the other foot, hurting Geoffrey deeply.

www.ingramcontent.com/pod-product-compliance
Ingram Content Group UK Ltd.
Pitfield, Milton Keynes, MK11 3LW, UK
UKHW020145250726
13967UKWH00002B/876

9 781915 424167